I0810391

IMAGES
*of America*

# NORWALK

**On the Cover:** The Huron County Courthouse and Jail proudly stand over the square around 1909. A large statue of Justice on top is a highlight of the skyline. The interurban kiosk houses a little traveler waiting on a trolley. This classic layout of the courthouse square still defines the city today.

IMAGES
*of America*

# NORWALK

Richard Kostoff and Mary Carabin

ARCADIA
PUBLISHING

ISBN 978-1-4671-2618-2

Published by Arcadia Publishing
Charleston, South Carolina

Printed in the United States of America

Library of Congress Control Number: 2017933996

For all general information, please contact Arcadia Publishing:
Telephone 843-853-2070
Fax 843-853-0044
E-mail sales@arcadiapublishing.com
For customer service and orders:
Toll-Free 1-888-313-2665

Visit us on the Internet at www.arcadiapublishing.com

*This book is dedicated to Platt and Sally Benedict—without their effort, this book would not have been written—and for the citizens of Norwalk past and present, both far and near in mind.*

# Contents


| | | |
|---|---|---|
| Acknowledgments | | 6 |
| Introduction | | 7 |
| 1. | The Early Settlement | 9 |
| 2. | The City Awakens | 13 |
| 3. | Norwalk on the Move | 23 |
| 4. | Goods and Services | 41 |
| 5. | Manufacturing and Industries | 67 |
| 6. | Schools and Churches | 77 |
| 7. | Historic Homes | 95 |
| 8. | Assemblies and Parades | 109 |

# ACKNOWLEDGMENTS

The authors would like to thank the members of the Firelands Historical Society, both past and present, for being a vast source of information. We would like to give a special thank-you to John Schumm. All photographs are part of the Firelands Historical Society collection and were taken by many different photographers.

# INTRODUCTION

The American Revolutionary War was the official beginning of the process of settlement for Norwalk, Ohio. During the war, the state of Connecticut saw very little military action but was busy manufacturing supplies for the Continental Army. These actions, of course, angered the British, and they sent raids out to destroy and cripple the manufacture and shipping of supplies. These raids got out of hand, with soldiers also burning private homes, schools, and churches, leaving citizens without any compensation to rebuild. The year 1792 was the year the "sufferers" were granted 500,000 acres of land called the "Firelands," located in present-day Huron and Erie Counties, plus sections in Ottawa and Ashland Counties. Many of the original sufferers never made the journey; however, one brave young man from Danbury, Connecticut, who grew up during the turmoil decided he would make the trip. Platt Benedict took his wife, Sally, and their children and made the journey by wagon. Settlers began arriving in the area as early as 1809. The War of 1812 had begun, and there were redcoats in the Ohio Territory. It was not very promising, and a few gave up and returned to Connecticut.

Huron County was formed in 1809 and organized in 1815. The village of Norwalk was formed in 1817 with the arrival of the Platt Benedict family. In May 1818, the county seat was officially moved from Avery to Norwalk. It sat on a feeder creek to the Huron River, with the town center above the floodplain. Platt Benedict made sure the city was attractive and planted maple trees along the streets. He encouraged an early industrial environment of carpenters, masons, and woodworkers that would later define the settlement. Progress was slow in Norwalk before the coming of the railroads in 1853. Then the population grew as more settlers arrived from the east. Many immigrants began arriving from Germany, Ireland, and other parts of Europe. The Civil War saw Ohio give its all, with Norwalk providing troops for the cause of the Union.

After 1870 and through 1890, the town grew into a thriving city. Most of the downtown today was built during this period. It was an unprecedented period of growth and industrialization. Norwalk had become a center of business, education, and culture. The very character of north central Ohio was centered in Norwalk, as it became a transportation hub for the interurban railroad lines. Sandusky, Huron, and Milan were to the north, Monroeville and Fremont were to the west, and Shelby and Mansfield were to the south. Of course, Cleveland and Toledo were each a few hours away by rail. Naturally, Norwalk was a comfortable stopover with hotels, restaurants, and shopping.

Norwalk took advantage of every opportunity for growth and expansion. It has a strong industrial past that it has not given up. The city has produced domestic goods from organs and pianos to furniture. The Norwalk Furniture Corporation still operates today. Early fortunes were made, and the city established banks and was a center of local commerce. Its opulence was displayed with the stately residences along Main Street. It was not just "picture postcard" ideal, but a hard-won triumph of the American spirit. The civic pride remains to this day.

Norwalk was where the Fisher family, who started as humble buggy workers on Benedict Avenue, helped to change the auto industry forever. The family's seven sons moved to Detroit and founded the Body by Fisher company, later helping establish General Motors. The Norwalk and Mead trucking companies added stable jobs and helped improve the economy during the mid-20th century. In 1912, John Ernsthausen and Rolla Fader started the Norwalk Truck Company, which would evolve into the Norwalk Trucking Line, with tractor trailers bearing the city's name nationwide. Profits from the company benefit the city today through the Ernsthausen Foundation, and the Norwalk High School mascot is the Trucker.

One of Norwalk's more famous residents was Paul Brown, born in 1908. He became a pioneer in American football, coaching for Ohio State University and then his namesake team, the Cleveland Browns. He was elected into the Pro Football Hall of Fame in 1965. The Summit Motorsport park draws large crowds every year to see races. The Maple City seems to love its "wheels" as it continues to be a busy crossroad near US 20 and Interstate 80. It still maintains one of the last drive-in theaters in Ohio: the Star View Drive In.

Many generations have contributed to the city's growth. This book presents a small look at their achievements. It is not just a history of Norwalk. This is more of a visual tour of the past, documenting many of the changes to the landscape. It is a celebration of the past. Most of the businesses and technology of the historic center are no more. Gone are the trolleys, many of the banks, churches, and services. The commercial center has moved to the city's north side. The residential neighborhoods have not changed since the original settlement. The Huron County Courthouse proudly stands on Main Street. One thing is for sure, the people seem to love their town no matter what direction it takes.

The 21st century poses many challenges to Norwalk. The city has always meshed well with new technology, from railroads to photography. It has survived difficulties and celebrated its triumphs. Each decade has left its mark of change on the city, yet its historic downtown, neighborhoods, and homes have a sense of permanence. Visitors from the past would recognize it with certainty. With a little care, the city can be preserved for future generations. Progress has always been welcome here, and we can only imagine what is possible in the next 200 years.

# One

# The Early Settlement

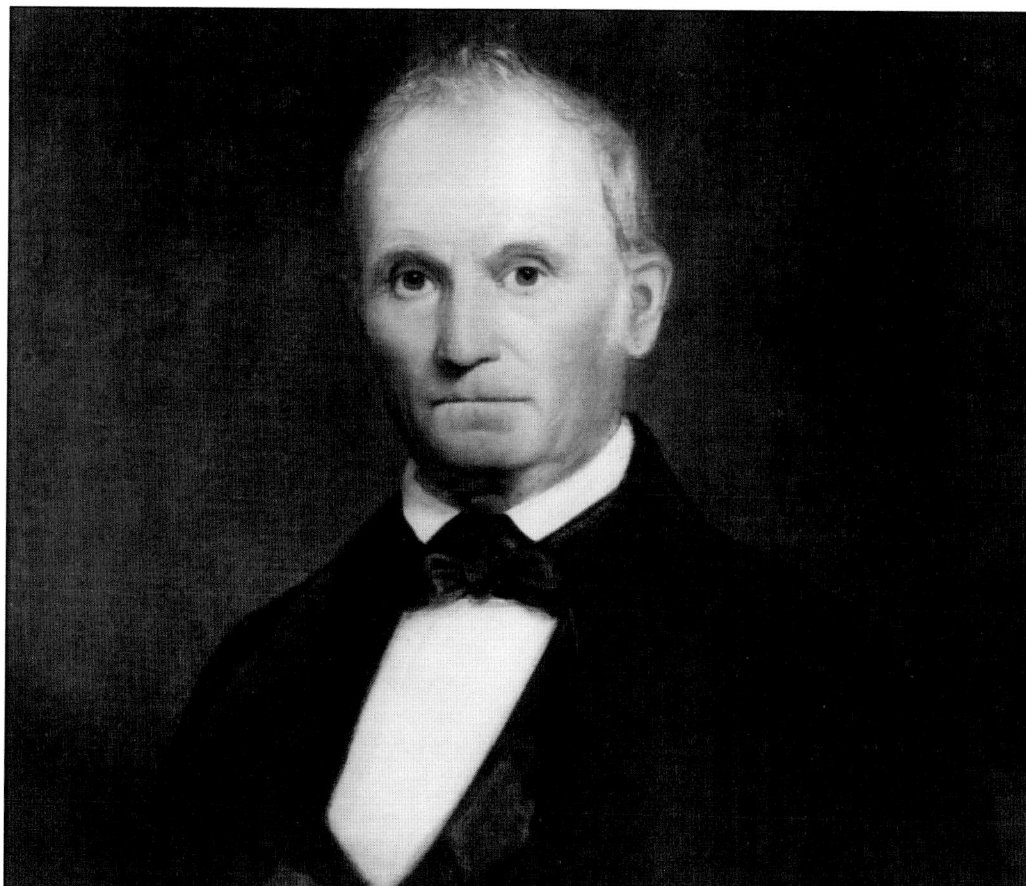

Platt Benedict was born in Danbury, Connecticut, on March 18, 1775. He was four years old when the British redcoats began to disrupt the town. Indeed, he was a true son of the American Revolution, and the spark that the British lit under his feet would later prompt him to move west. In 1817, Benedict made the seven-week journey to the Ohio wilderness by ox and wagon with his wife, Sally, their children, and a few household goods. Obviously, this was for the brave and strong. He was both, with a strong sense of vision for the settlement in the vast forest. Benedict was a pioneer in the classic sense, and his vision produced the city seen today. He planted maple trees along the streets, giving Norwalk its nickname "the Maple City" in 1851. He helped ensure that his settlement would grow into the handsome city it is today. He lived to see the end of the Civil War and died October 25, 1866.

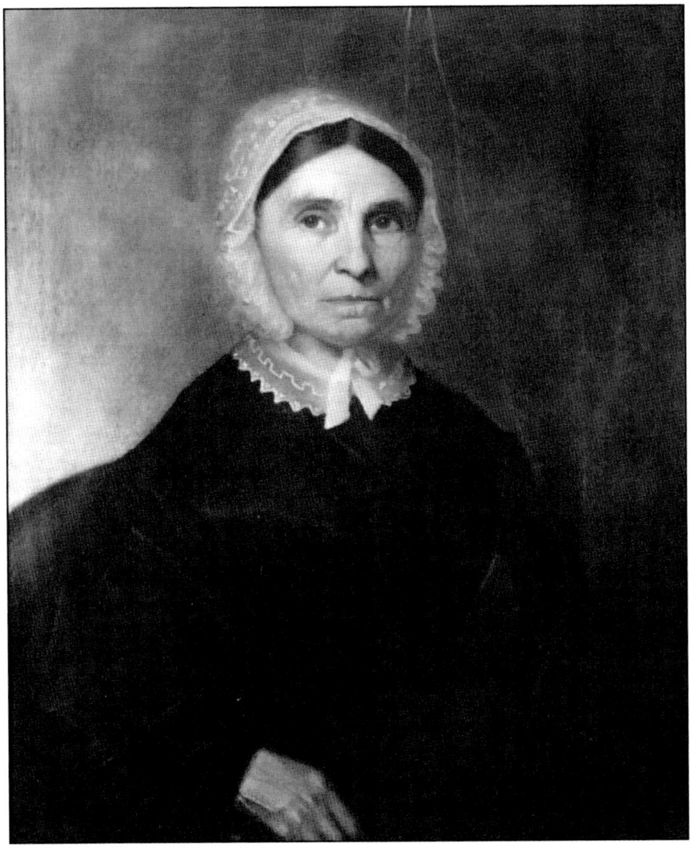

Sally DeForest Benedict was born on August 27, 1777, in Wilton, Connecticut. She set out with her husband, Platt, and children for the difficult and challenging journey through the wilderness. She was a true daughter of the American Revolution, enduring the harsh conditions of north central Ohio. She died on June 24, 1852.

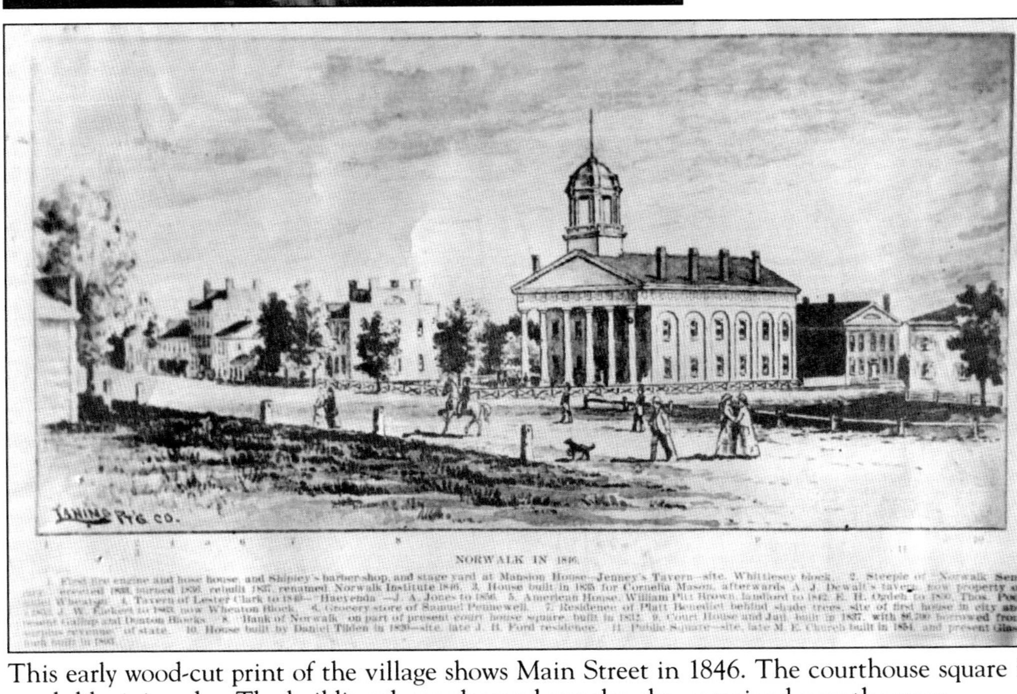


This early wood-cut print of the village shows Main Street in 1846. The courthouse square is much like it is today. The buildings have changed, yet the plan remained over the years.

This is an early photograph of the Huron County Courthouse and Jail. This courthouse was later razed for a larger facility as the city grew. The snow on the ground is evident of the long winters of northern Ohio.

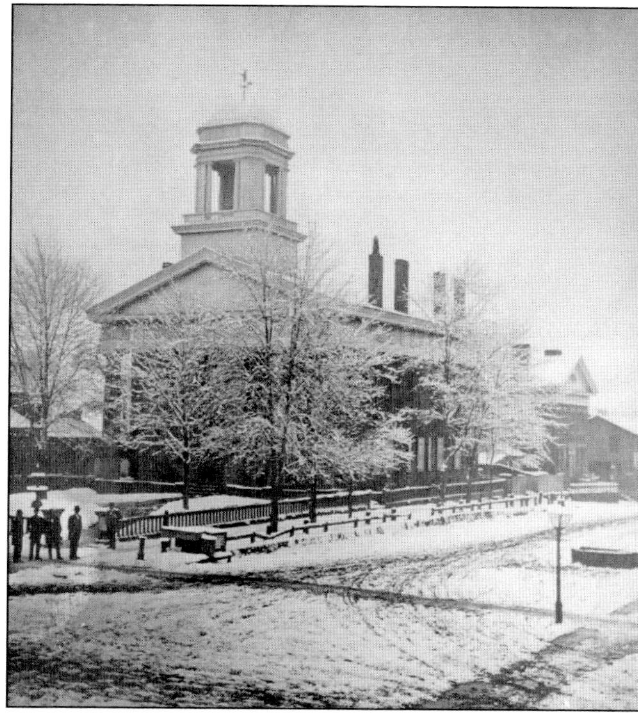

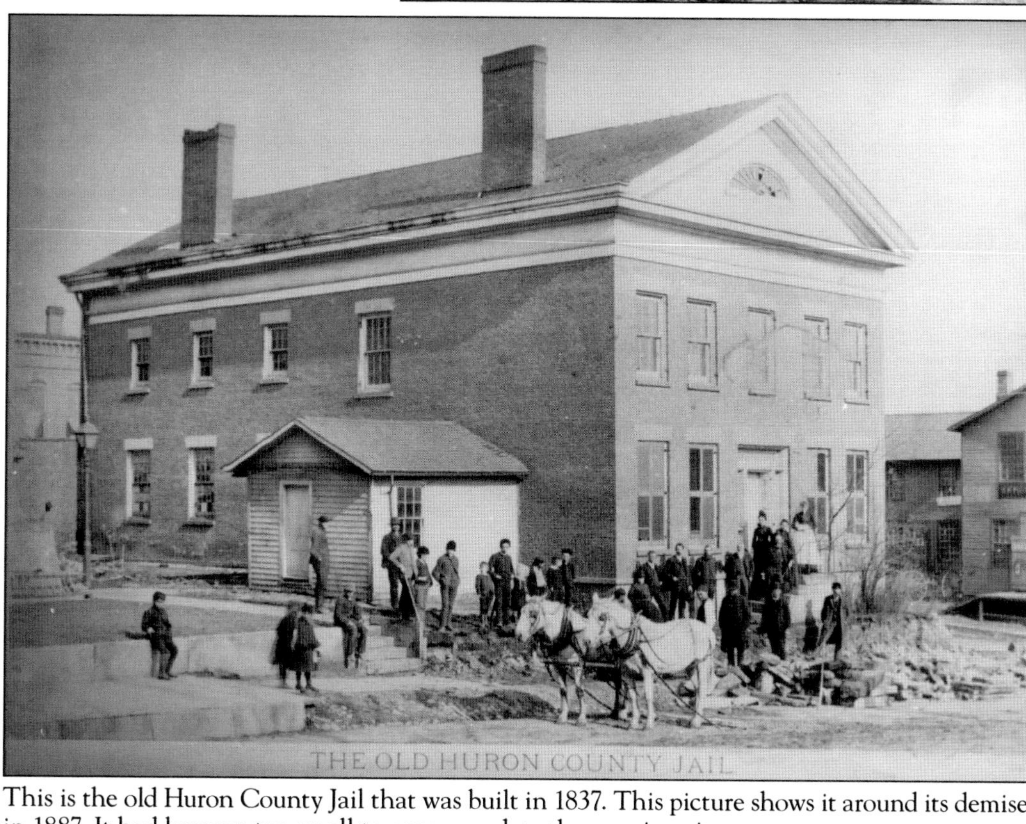


This is the old Huron County Jail that was built in 1837. This picture shows it around its demise in 1887. It had become too small to accommodate the growing city.

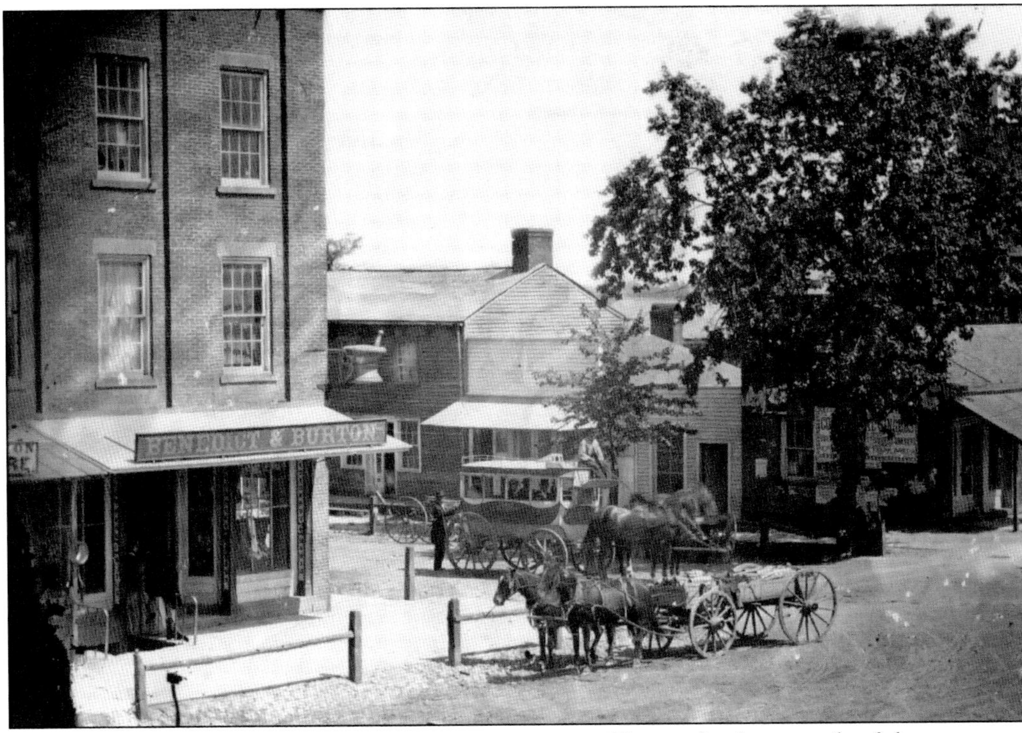


This early photograph of the Benedict and Burton drugstore at the corner of Main Street and Whittlesey Avenue shows a stage coach, which was the main means of transportation before the railroads. The Whittlesey Building, built in 1854, is one of the oldest commercial structures still standing; however, its upper floor has been removed.

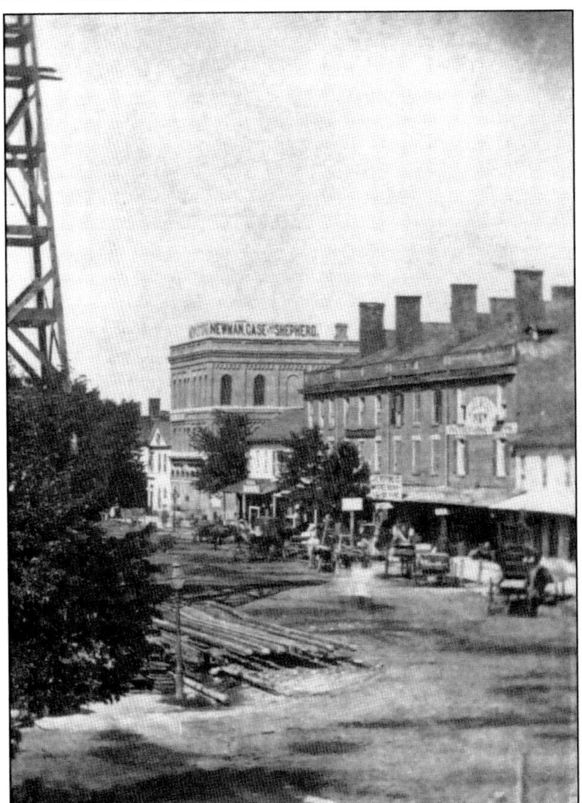

This 1863 picture shows the north side of West Main from the old Mansion House hotel to past Hester Street. It looks like it might have been a busy shopping day with all the horses and wagons. The tall structure at left is unidentified.

# *Two*

# THE CITY AWAKENS

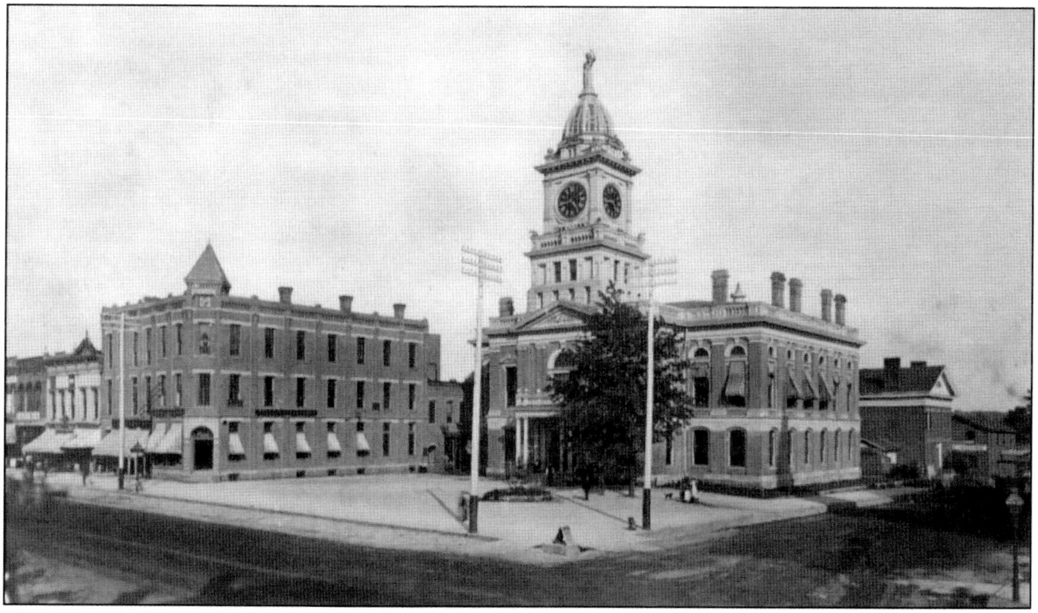

The new 1882 courthouse was needed as the city grew and needed more space. The Victorian-era fashion for ornate details and eye-catching beauty is well represented here. A large statue of Justice is standing on top. None of these buildings are standing today, including the original Huron County Jail and the bank, but this classic layout of the courthouse square still defines the city.

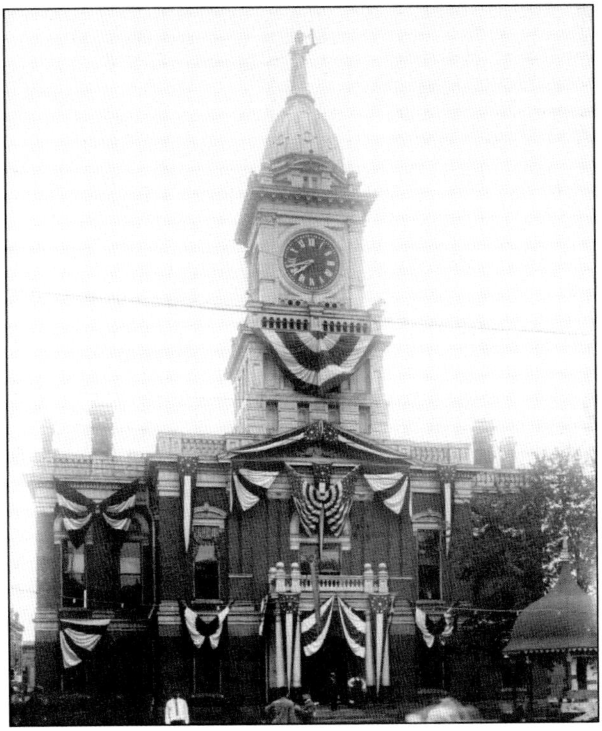

Here is the proud courthouse dressed up in bunting for a celebration. The details of the large clock with Roman numerals and large Justice statue are visible. This courthouse was completed in 1882 and served the city until 1912.

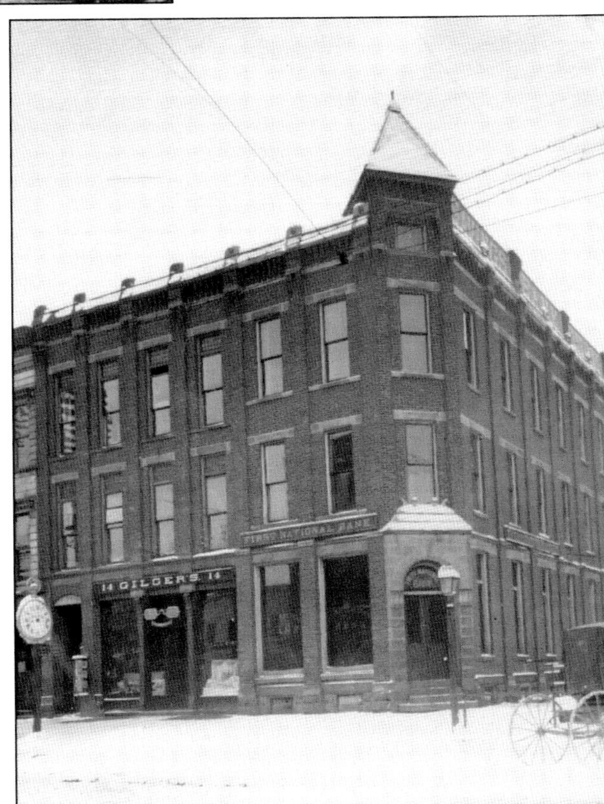

This is the First National Bank in the winter, just to the east of the courthouse. The building would later be replaced by a larger structure. This was the beginning of the Golden Age of American architecture. Fortunately, most of these buildings are still standing in Norwalk.

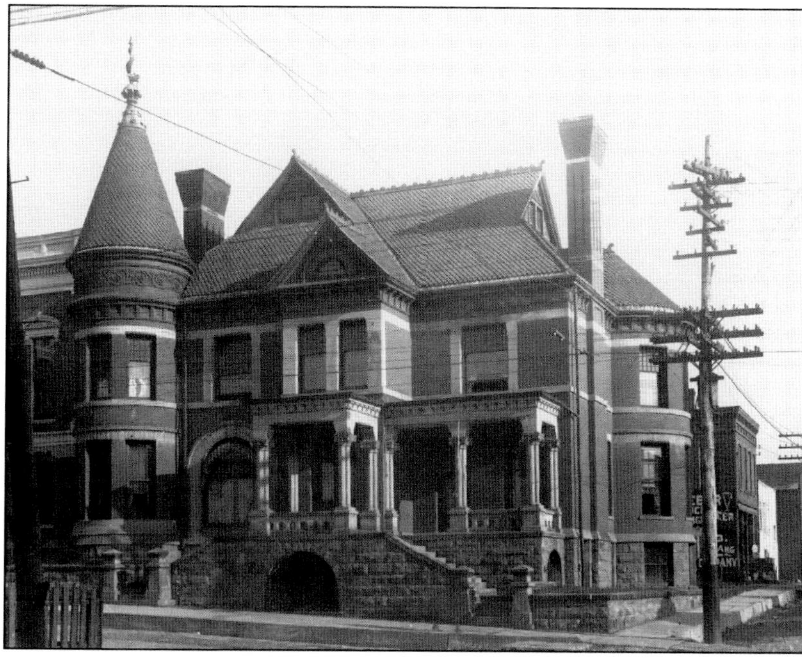

In 1887, the new Huron County Jail was built. The details of the building were ornate and gave a commanding presence to the city, complete with the dragon atop the spire. It was also the residence of the sheriff and his family. The cells are to the rear. The sheriff's wife would cook for the prisoners.

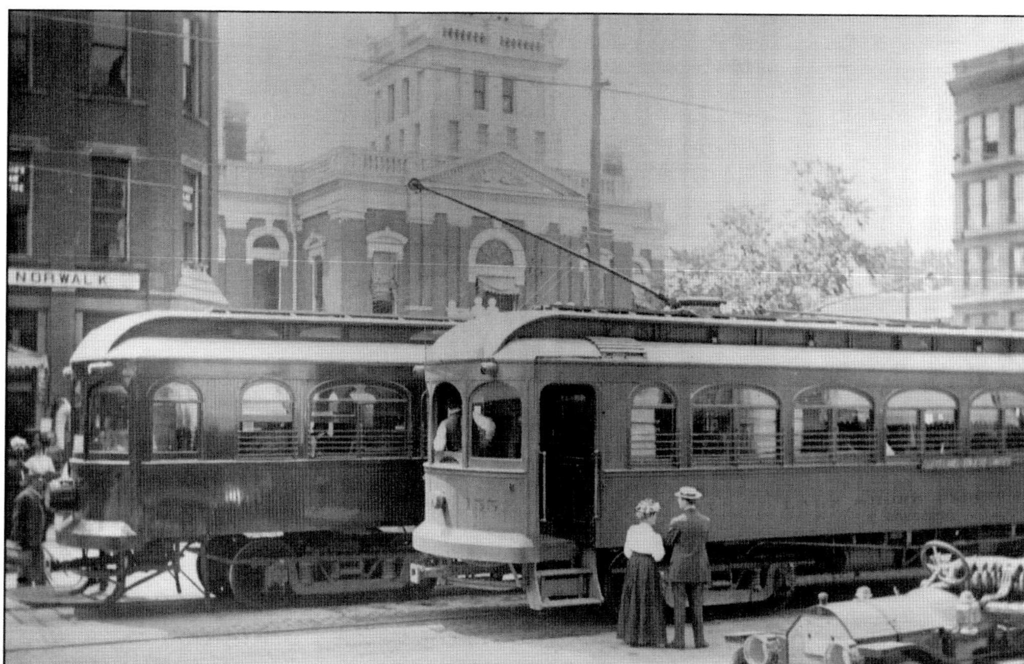


This 1909 photograph illustrates the importance of the city as an interurban trolley hub. It shows the courthouse square with the Glass Block Building on the right. The city's central location provided a local travel industry boom. The automobile promised more progress as Norwalk became a city on the move.

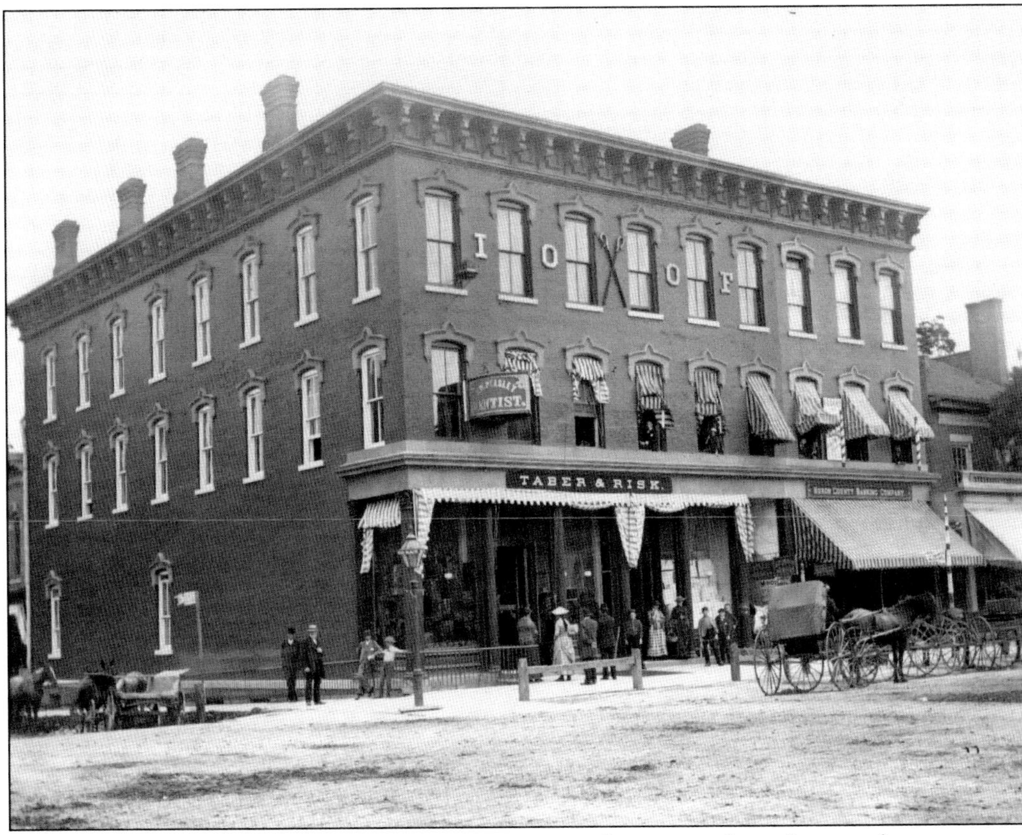


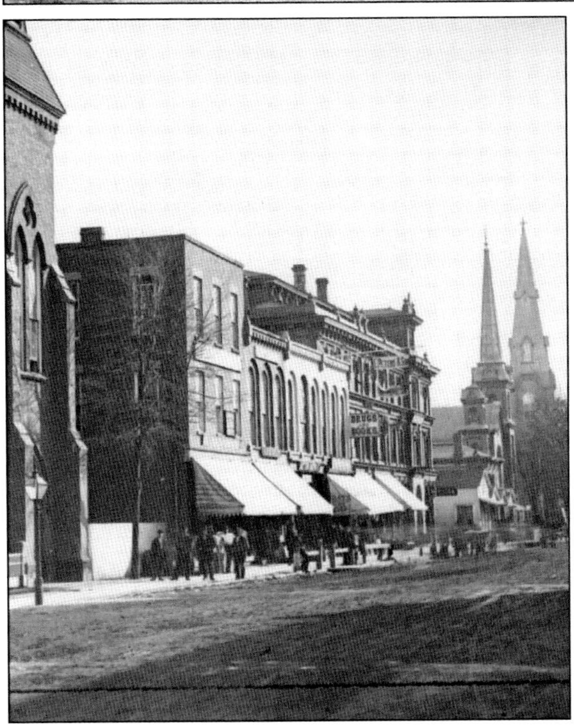

Just across from the courthouse on Main Street and Whittlesey Avenue is this classic building. It housed the Taber & Risk Company, a successful department store locally owned and operated. Notice the dentist office on the second floor. The beautiful cornice is well maintained to this day.

This view looks down West Main Street in the 1880s. Notice the street is still unpaved. In the summer, the street would get dusty when it was dry and muddy when it rained. None of the churches are standing today. The St. Charles Hotel is partially standing today and known as Berry's Restaurant.

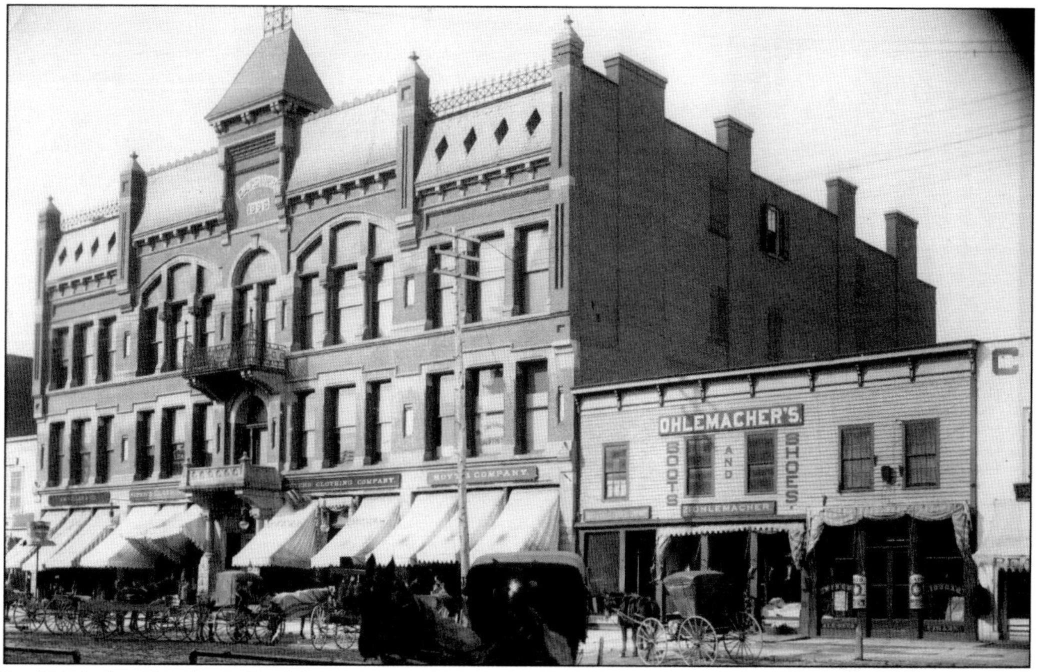


In 1885, the Gardiner Building rose to four stories. This large structure served many functions, including retail on the street level, an opera house that seated 900 on the third floor, and a banquet room and dressing rooms for entertainers. Vaudeville shows were popular until the motion picture replaced them. The building later served as a bank and is proudly standing today.

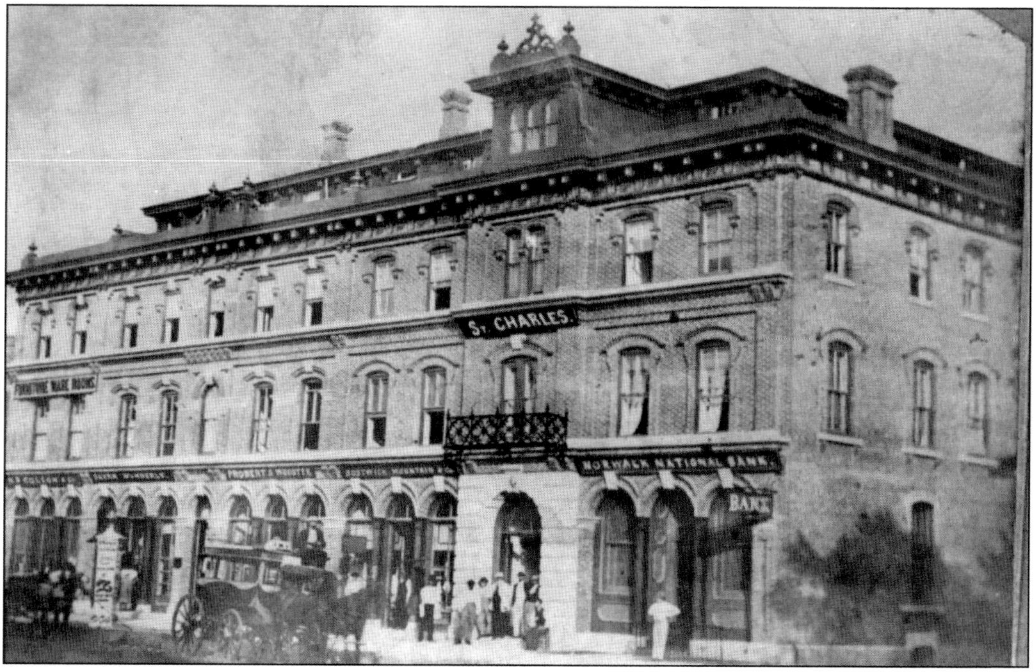


When it opened in 1868, the St. Charles Hotel was considered one of the finest in northern Ohio. It had rooms for 75 guests, a 100-seat dining room, and carriages that met every train at the two passenger depots to provide transportation to and from the hotel.

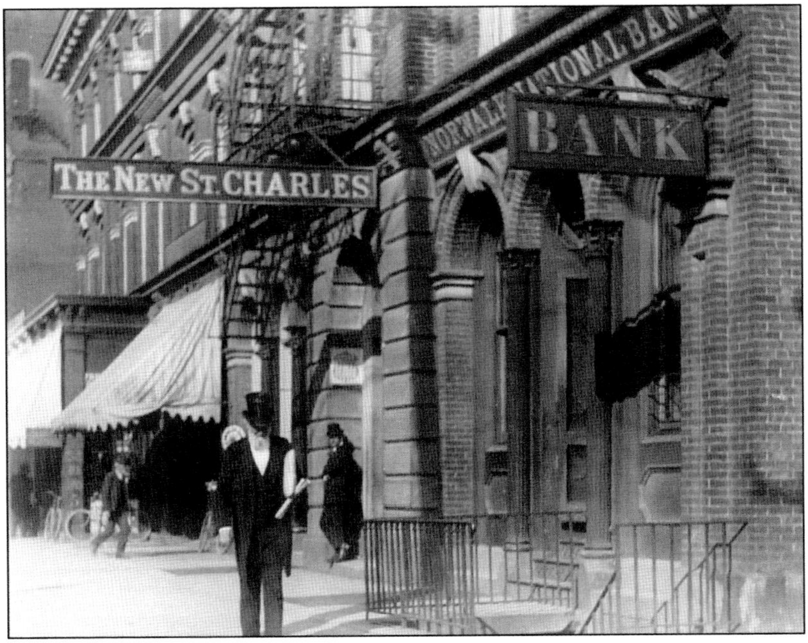


A gentleman sporting the fashion of the day strolls past the St. Charles Hotel. Notice the iron columns and the subterranean stairway at street level.

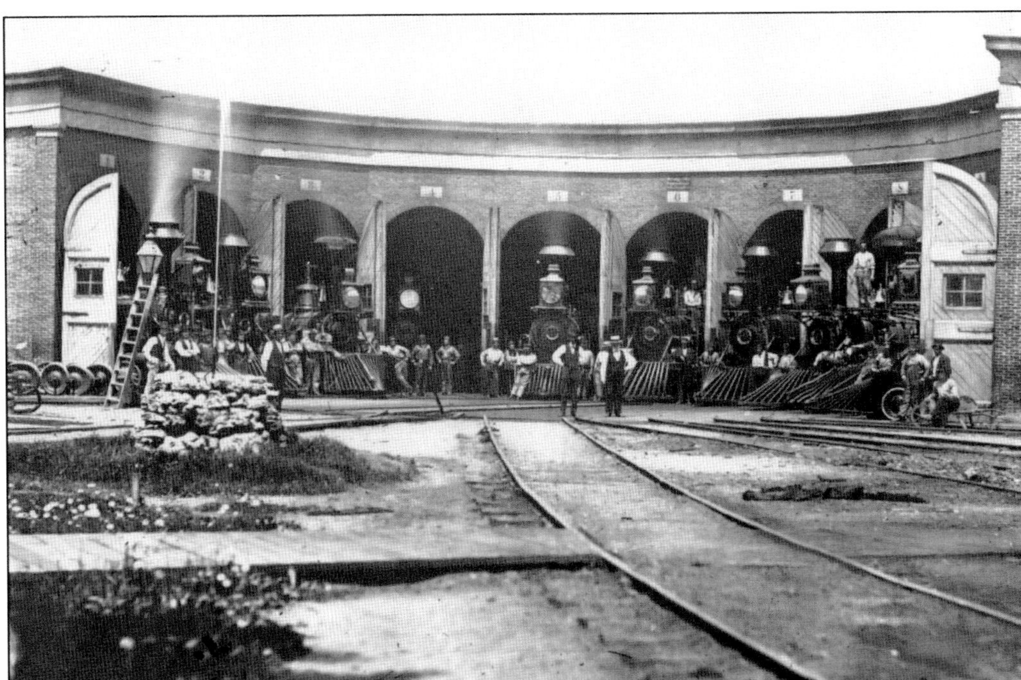

In 1853, the railroad roundhouse repair shop for the Toledo, Norwalk & Columbus Railroad was built on land between Whittlesey Avenue and Prospect Street. It soon was purchased by the Michigan & Southern Railroad. By 1879 this was a busy place, with about 700 men employed. These men, carpenters, blacksmiths, and painters, repaired cars and engines and built new passenger and freight cars. Unfortunately for Norwalk, in 1899, the company was sold to the New York Central Railroad, and it moved the shops to Collinwood, Ohio.

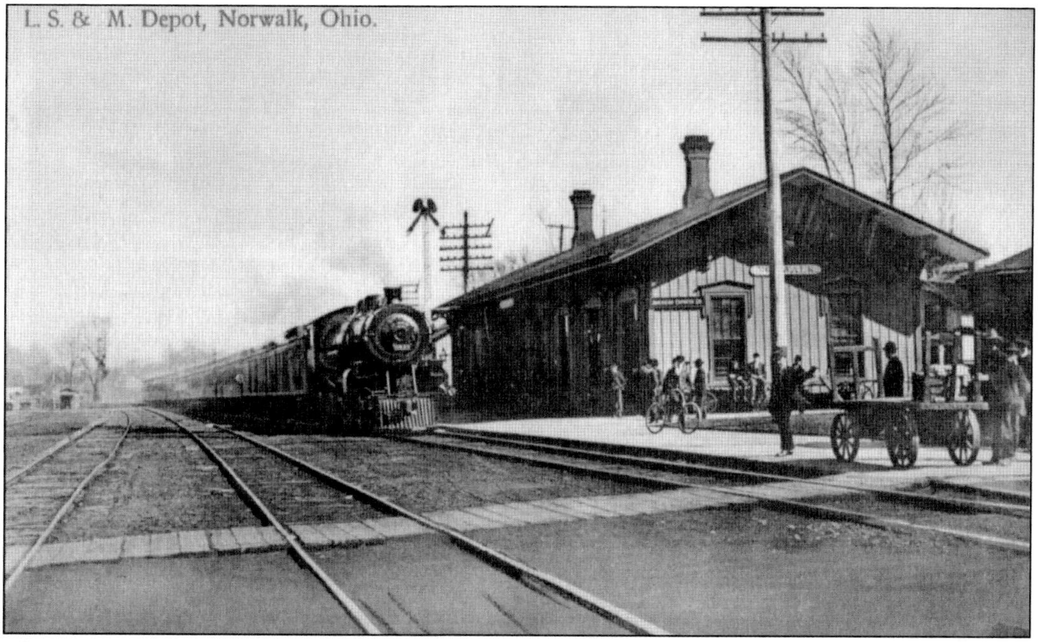


This is Norwalk Station on the north side of town, with a large passenger train arriving. The steam engines filled the city with a commotion of noise and steam.

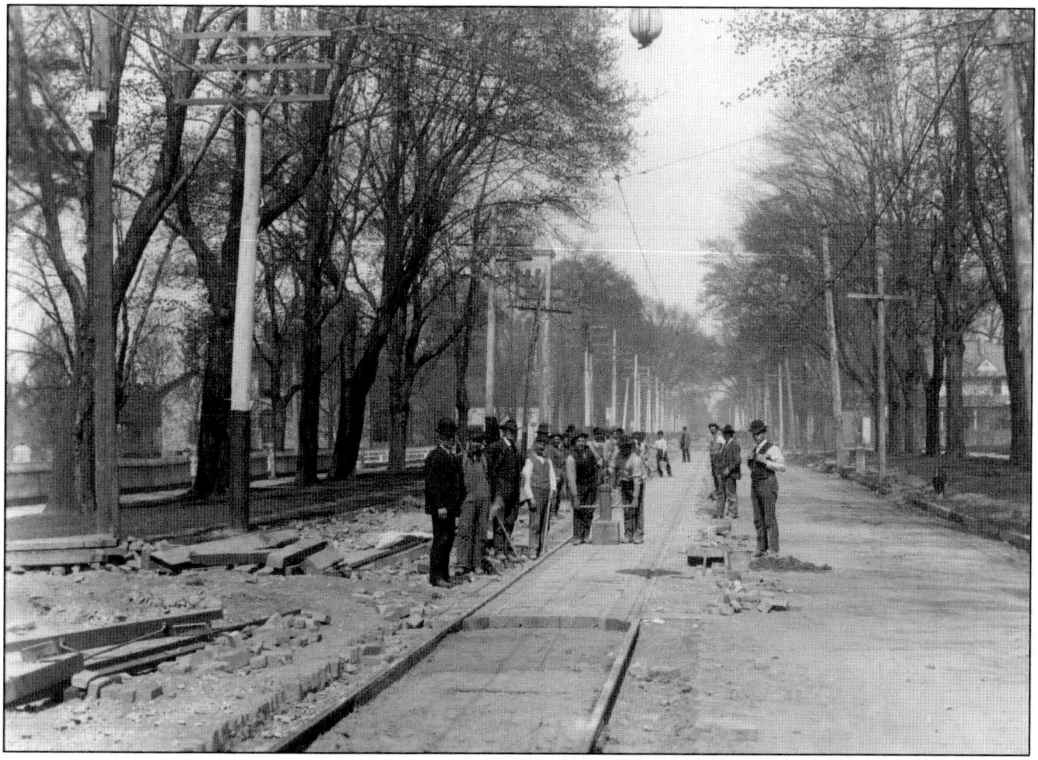

A Lake Shore Electric Railroad crew is busy laying new 100-pound T-rail and special "nosed" brick paving on West Main Street in 1908. The first rail was laid in 1893. Being the local interurban hub helped Norwalk to grow.

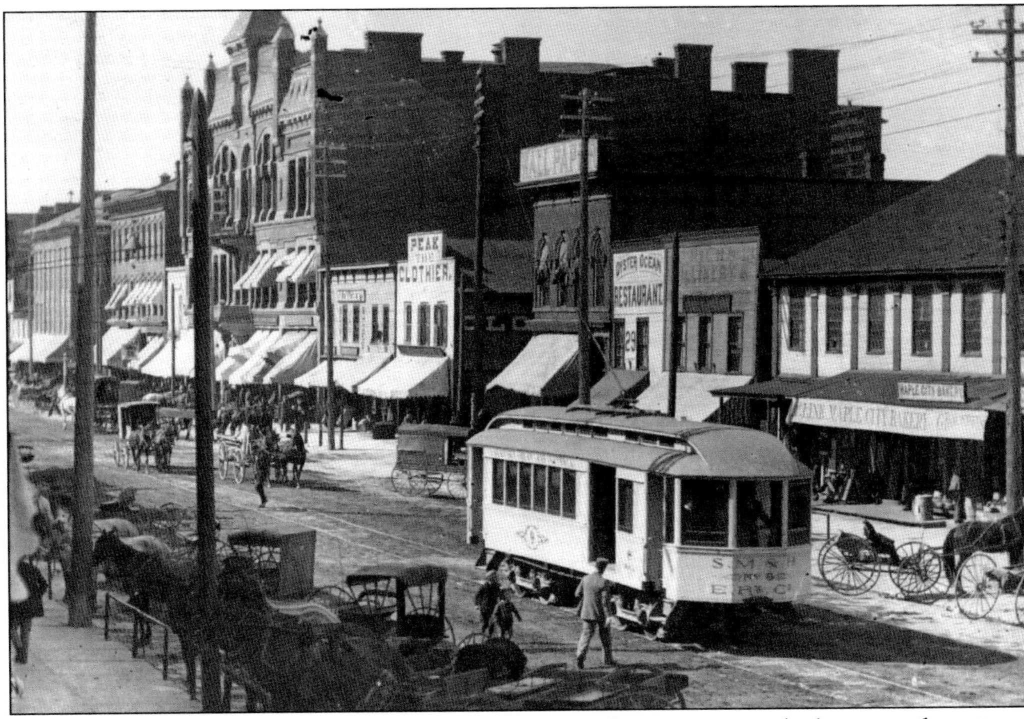


Here is an early scene on Main Street showing an interurban car among the horses and carriages. The skyline would quickly modernize as the 1890s began. This car would travel to Milan via old State Road.

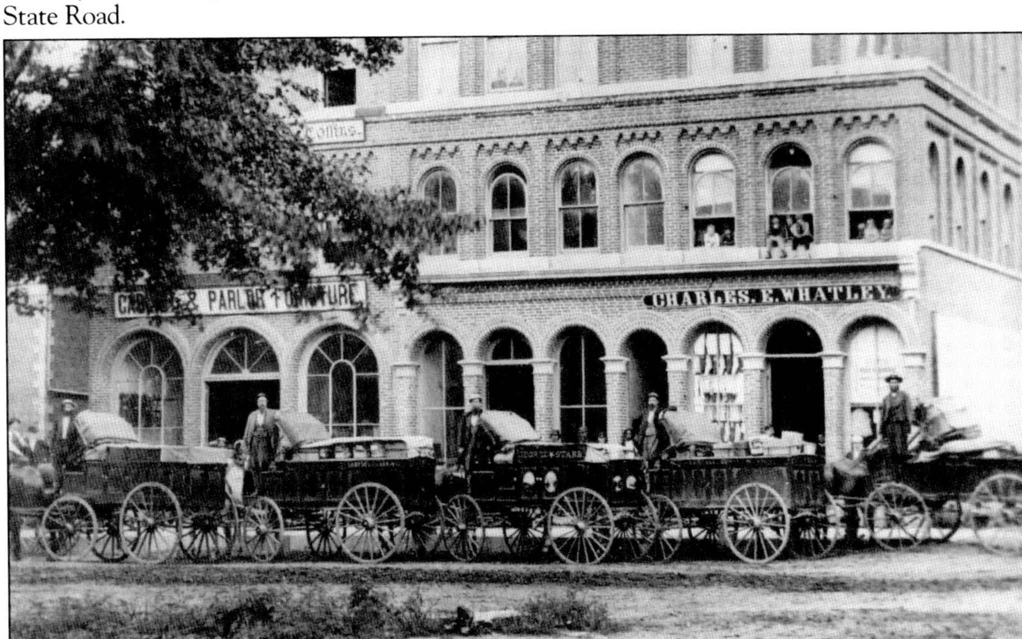


Traveling salesmen and their "sample wagons" line up in front of 26–28 West Main Street near Hester Street, perhaps preparing to show their wares or getting ready to travel. It is possible that they spent the night at the St. Charles Hotel, which was across the street.

Here is the Glass Block Building, erected in 1893. This was the tallest commercial building, standing six stories counting the dome. Originally the site of the Methodist church, it was razed in favor of a modern department store. Local merchants Harry Hoyt and Caleb F. Jackson opened the new store at Benedict Avenue and West Main Street. It was made of brick, brown stone, iron, and an unusual amount of plate glass windows, giving it its name. It was state-of-the-art for its time, with an elevator and special fire protection. A classic department store, it had everything that Victorian shoppers were looking for, including a grocery and lunch counter in the basement. This was perfect one-stop shopping that attracted interurban shoppers to the city.

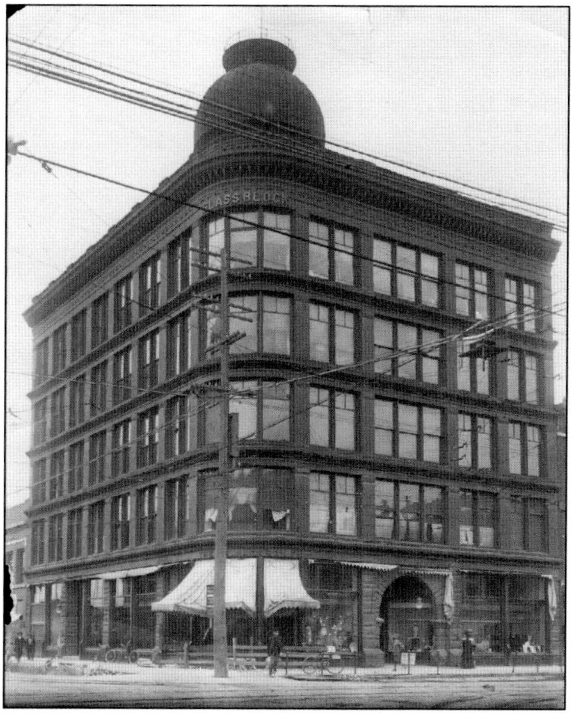


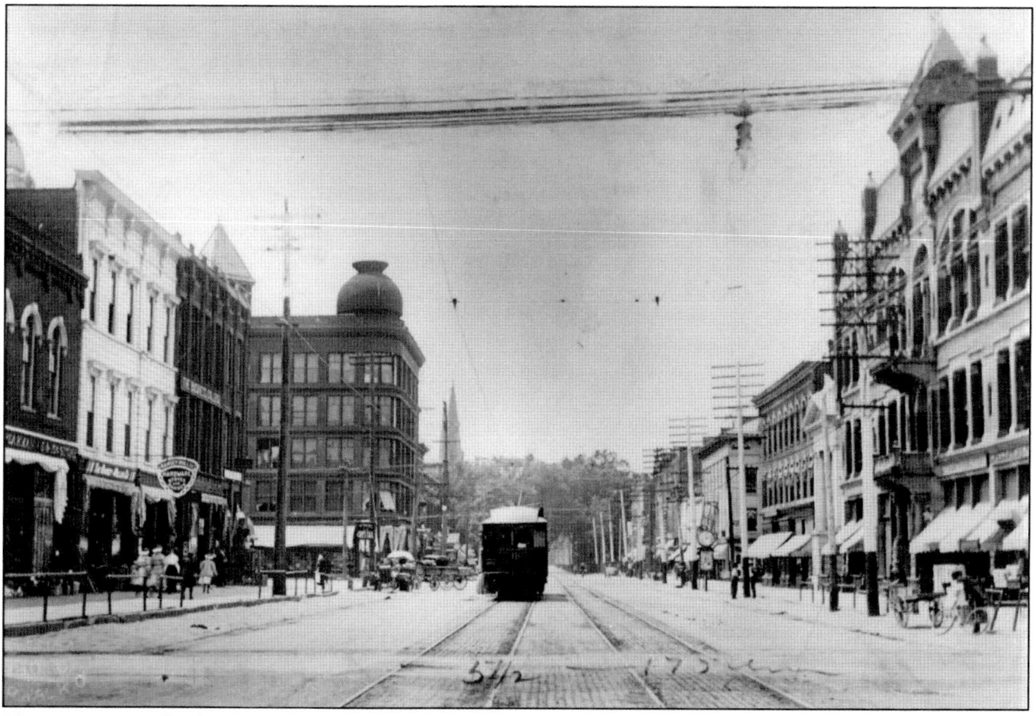

Here is a view looking west on Main Street. The skyline of the city begins to define itself with the Glass Block Building on the right and the Gardiner Building to the left, as well as the top of the courthouse in the top right corner. The interurban cars would become a distinct feature as well in the coming decades.

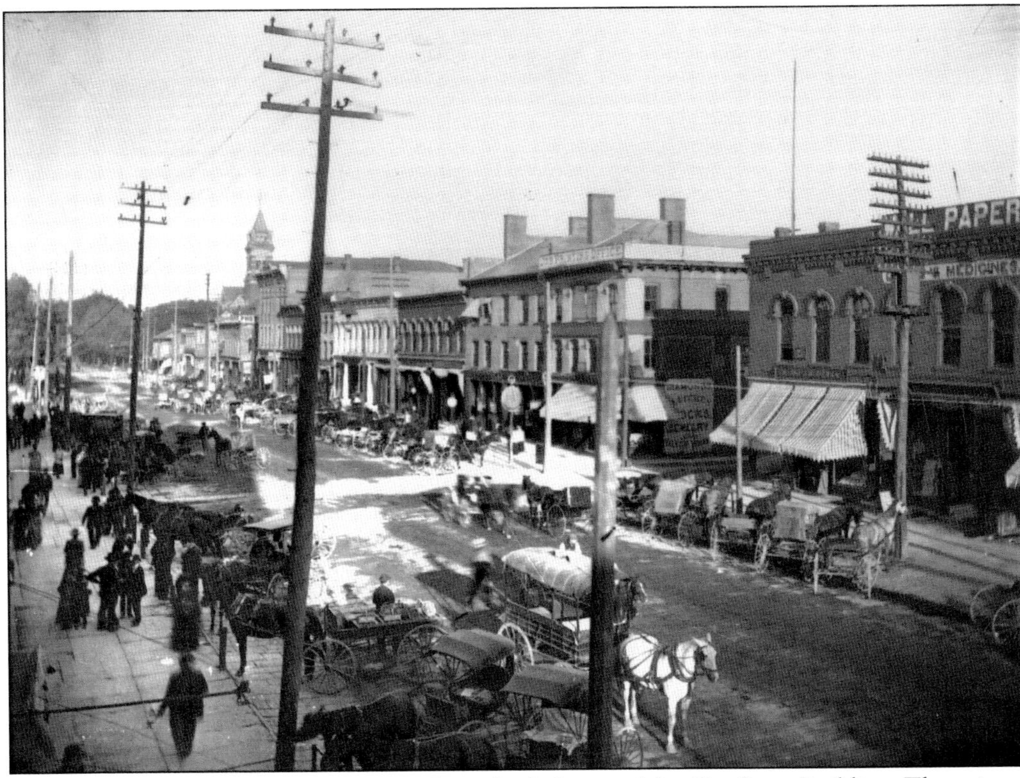


This view looks over East Main Street from the balcony of the Gardiner Building. The spire of Norwalk High School is a proud part of the skyline. The horse-and-carriage traffic is already heavy as business thrives in the growing city.

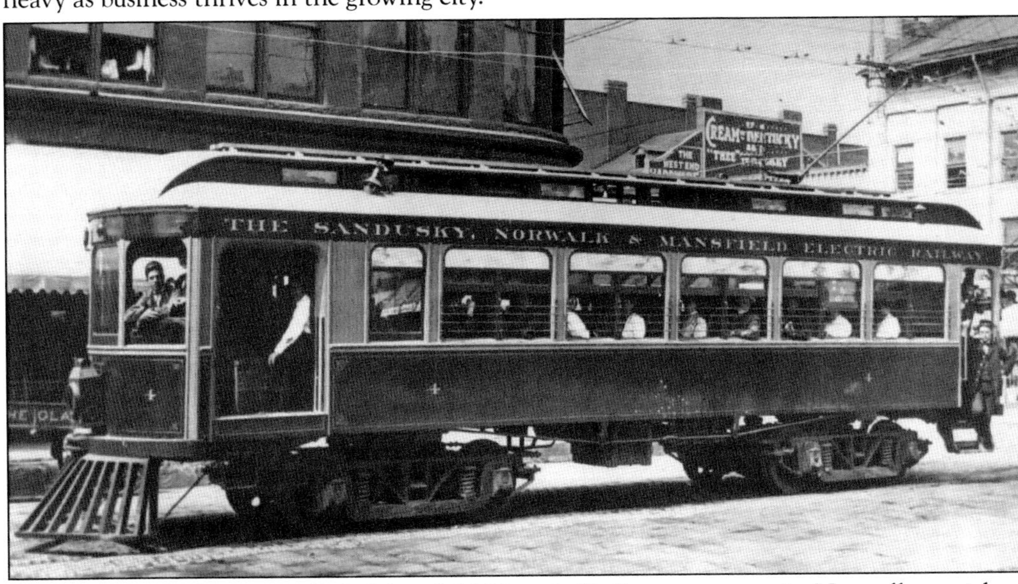


This first Sandusky, Norwalk & Mansfield Electric Railway car stops in Norwalk to pick up passengers. This must have been a very desirable mode of travel in horse-and-buggy times. This photograph was taken in July 1905. The interurban provided service for farmers to get their milk and cream to market, and also carried mail between some communities.

*Three*

# Norwalk on the Move

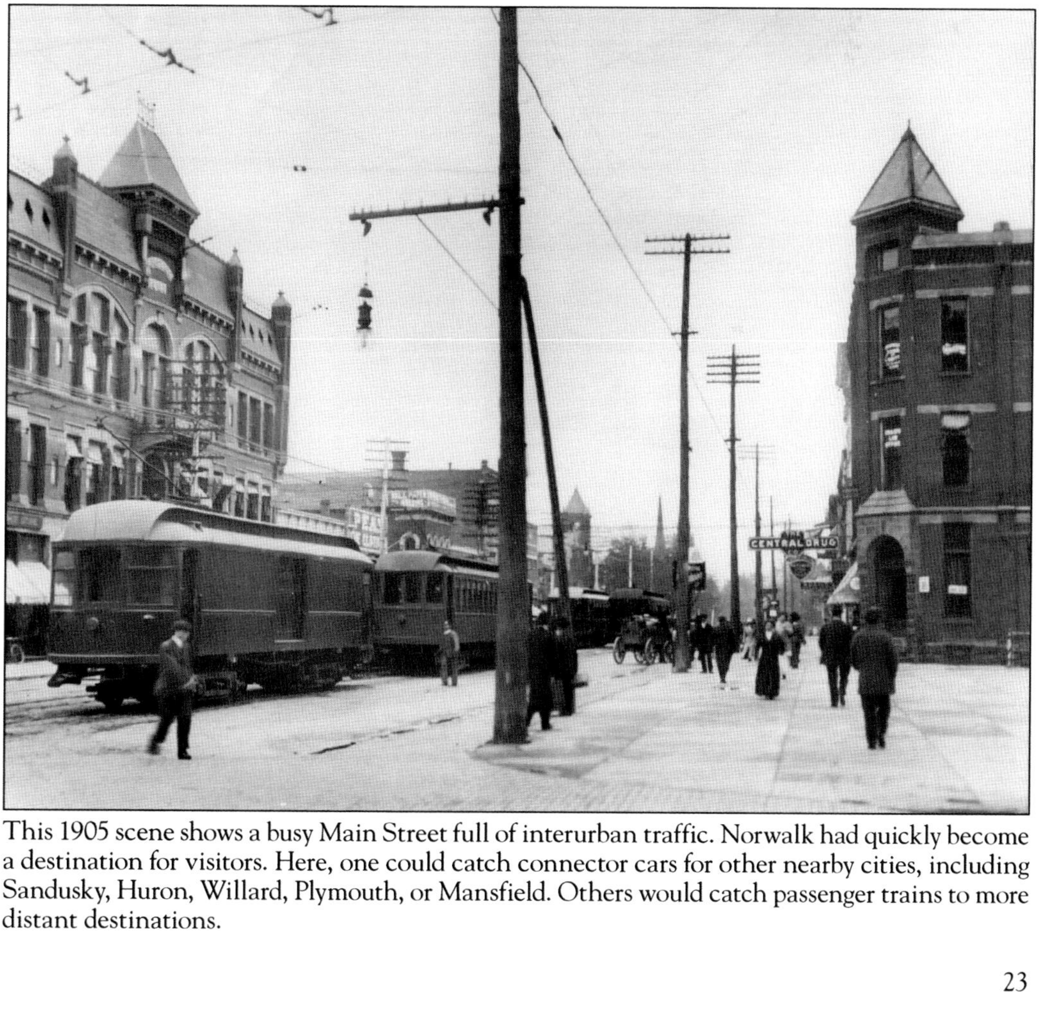


This 1905 scene shows a busy Main Street full of interurban traffic. Norwalk had quickly become a destination for visitors. Here, one could catch connector cars for other nearby cities, including Sandusky, Huron, Willard, Plymouth, or Mansfield. Others would catch passenger trains to more distant destinations.

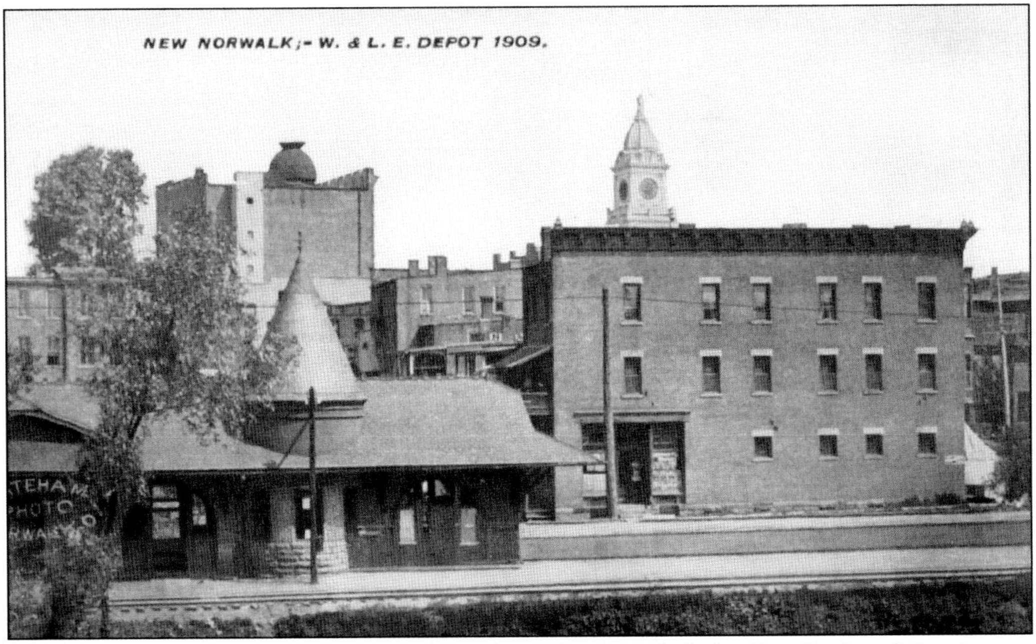


Here is an unusual view of the city from the Wheeling & Lake Erie Railroad Station on Benedict Avenue.

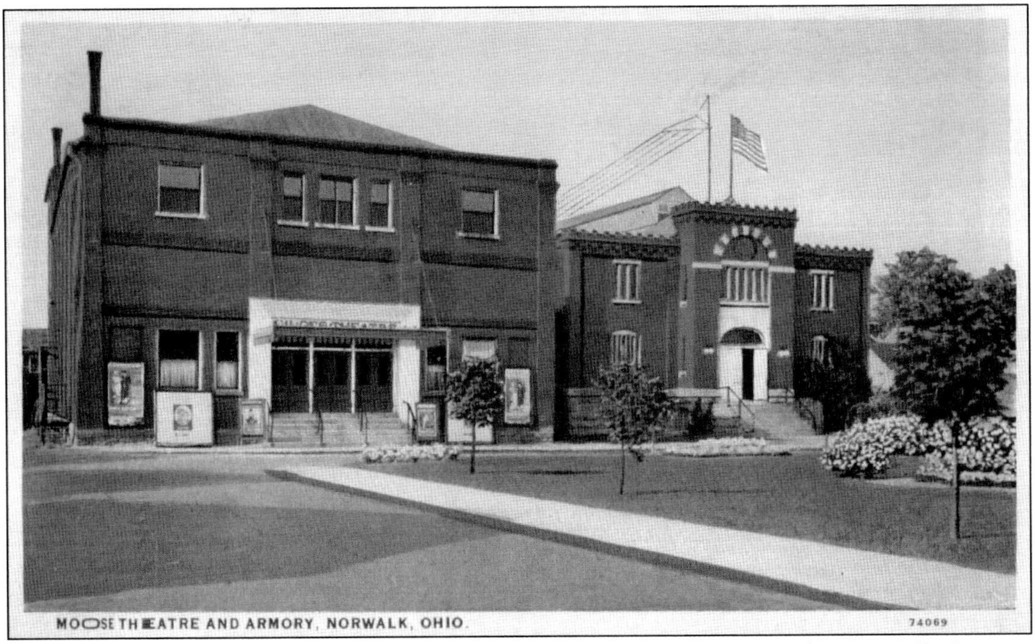


The redbrick Gilger Theater was located at 34 Monroe Street, next to the Norwalk Armory building, and was built in 1903 by William Gilger. It had a large stage and excellent orchestra, which attracted many theater companies. Live drama eventually gave way to silent movies. Sometime after World War I, it was sold to the Norwalk Moose Lodge, which continued to run it as a movie theater until it was sold to the Schine movie chain. It ceased to exist after the new Shine Theater was built on West Main in 1941. It later was used for businesses, and due to a welder's torch, the building burned to the ground in 1959.

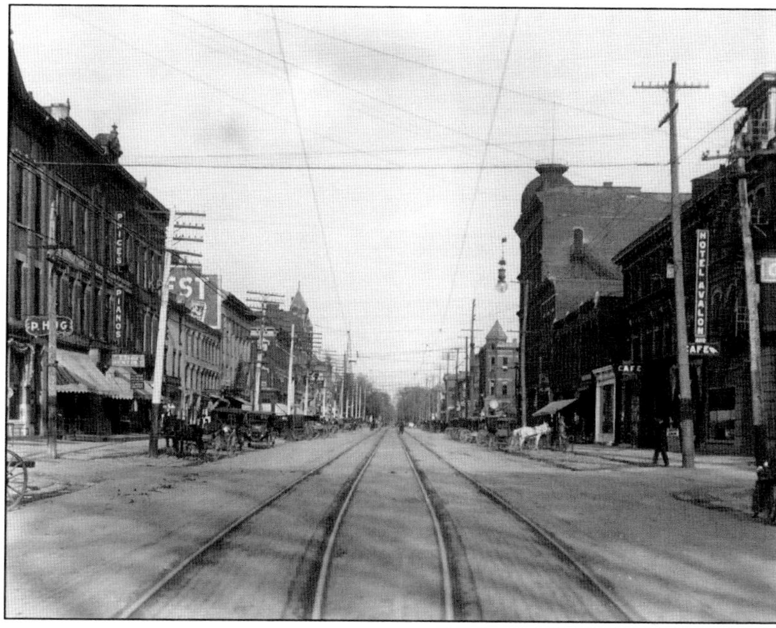


This scene looks east on Main Street in 1909. The St. Charles Hotel has become the Avalon Hotel. The Glass Block Building dominates the skyline.

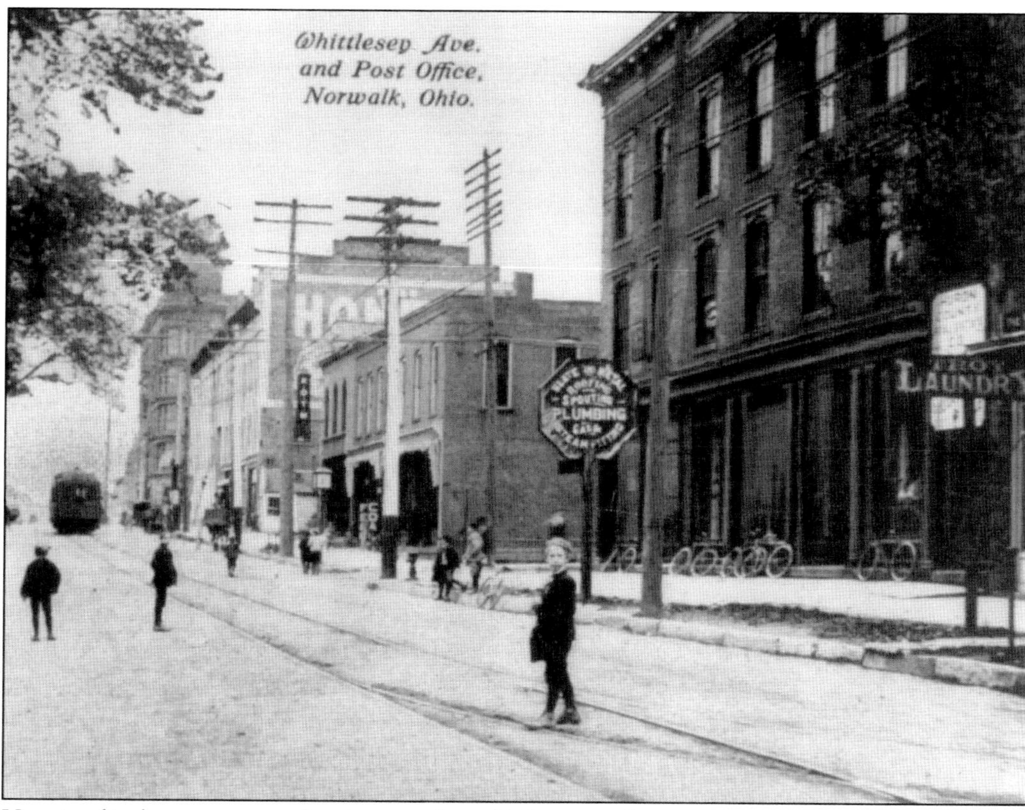


Here is a lively street scene showing carefree children watching a passing interurban car in 1902. This looks south on Whittlesey Avenue to Main Street.

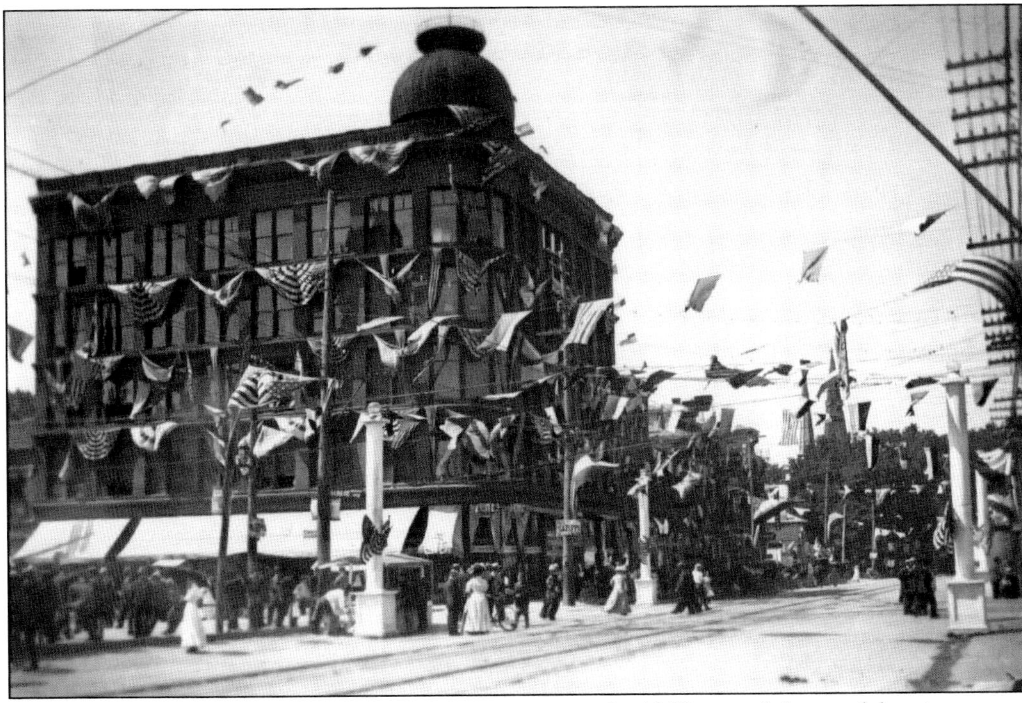

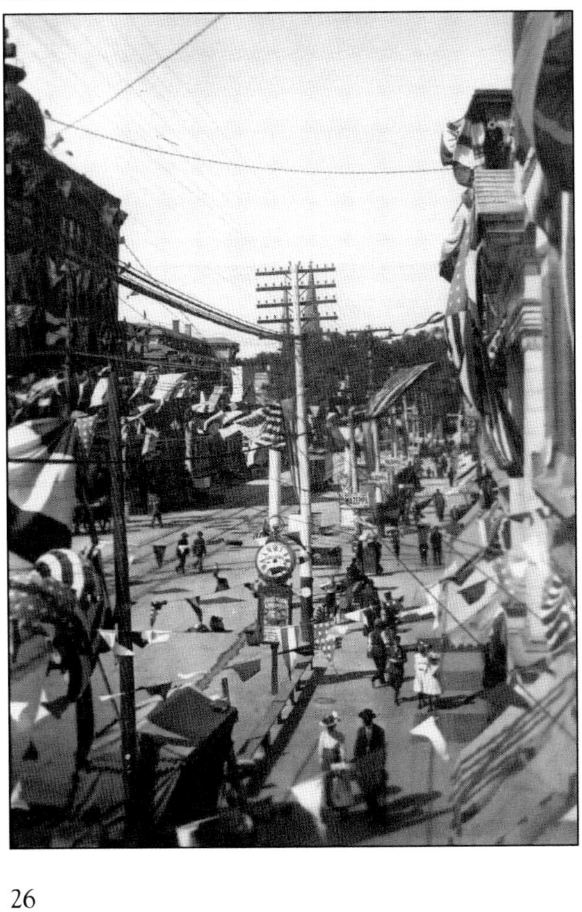

In 1909, a week-long celebration took place in Norwalk from July 18 to 25. It was to commemorate the founding of the first permanent settlement in Norwalk Township, of which Norwalk is a part.

Looking west on Main Street, it appears that all stores are celebrating in 1909, including the Glass Block Building.

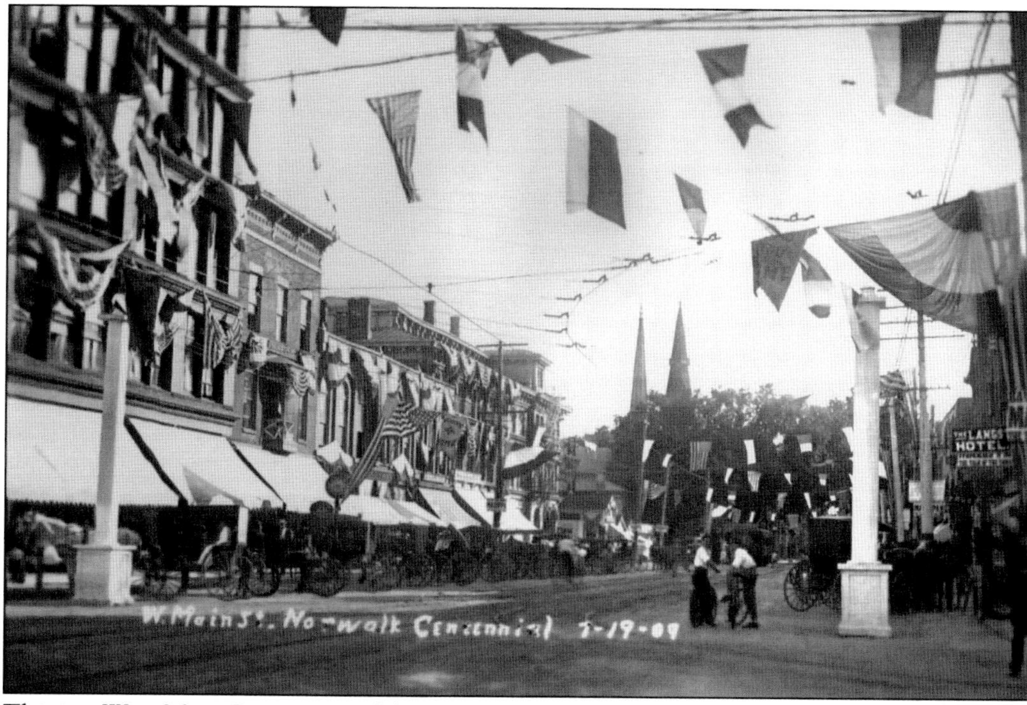


This is a West Main Street view of the centennial in 1909.

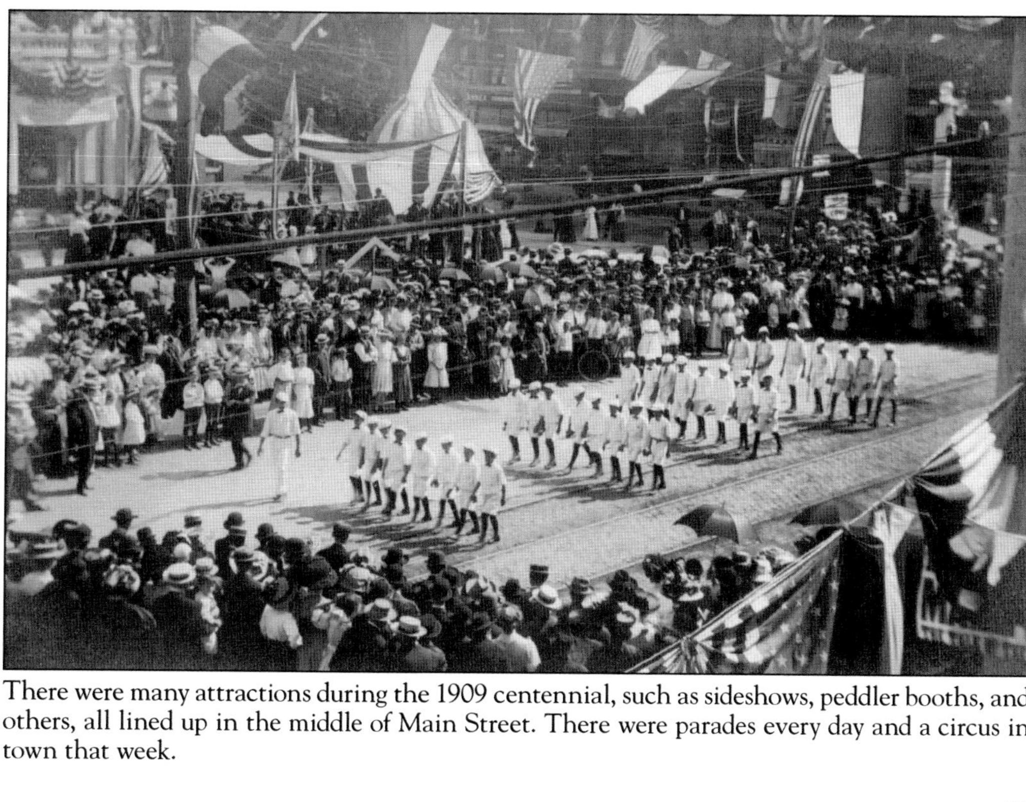

There were many attractions during the 1909 centennial, such as sideshows, peddler booths, and others, all lined up in the middle of Main Street. There were parades every day and a circus in town that week.

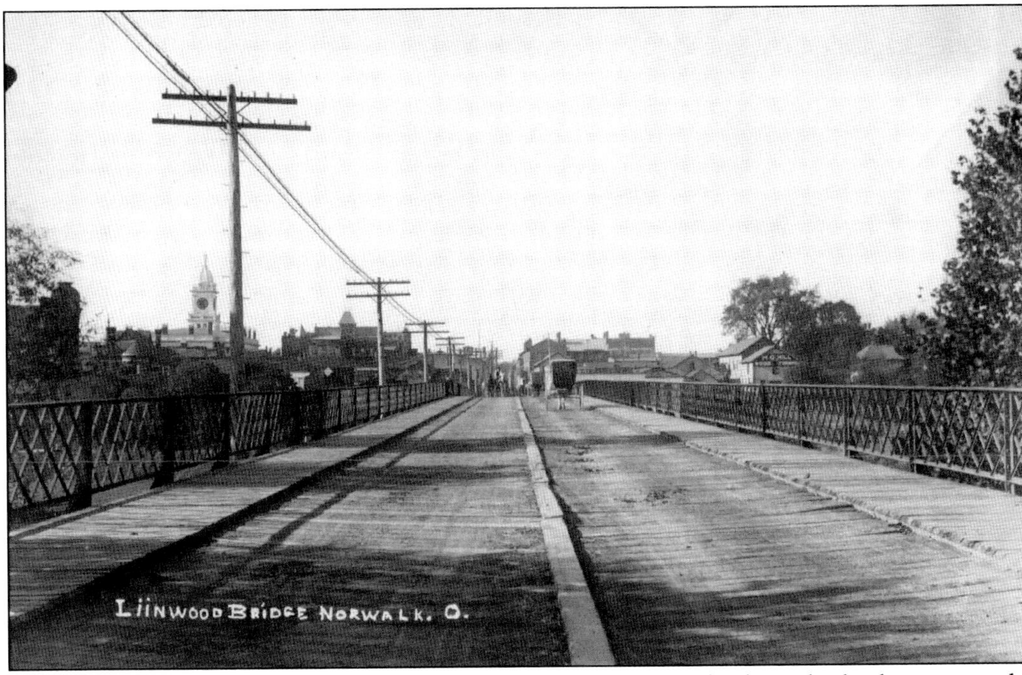


This is a peaceful view of the Linwood Avenue, or "high level" bridge. The bridge crosses the industrial area above Water Street. The skyline is beautifully captured here.

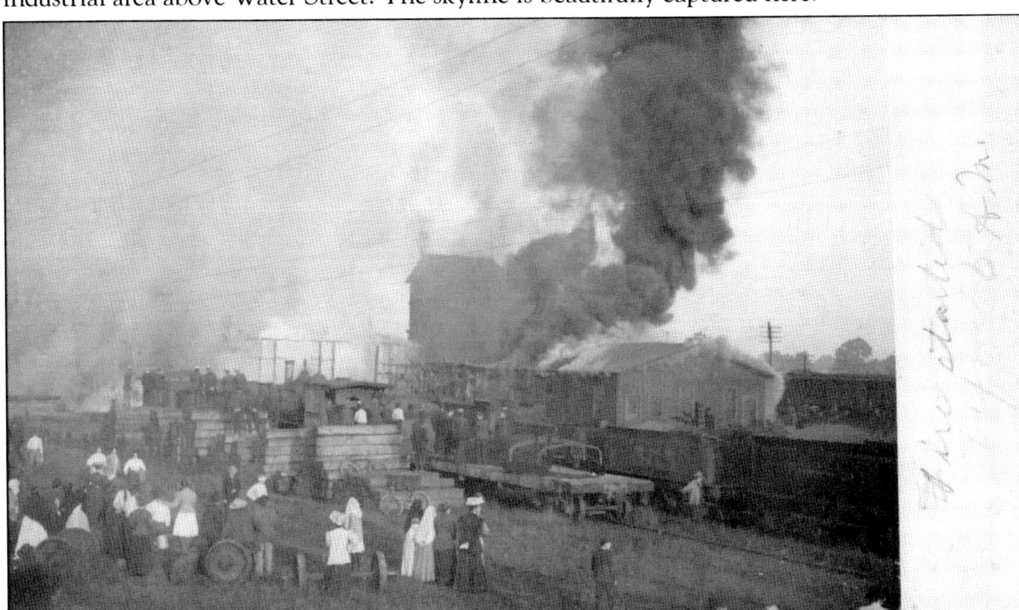

A true disaster struck the city around 5:00 a.m. on August 24, 1908, when fire nearly destroyed all of the Wheeling & Lake Erie Railroad shops. The fire was believed to have started in the blacksmith shop. The railroad shops were built in 1877 between Pleasant and North West Streets. They employed around 400 people, and because Norwalk was the division point in the line, many of the trainmen made Norwalk their home. After the fire, the company decided not to rebuild in Norwalk and moved the operation to Brewster, Ohio.

Tragedy strikes as the Huron County Courthouse was burned in a fire in 1912. This marked the beginning of changes to the skyline. This amazing photograph shows the clock tower in flames.

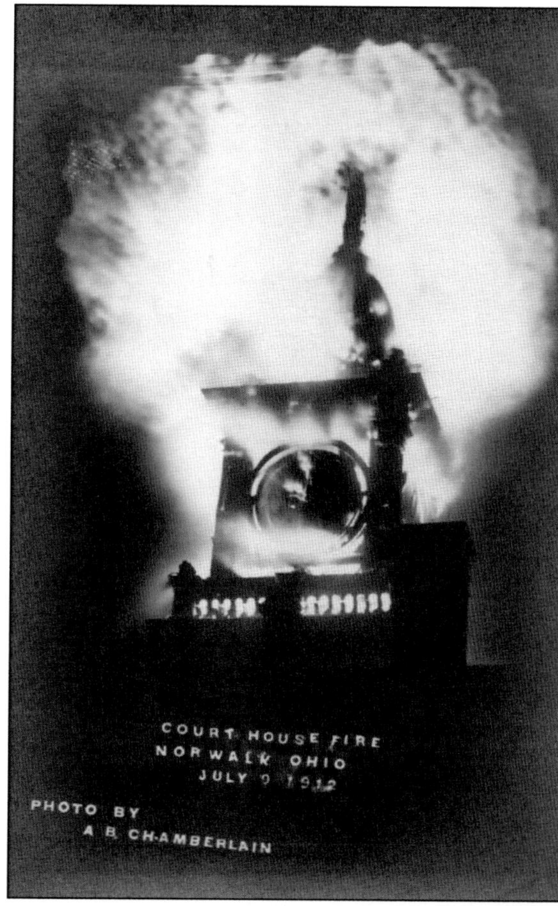


Curious onlookers stare in disbelief at the ruins of the courthouse. Daily life continued despite the tragedy.

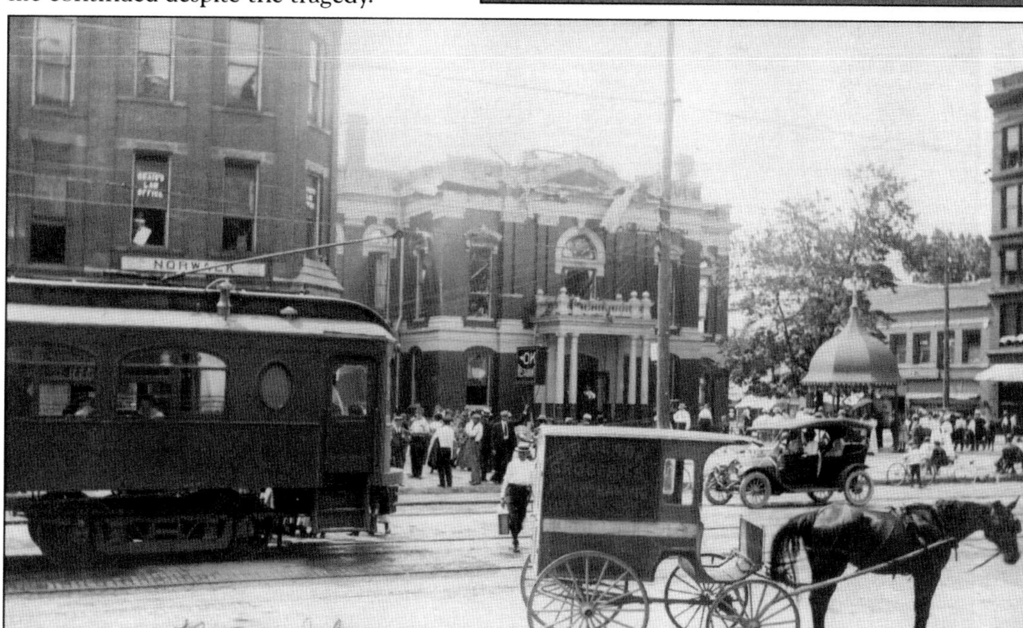

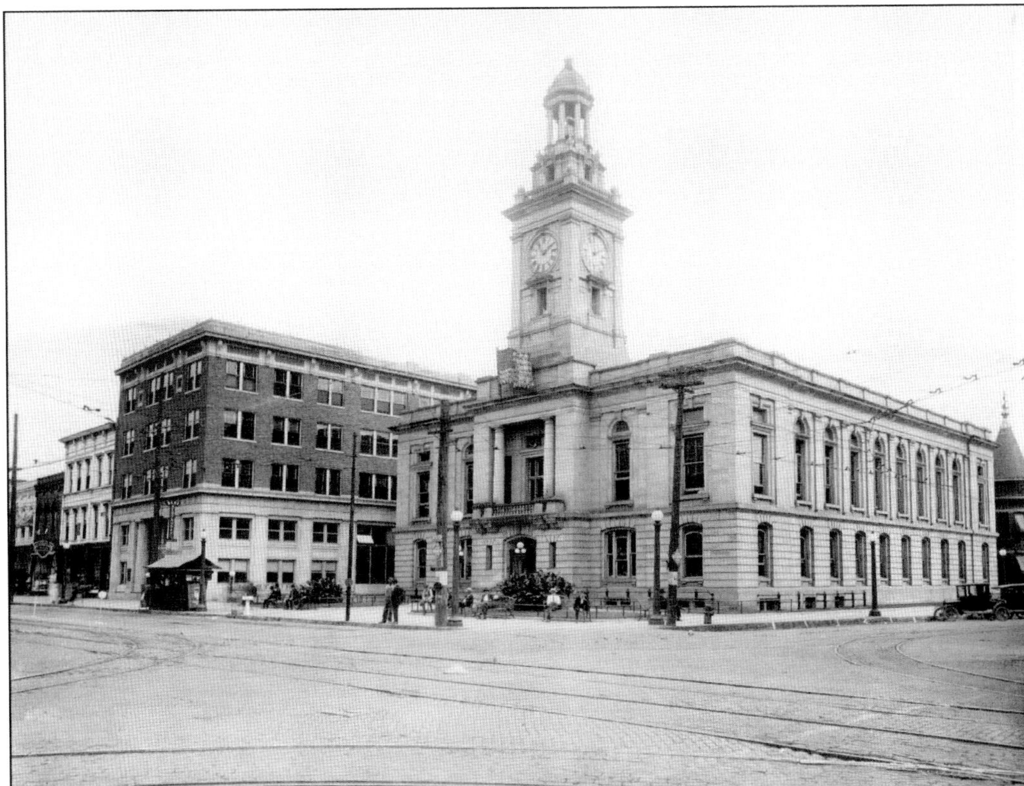

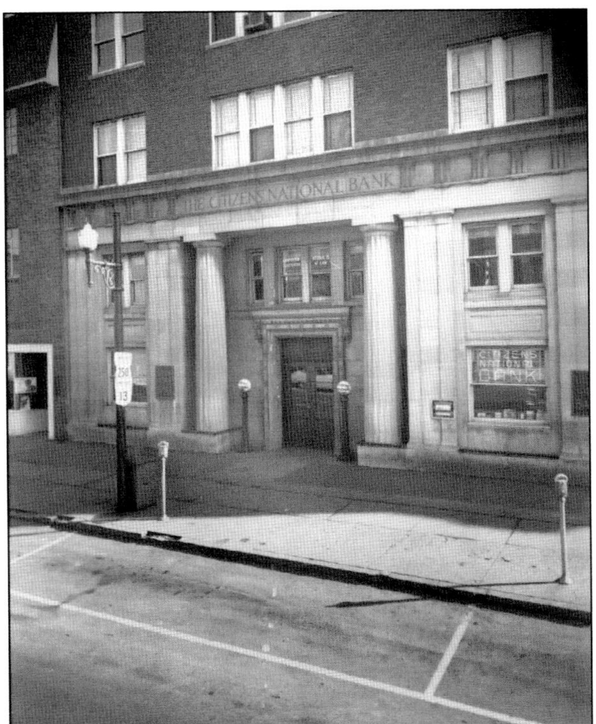


In 1913, the third Huron County Courthouse arose from the ashes. The new courthouse updated the older Victorian style to a more modern Neoclassical style that has become a symbol of the city itself. The illuminated electric flag proudly shines over the square.

This is the new Citizens National Bank of Norwalk, which opened in about 1922. The Neoclassical entrance gives the building a commanding presence on Main Street. The Doric columns match the courthouse.

Just across the street, tucked neatly between B.C. Taber and the Gardiner Building, is the Huron County Banking Co. It was a wonderful Neoclassical structure. Its eye-catching Ionic columns offered a sense of the wealth and prestige of the growing city.

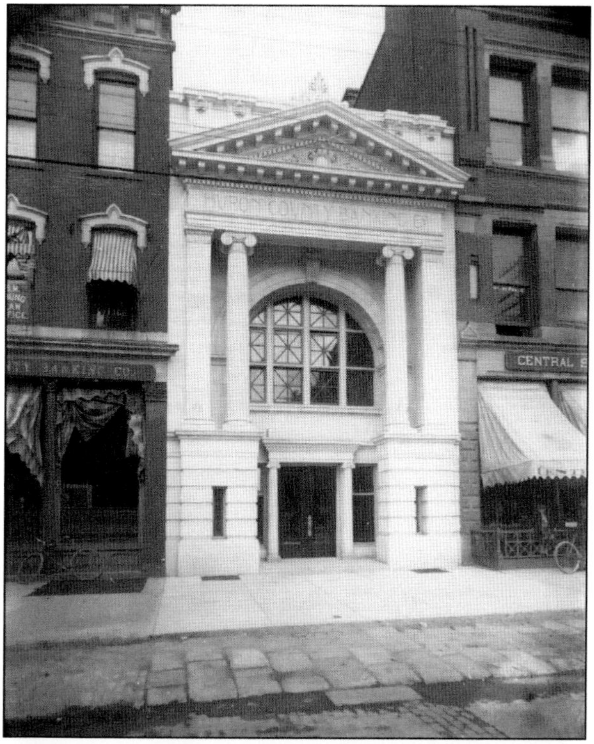


The Huron County Bank eventually expanded to the first floor of the Gardiner Building. Here, Norwalk businessmen Worthington Pratt and Ben Wood enjoy a friendly chat in 1930.

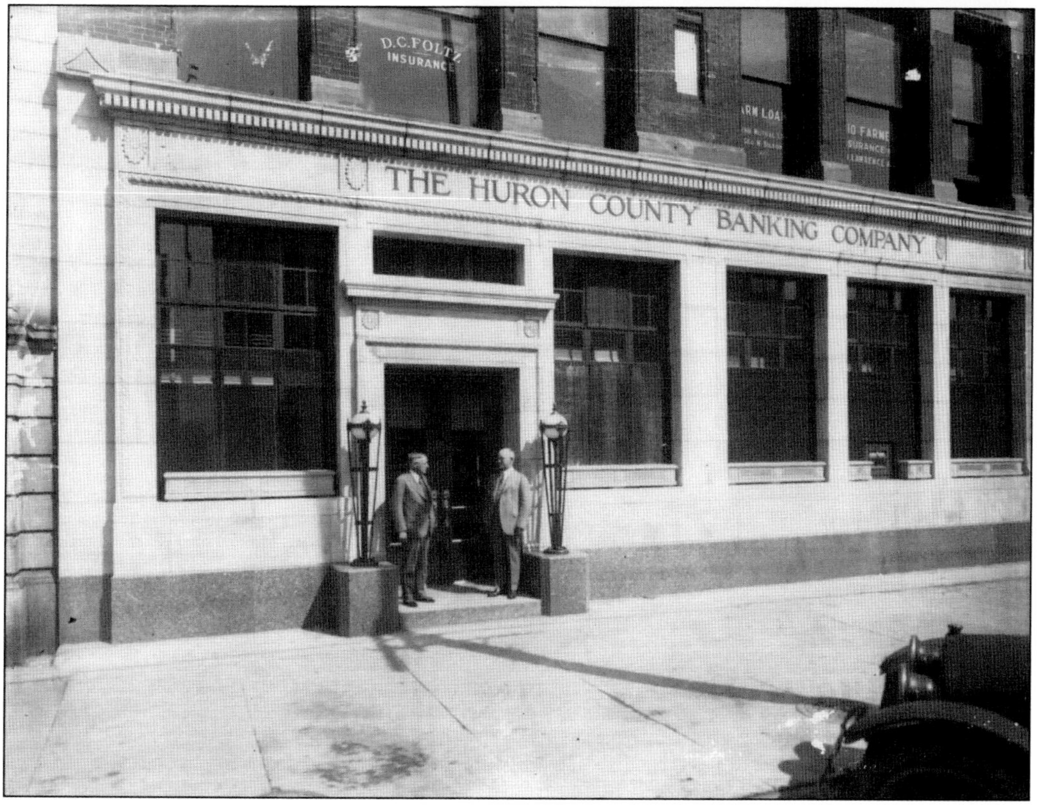

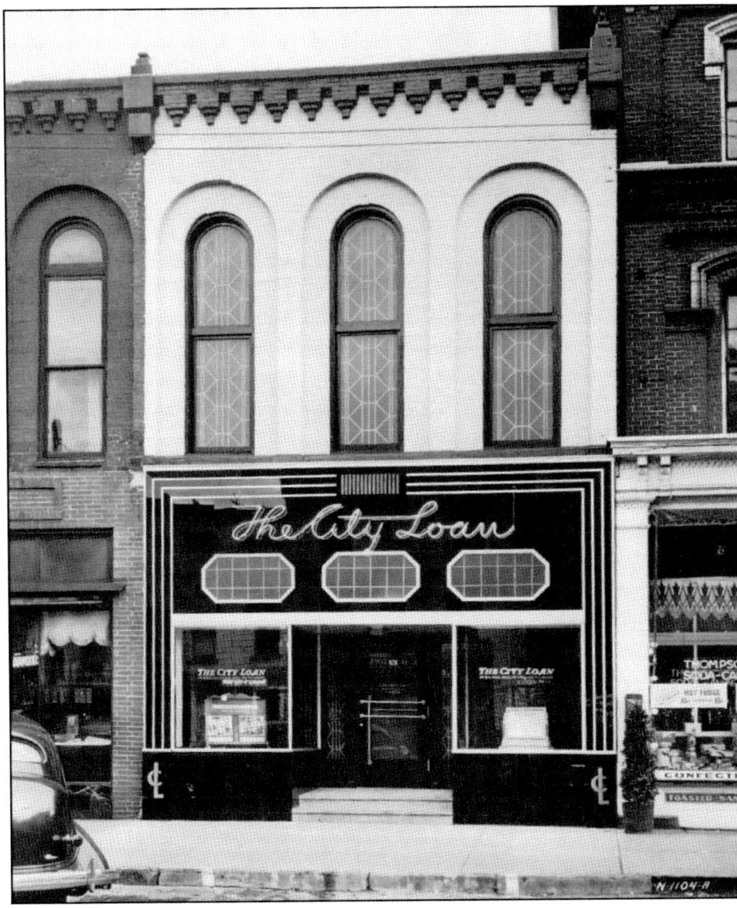


The City Loan proudly stood on West Main Street around 1940. It brought with it a modern Art Deco facade to a nearly century old Victorian building. It is faced with structural glass block, which gave the building a sleek and shiny appearance.

This c. 1920 postcard shows the Linwood Avenue bridge with the new courthouse towering over the skyline.

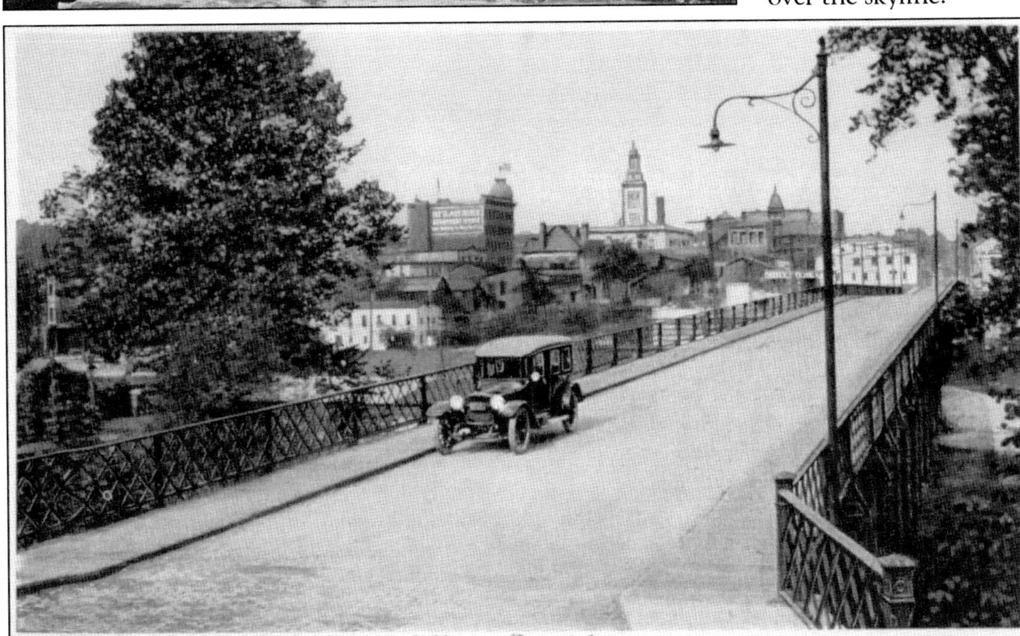

On Sunday, August 5, 1923, at 12:30 p.m., workmen were filling the carbide-ammonia container of a Glass Block Building refrigeration unit under the sidewalk on West Main Street. The substance exploded, killing Leo Schlacter and Charles Whitter. Elizabeth Sipple was waiting for a streetcar to take her to West Main Street and was thrown into the basement wreckage and died the next day. The building was badly damaged, with many windows shattered. The store operated a few more years and eventually closed.

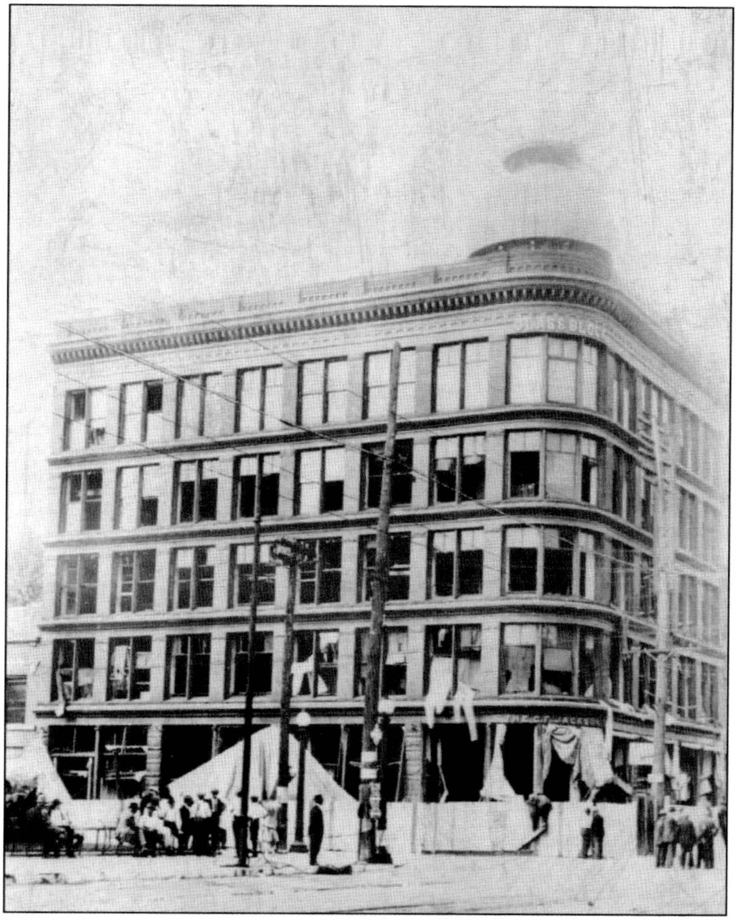

This was the aftermath of the Glass Block explosion. This was a big setback for the growing city.

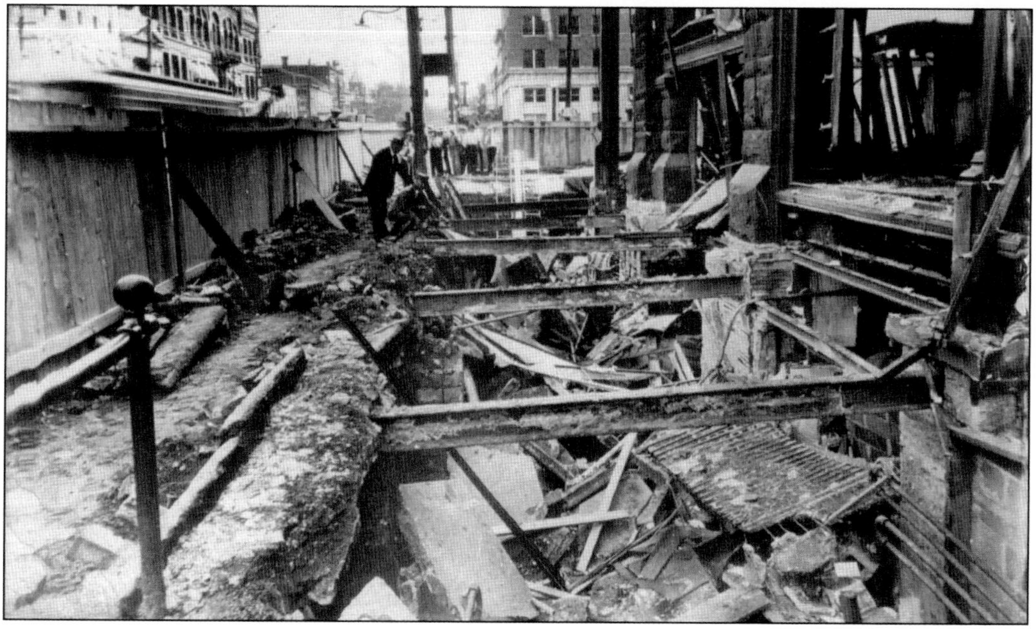

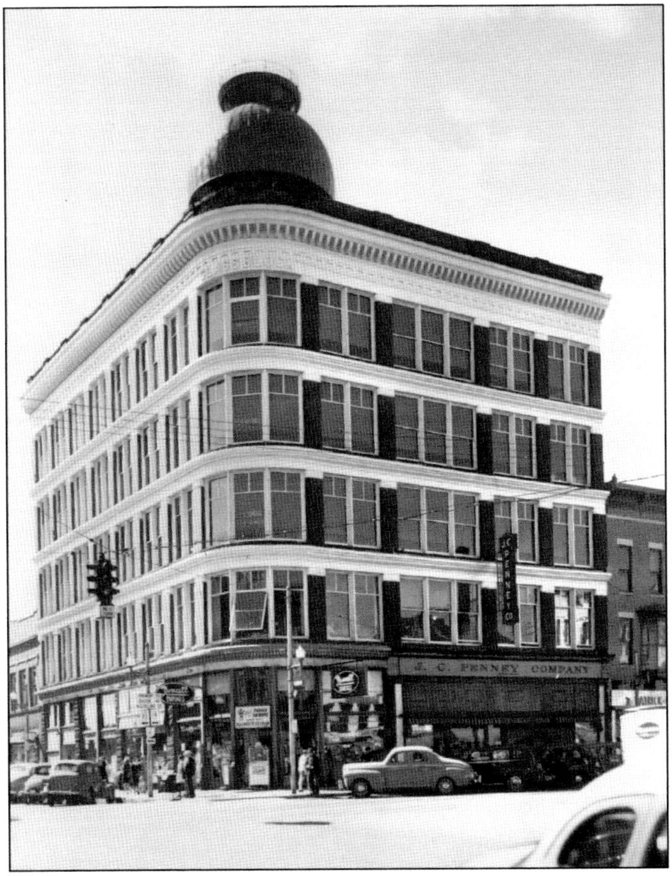


Here is the Glass Block Building in the 1940s, patched up with a coat of white paint. The J.C. Penney Company occupied the first floor for a few years, as did Rexall Drug. A raincoat factory occupied the upper floors for a time. In 1950, the dome was removed. In 1952, the top three floors were removed, as the structure became unstable. In 1959, a fire damaged the basement and first floor. The building is still standing; however, it has dramatically changed.

In this view looking out over East Main Street at the courthouse square is the progressive, modern city filled with automobiles. The buildings have an elegant and sophisticated presence. The new structures harmonize well with the older ones. On the right, Taber and Risk had become B.C. Taber, with an ornate canopy above the entryway.

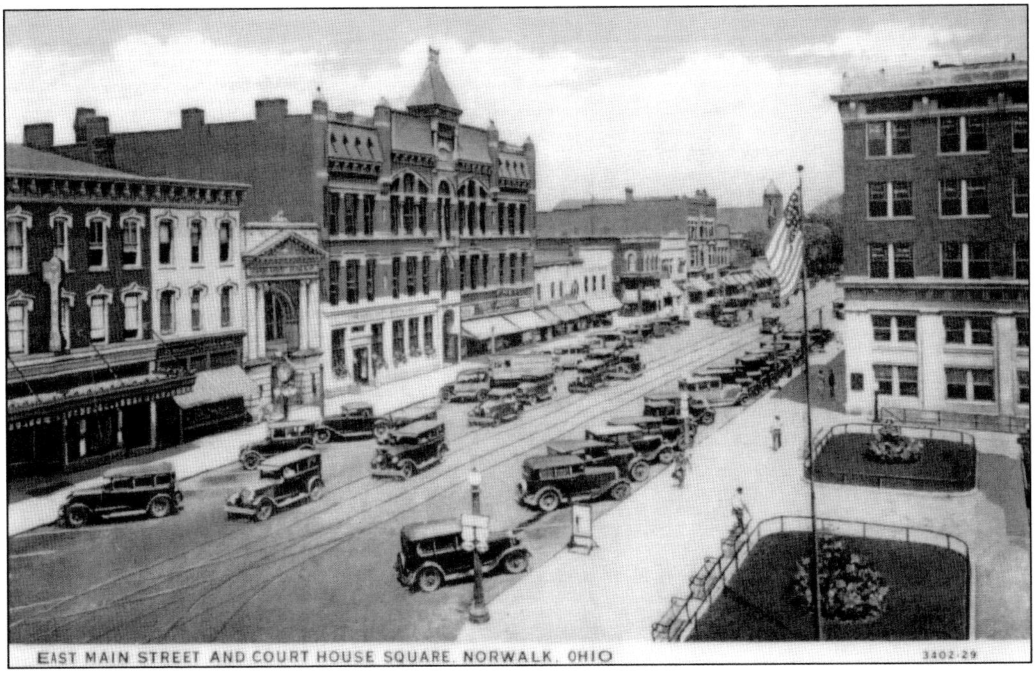

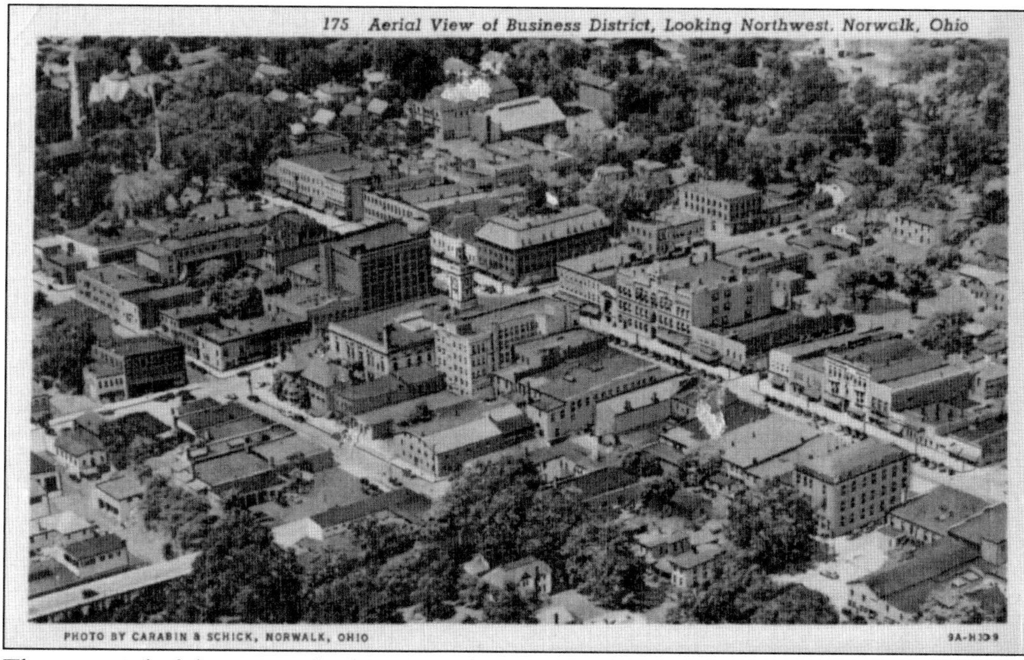


This postcard of the city in the late 1930s shows the progress of the blossoming metropolis.

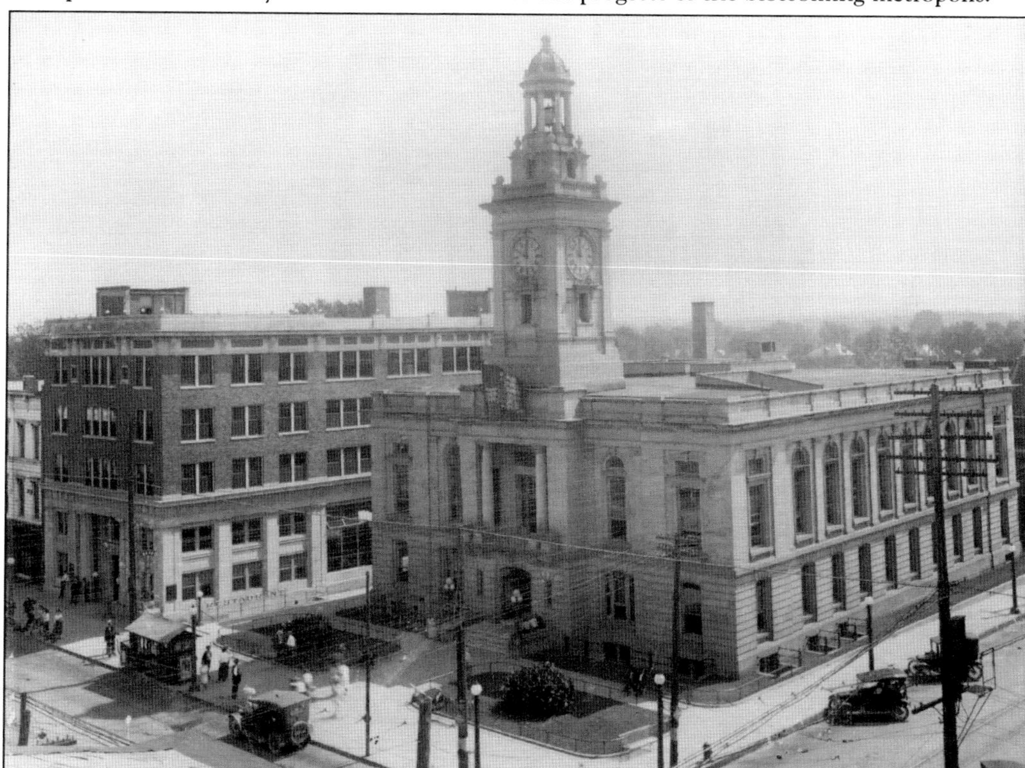

The courthouse proudly looks over the square. Notice the cars parked on Benedict Avenue. Traffic control was still minimal in the 1920s.

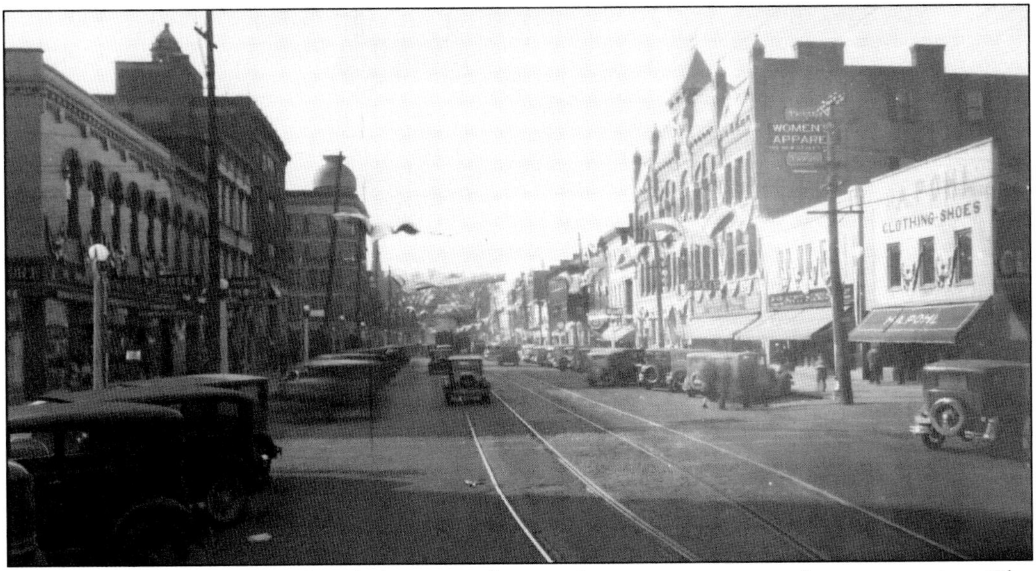


The automobile quickly replaced the interurban as the primary means of transportation. The tracks are still there, yet they would soon become a thing of the past. Many of the businesses seen here prospered in the city for decades.

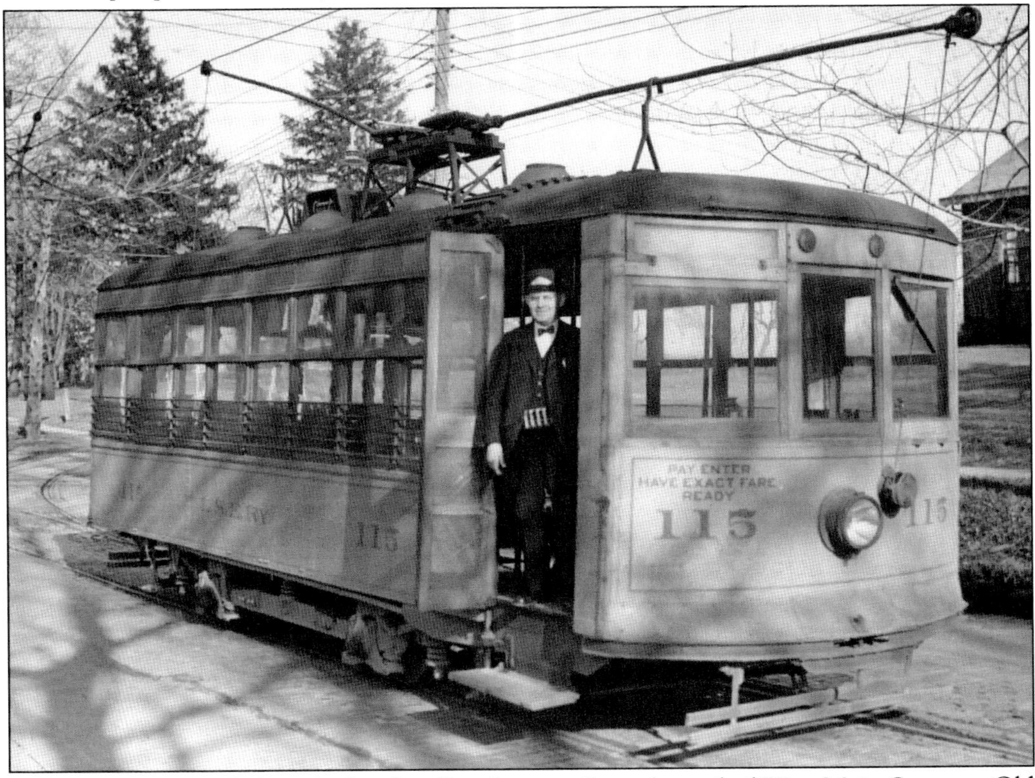


This is Norwalk' s "dinky," the local trolley that ran from the end of West Main Street to Old State Road on East Main Street. Fred Gassman was the motorman from 1905 until its last day on May, 15, 1938. It operated every half hour from 6:30 a.m. to 11:00 p.m. The fare was a nickel or six rides for a quarter. Exact change was required.

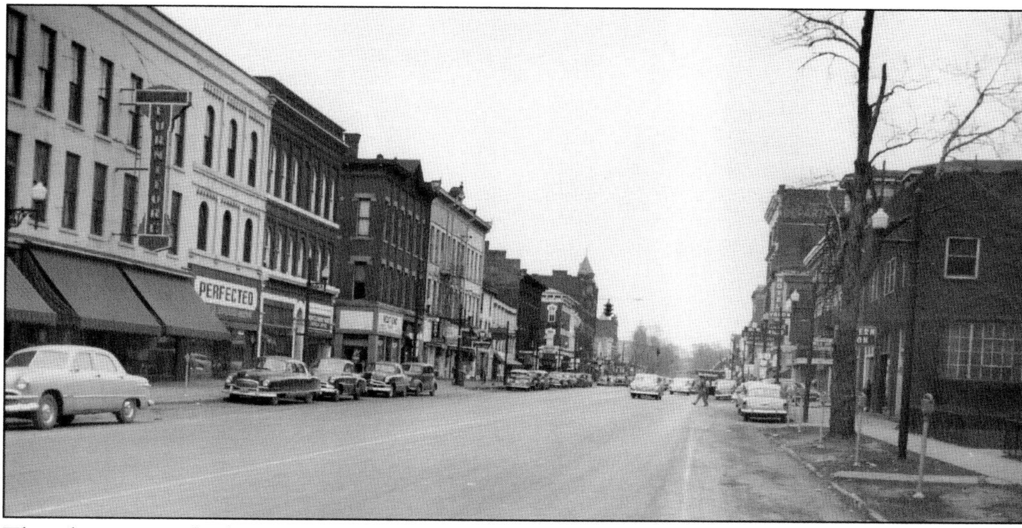


This sleepy view looking east on Main Street is one of the few street scenes with light traffic. This was possibly taken during World War II or just after.

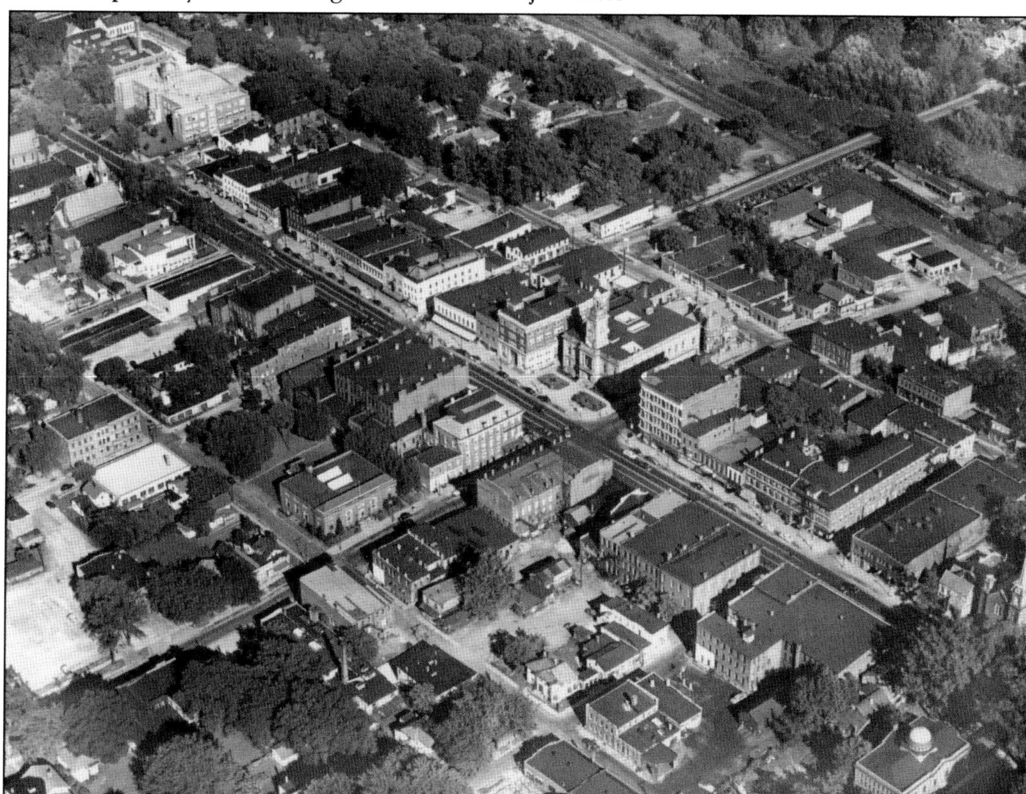

Looking southeast, this splendid view shows the city in the early 1950s, as the Glass Block Building has its dome removed. The city blocks are filled with buildings. Parking was at a premium. The urban center was compact and tidy. This image shows just how large the Avalon Hotel was, as Hester Street ran to West Seminary Street, and the hotel ran its length. The city had a lot of green space as well, with many maple trees.

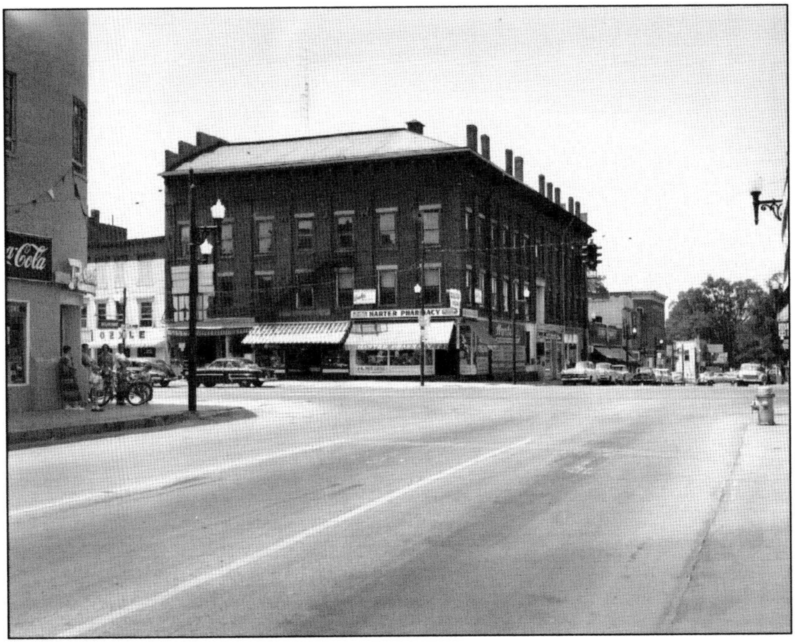

Pictured around 1950, the Glass Block Building is now two stories, and the Whittlesey Building across the street would soon have its third floor removed. Harter Pharmacy still occupies the corner of Whittlesey Avenue and Main Street.

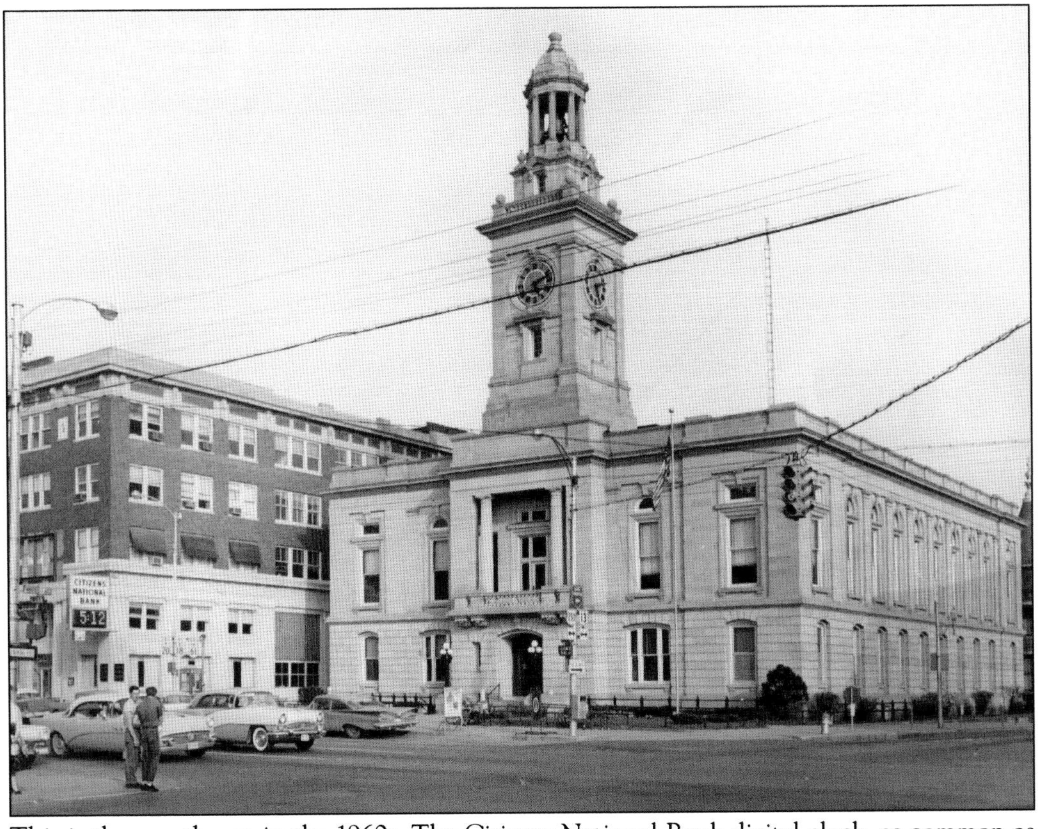


This is the courthouse in the 1960s. The Citizens National Bank digital clock, as common as it is today, was quite the novelty when it was introduced. Another note of interest are the four segments on the traffic signal. The bottom one was the walk light, which also buzzed.

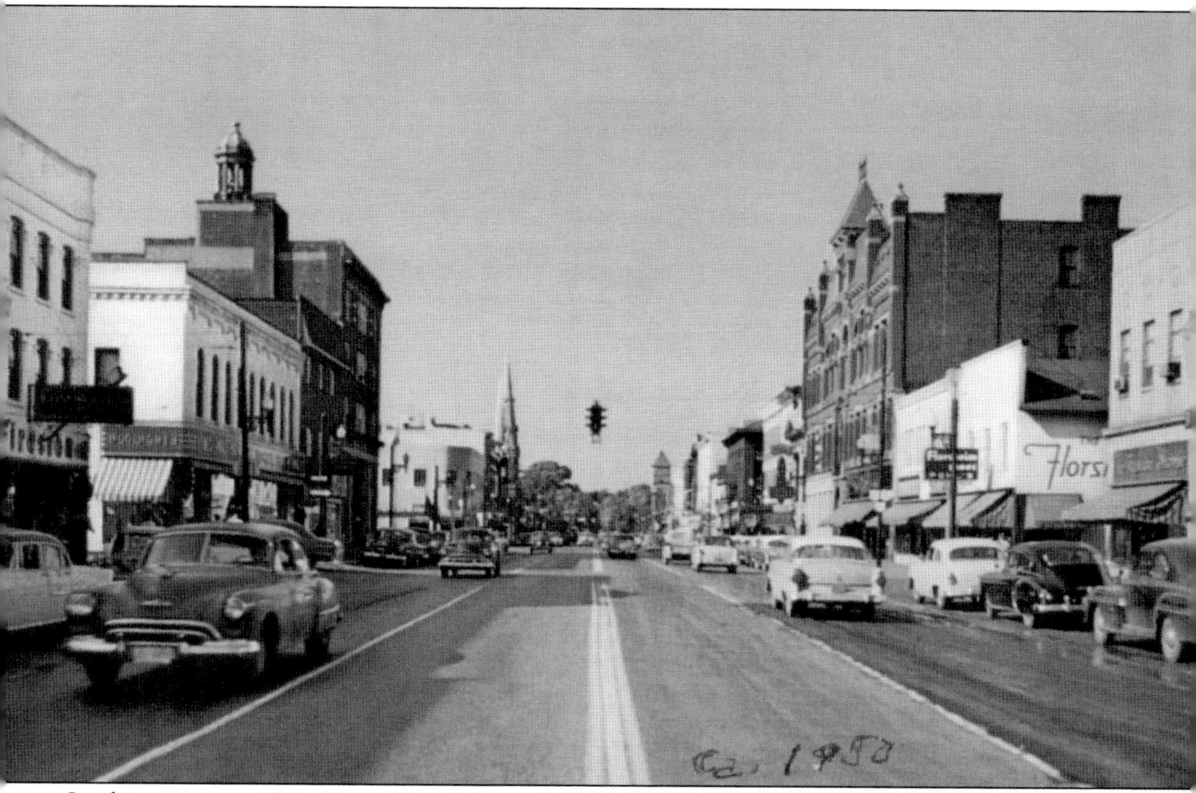


Looking west on Main Street from Linwood Avenue are many familiar businesses. Woolworth, Firestone, Pohl's, and Florsheim Shoes dot the commercial district. Later, the retail center would move to the north of the city. The church spires on the right are the only thing missing today. Otherwise, it is heavy traffic as usual with four lanes on Main Street.

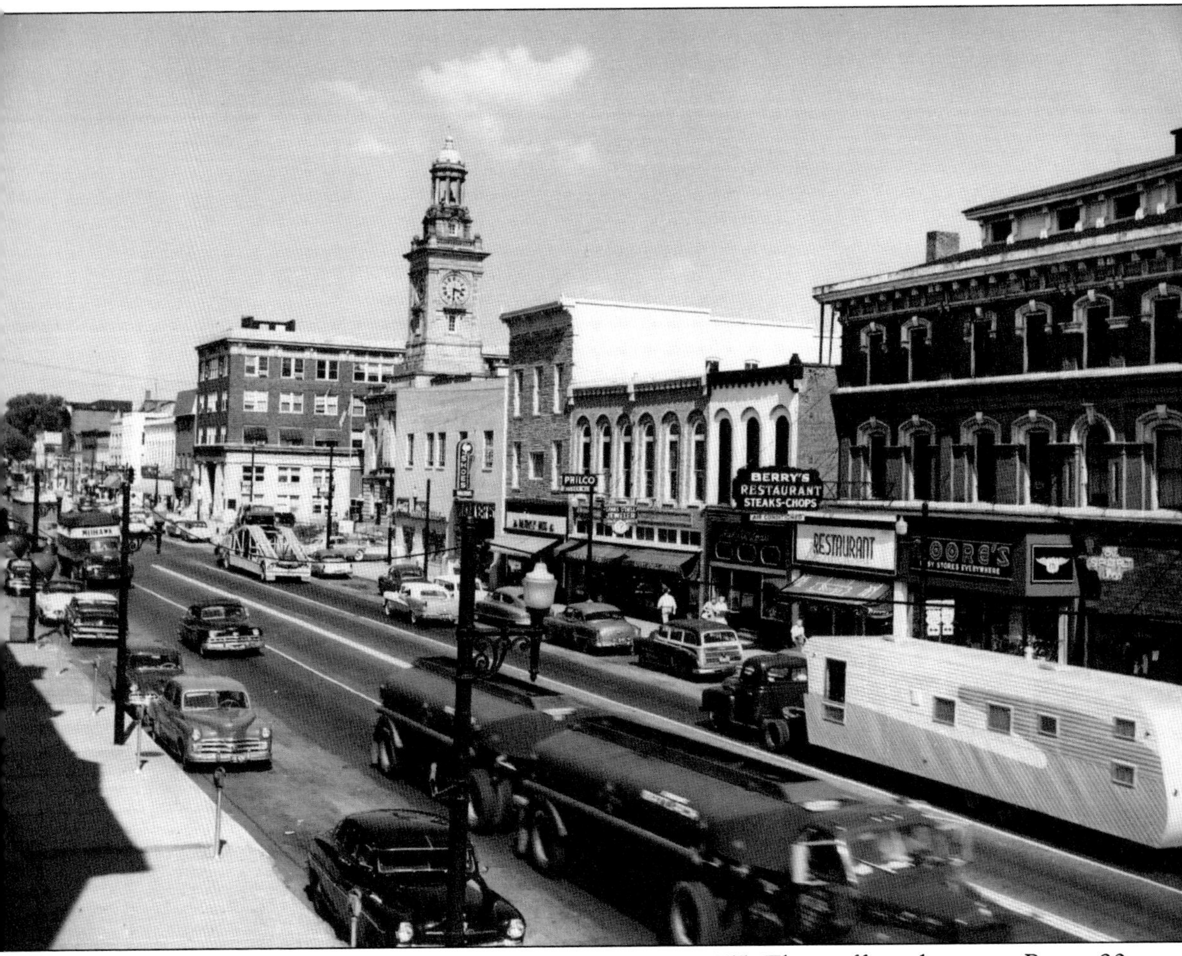


Here is another view looking east on Main Street in 1955. The traffic is heavy as Route 20 runs through the center of town. This shows the vital local economy booming downtown. A few years later, the bypass would change the flow, and crossing the street would not seem so intimidating.

# *Four*

# Goods and Services

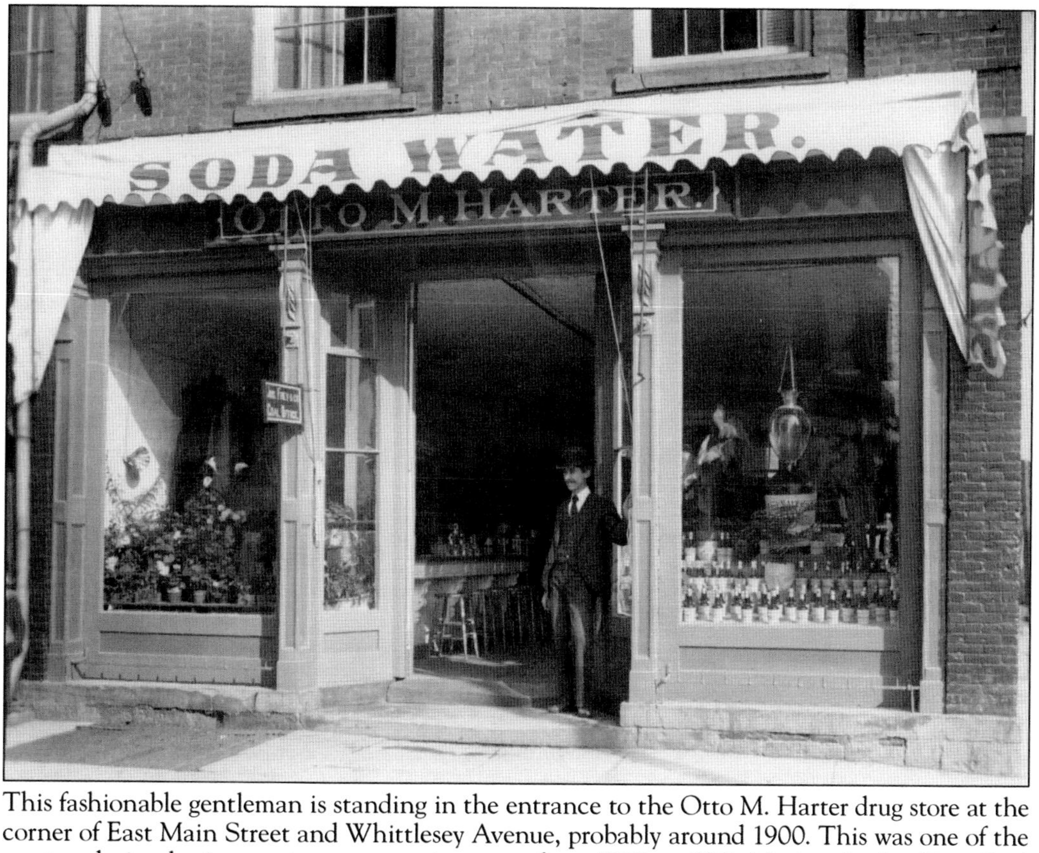


This fashionable gentleman is standing in the entrance to the Otto M. Harter drug store at the corner of East Main Street and Whittlesey Avenue, probably around 1900. This was one of the most enduring businesses in town, staying open from 1897 to 1962. Notice the Jos. Frey Coal sign to the right of the doorway.

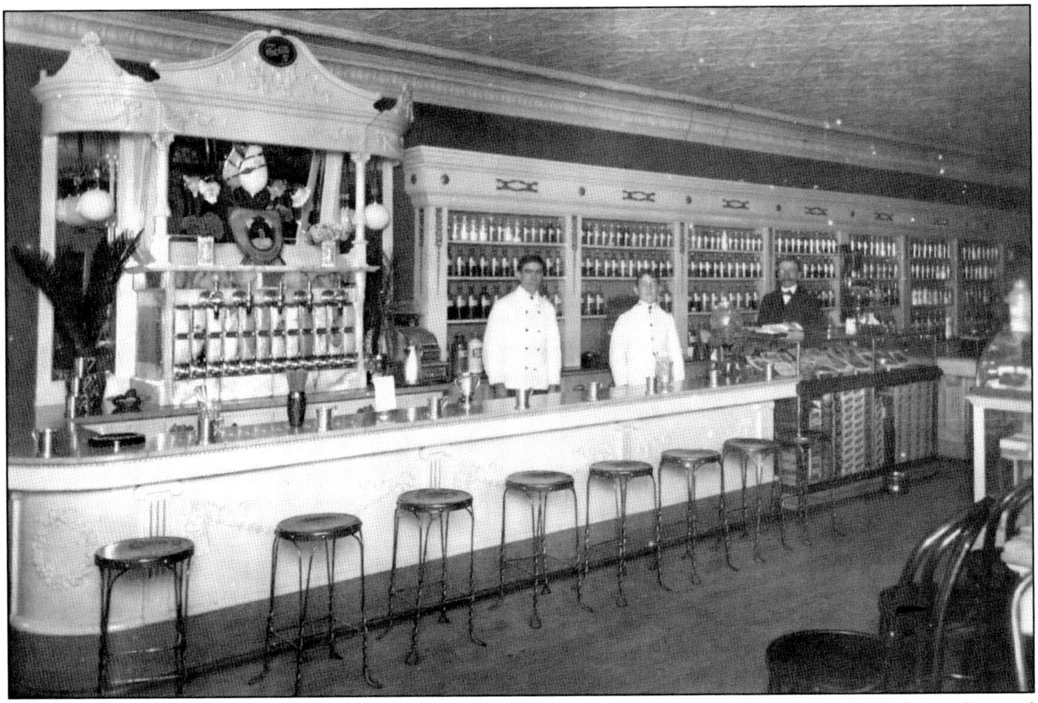

This is what Harter Drug looked like from inside. The soda fountain is prominent, with uniformed staff to serve refreshments.

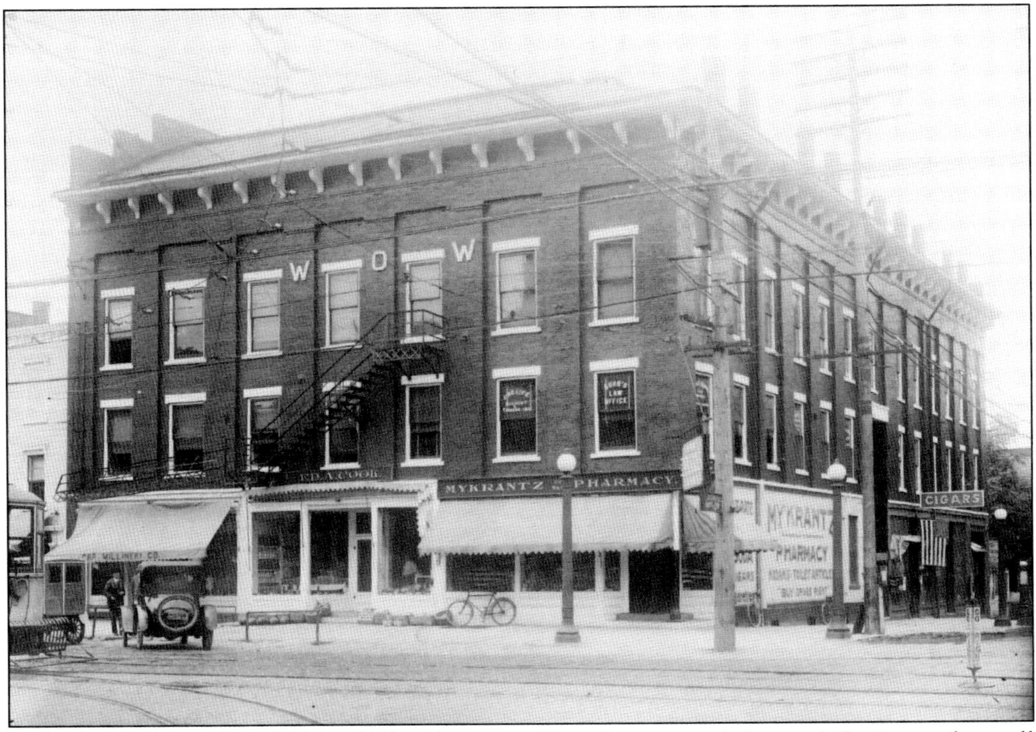


This is the Whittlesey Block with the pharmacy. Bicycles, automobiles, and the interurban, all pictured here, were the primary modes of transportation in the city.

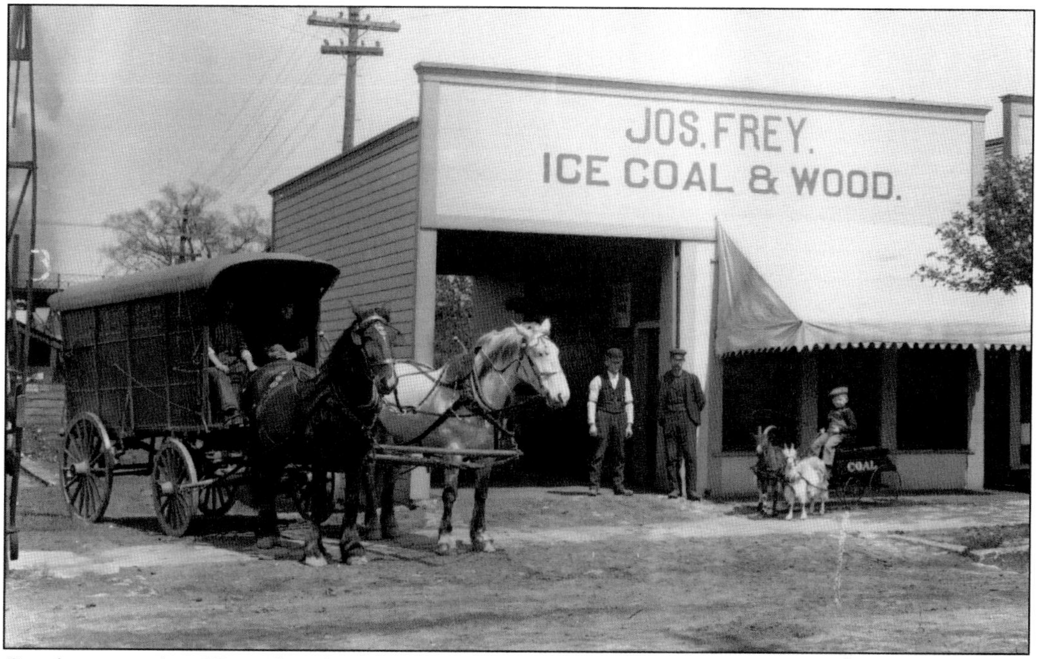


On the east side of Benedict Avenue was Jos. Frey. Ice Coal & Wood. These commodities were vital to life in early 20th century Norwalk. Before the age of electricity, this was an expected delivery. Most of the ice came from Lake Erie when it was frozen each winter. It was stored in large underground vaults and distributed all year. The little boy, Arthur Frey, with his goat wagon is a charming mascot for the company.

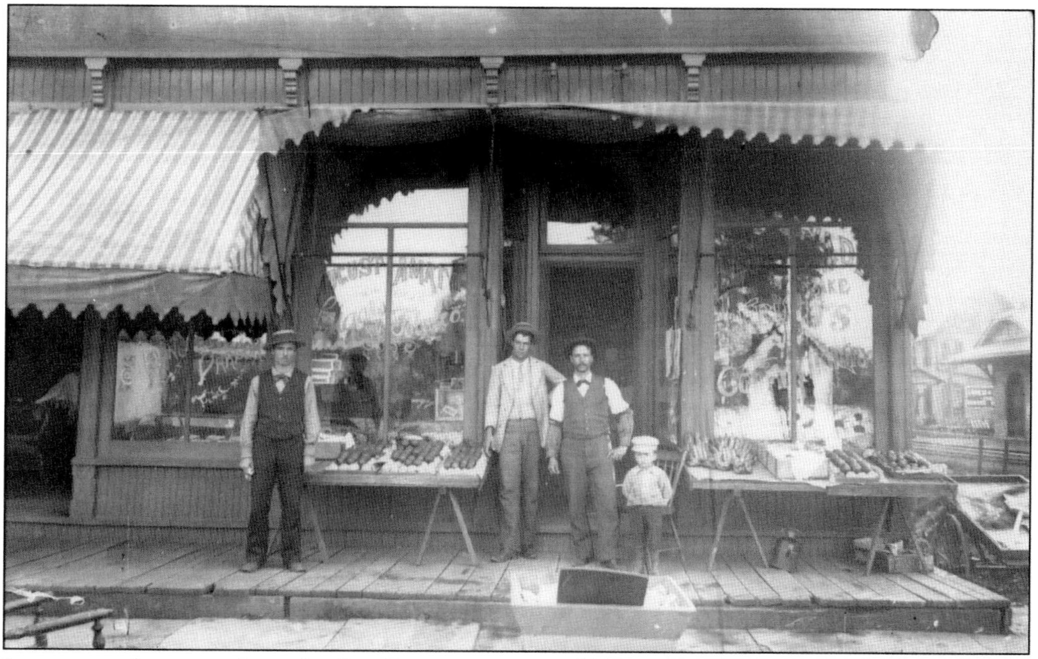

Just across the street from the Jos. Frey company at 54 Benedict Avenue was the fruit store of August Amato. A tantalizing arrangement of fruit is displayed on the street. On the far right is the Wheeling & Lake Erie Railroad station.

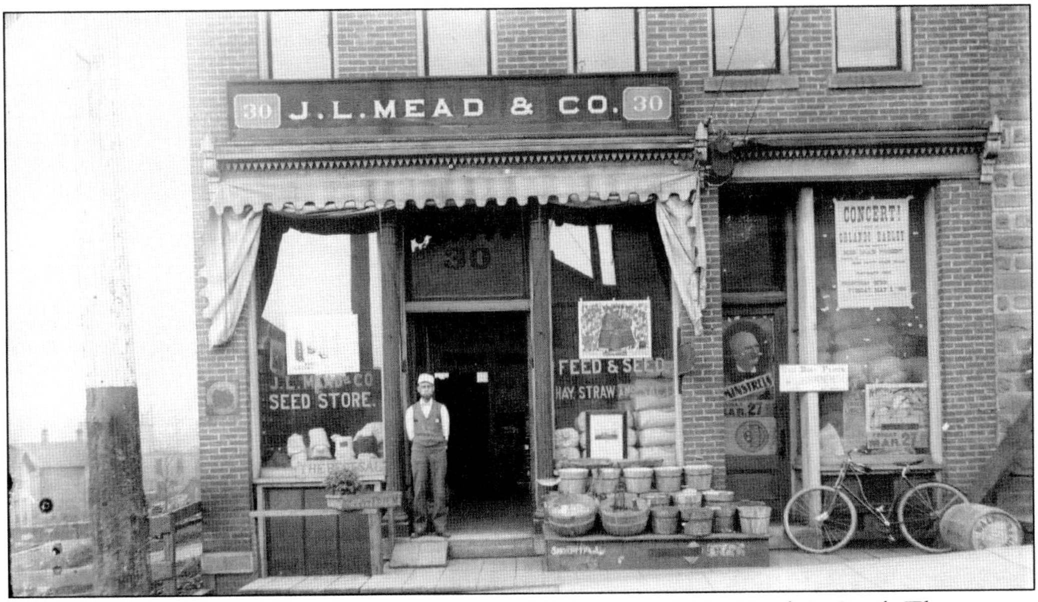


Just up the block at 30 Benedict Avenue was J.L Mead and Co. Feed & Seed. There is an advertisement for minstrel shows, which were common at the time.

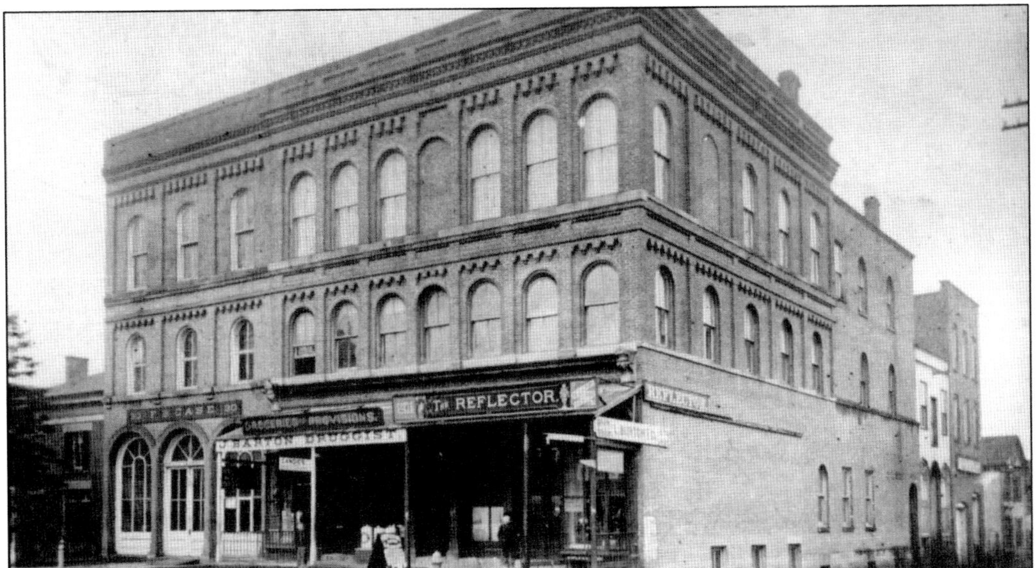


The *Huron Reflector* office was at one time located on the corner of West Main and North Hester Streets. The first issue of the *Huron Reflector* was published on February 2, 1830, by Samuel Preston and George Buckingham. The first office was at 9 West Main Street. In 1836, Preston built a house at 38 West Main Street (now the Firelands Museum) for his daughter Lucy, who had married Frederick Wickham. The family was to have the first floor and the basement for their use. The newspaper moved out of the house when both it and the growing family needed more room. At that time, Lucy's husband took over the editorship, and it stayed in the family until it was purchased by R.C. Snyder in 1913. The paper got its name from the reflection of a reflector lamp or candle that was seen on a wall. It was decided that *Huron Reflector* was a good name, as it would "reflect" the news.

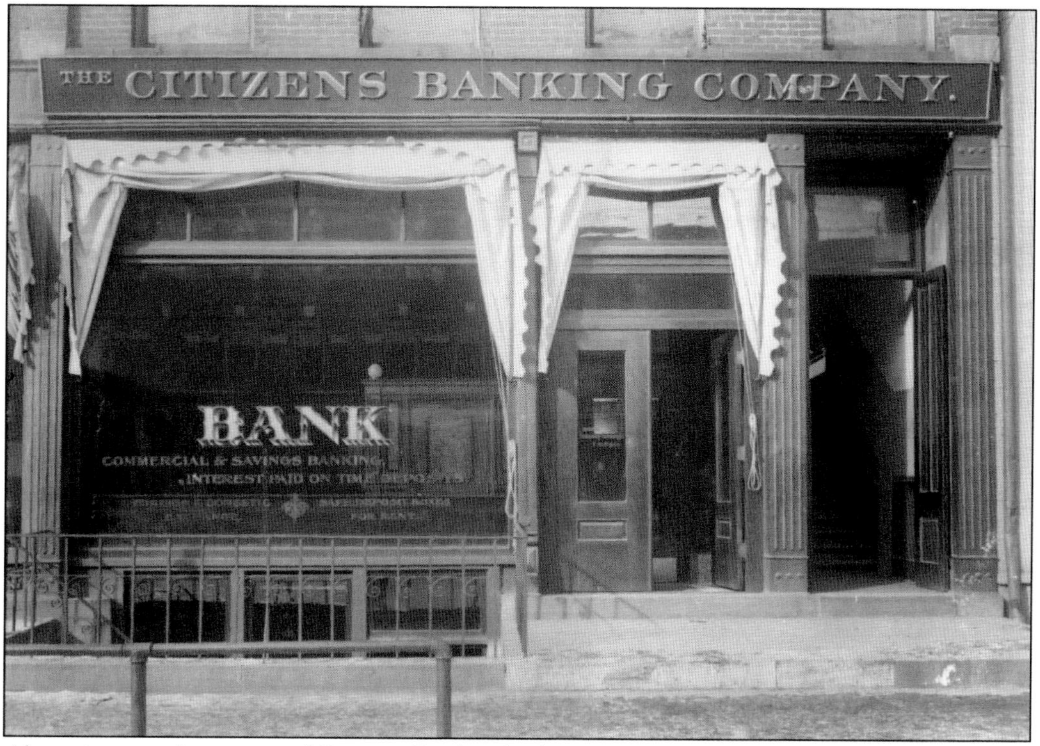


Above is an early picture of Citizens Bank, which opened in 1902 at 16 West Main Street. In December 1918, Citizens Bank absorbed the Norwalk National Bank, which was one of the strongest and oldest financial institutions in Ohio. A new building was erected at the old National Bank's location at 12 East Main Street. The bank opened in about 1922 as the Citizens National Bank of Norwalk. Below is a glimpse of the early Citizens Bank interior, with its ornate ceiling and scrollwork.

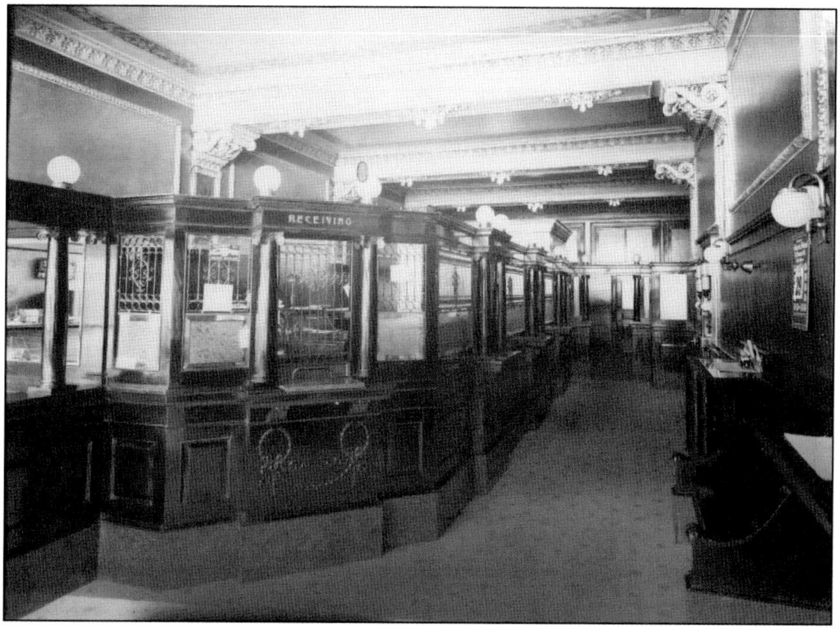

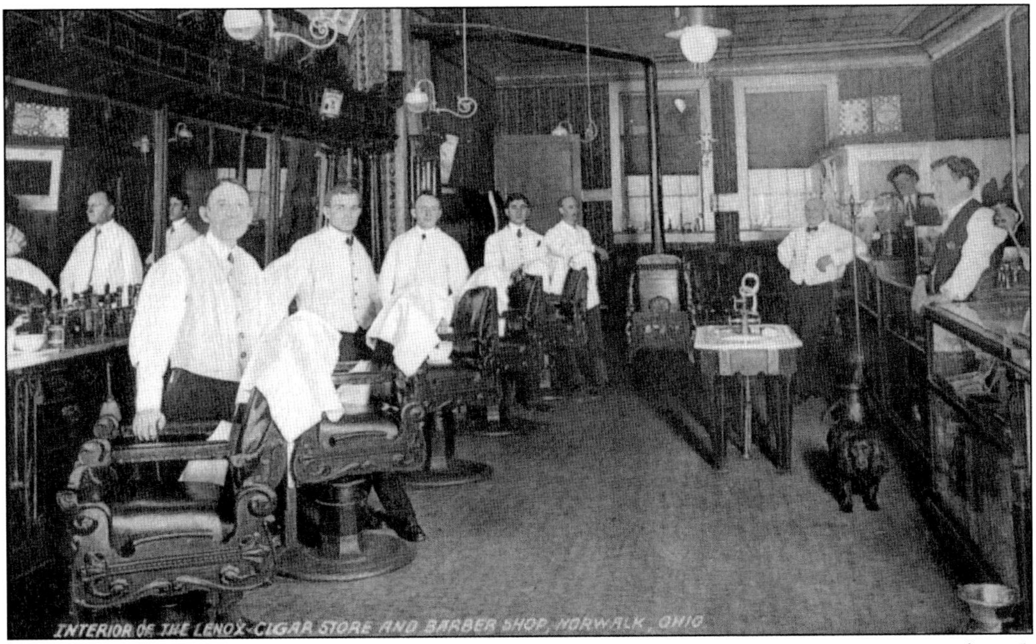


This is the interior of the Lenox barbershop and cigar store at 9 Whittlesey Avenue around 1915. The owner was F.F. Gregory. This was a required stop for Norwalk gentlemen. Barbers not only cut hair, but also shaved and cut beards. Some men even kept their own shaving mug with their name imprinted at the shop. Of course, the barber used a straight razor to do the job.

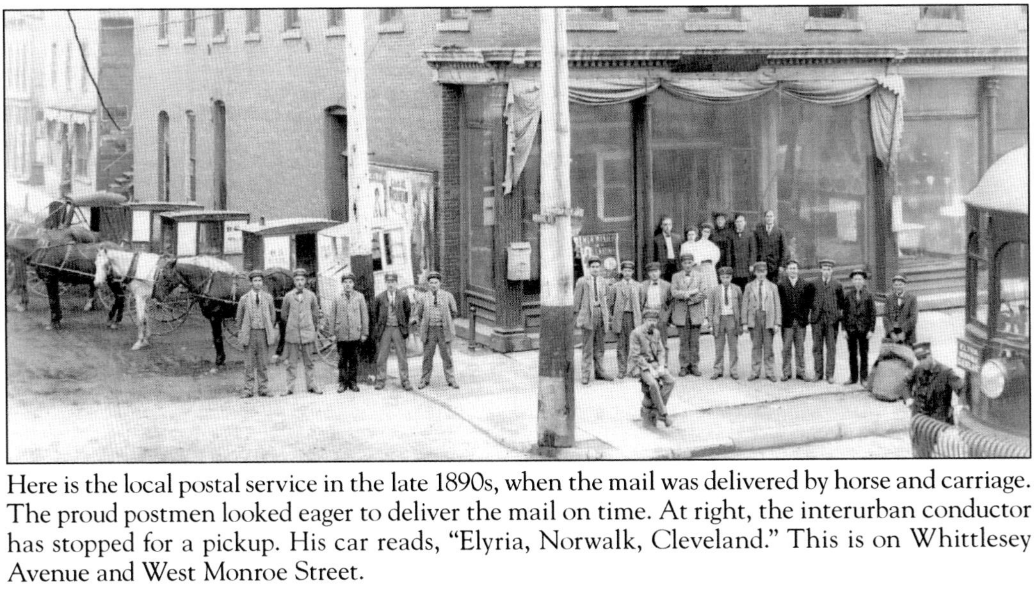

Here is the local postal service in the late 1890s, when the mail was delivered by horse and carriage. The proud postmen looked eager to deliver the mail on time. At right, the interurban conductor has stopped for a pickup. His car reads, "Elyria, Norwalk, Cleveland." This is on Whittlesey Avenue and West Monroe Street.

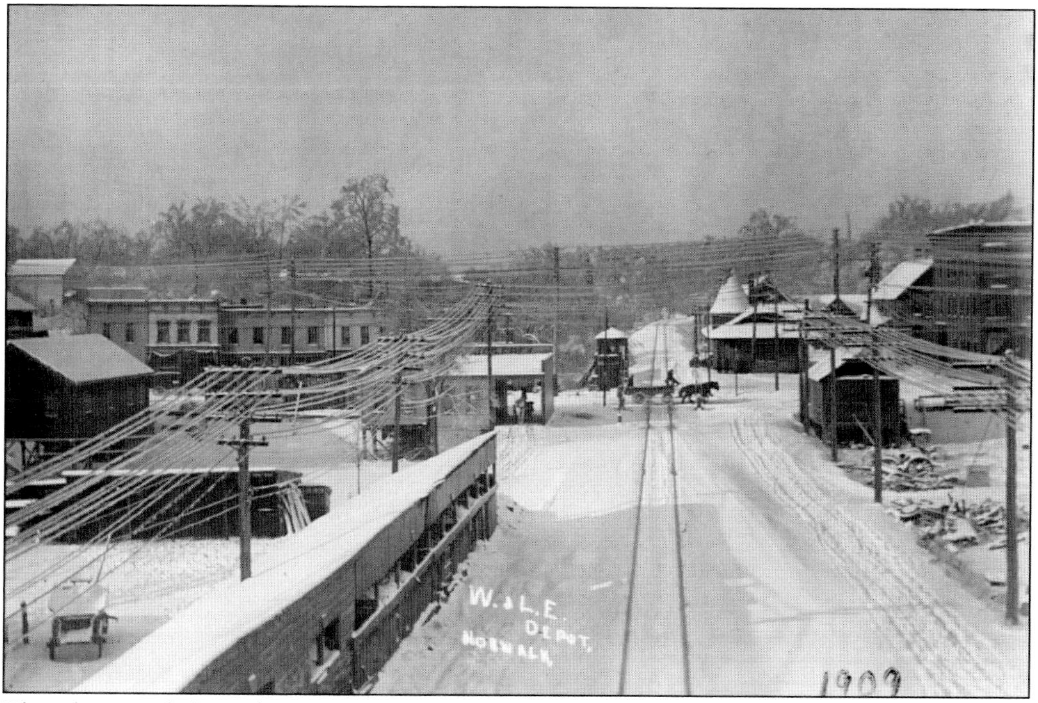


This photograph from the 1909 snowstorm looks west from the Linwood Avenue bridge. Across from the Lake Erie Railroad station is a horse-drawn cart crossing the tracks on Benedict Avenue. The Joe Frey coal yard is at left.

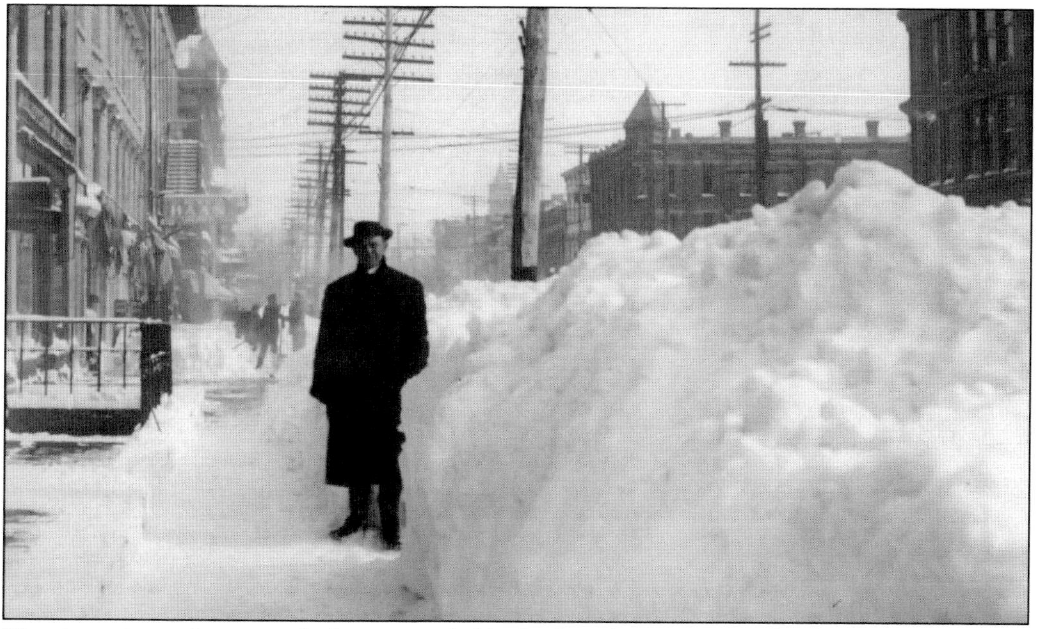

Here is a winter picture, with the snow piled high along Main Street. The digging out was done by hand.

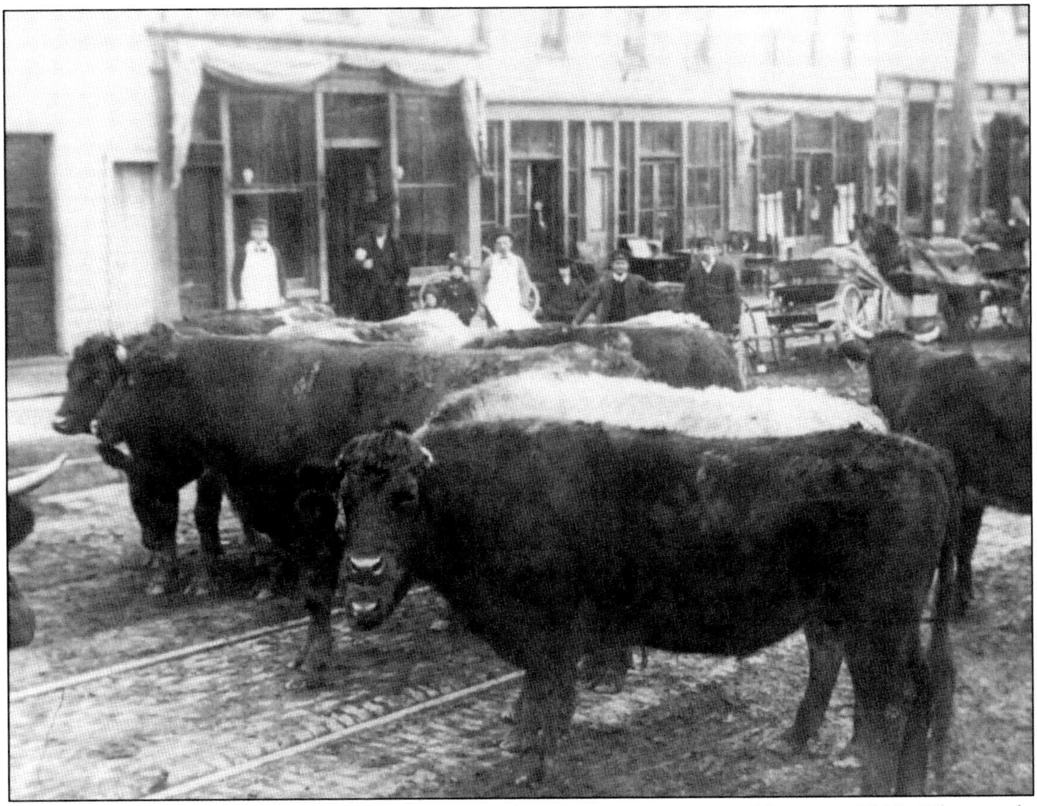

The F.A. Lieber Southside Market at 62 Benedict Avenue is pictured here in 1908. The cattle were purchased through the Chicago Stockyard and brought to Norwalk by train. They were herded by dogs and herdsmen to Fred Lieber's farm on Old State Road, a distance of about three miles. The cattle were then butchered, and their meat was sold in his market.

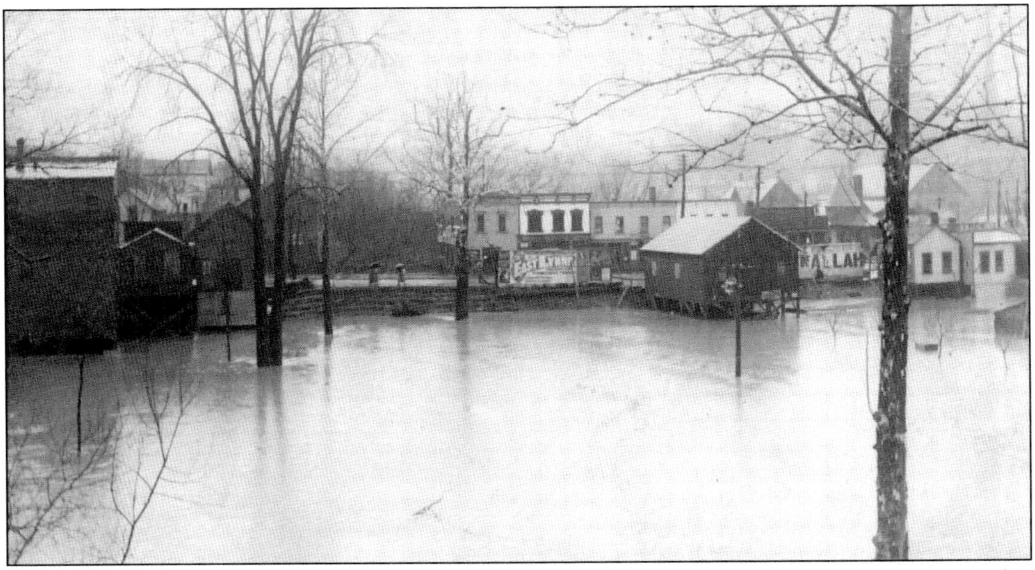

The great flood of 1913 affected Norwalk Creek, a small tributary to the Huron River. It also inundated the industrial lowlands around Water Street.

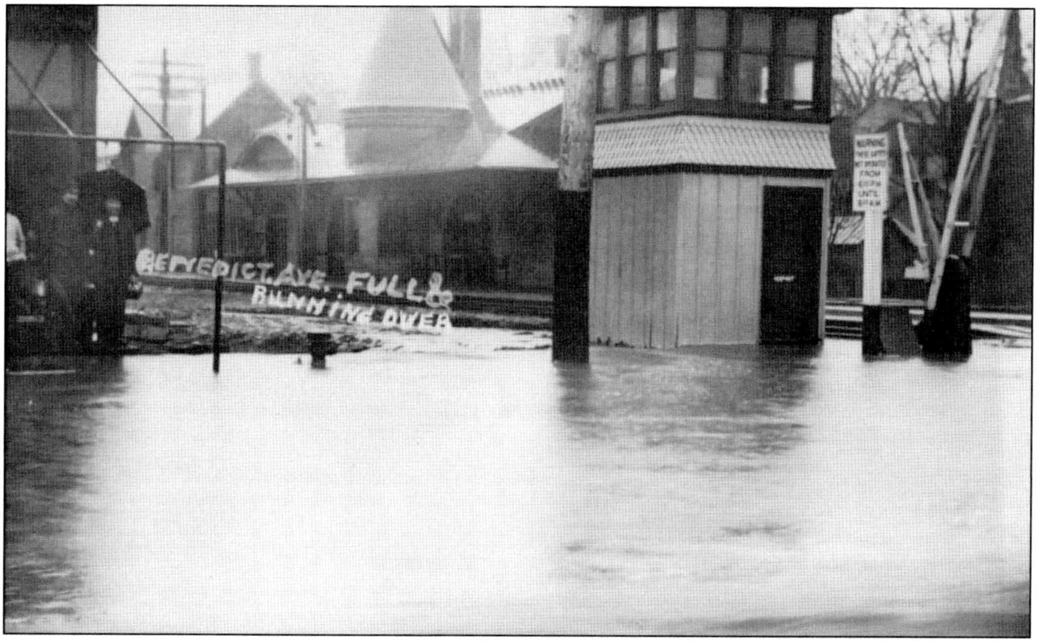


A water-covered Benedict Avenue is pictured here as onlookers nervously observe the rising water. Note the railroad crossing house, which was manually operated. The crossing attendant only manned it from 6:00 p.m. to 6:00 a.m. Extra care had to be taken around the busy train traffic. The trains were quite noisy when they passed through, which was all the warning one needed.

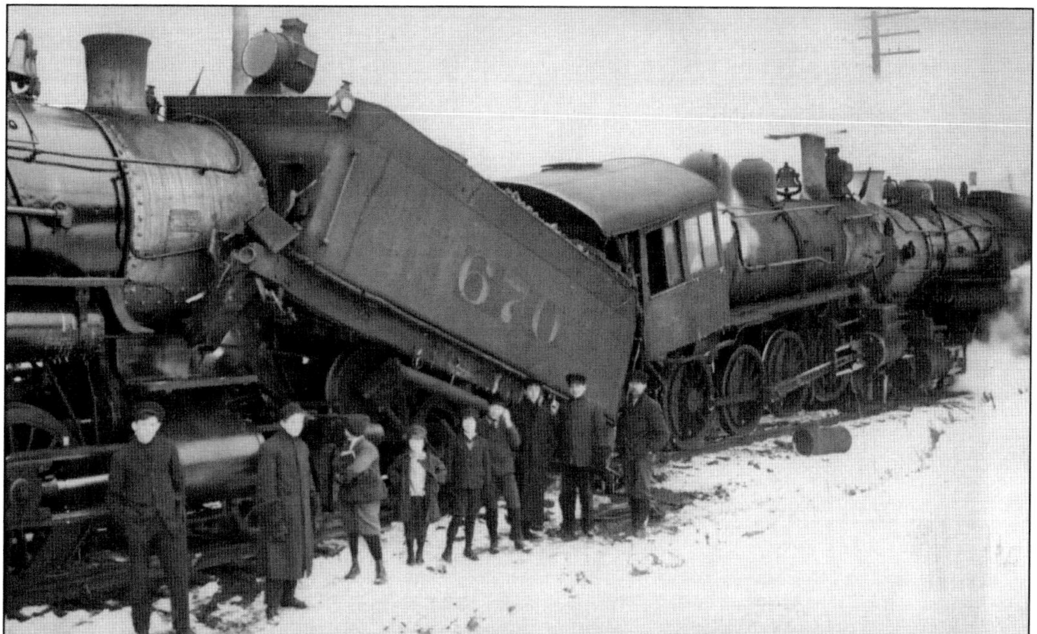


This is one of the many train wrecks that always gathered spectators. This 1910 Wheeling & Lake Erie derailment took place near Woodlawn Avenue.

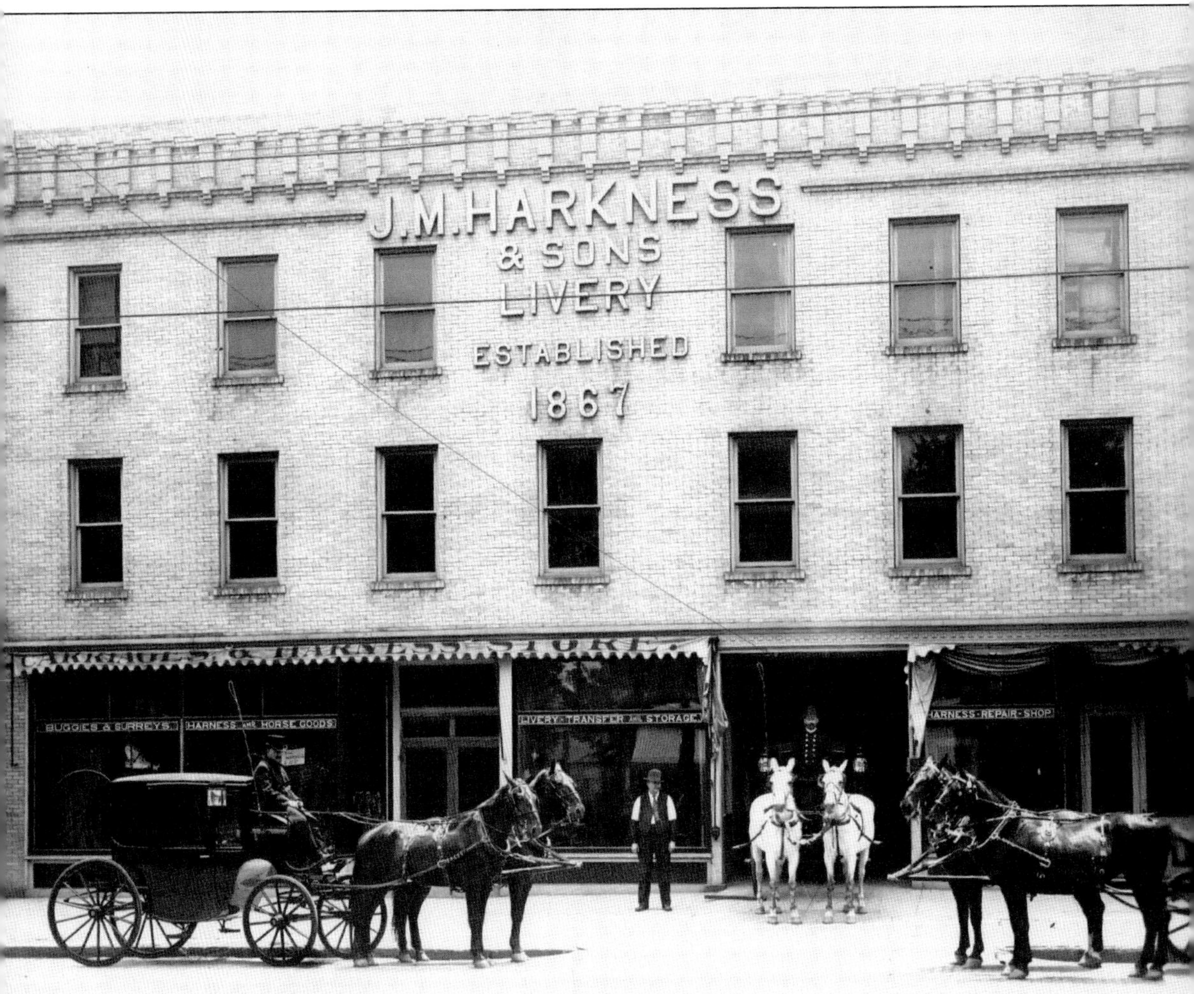


At 60–64 East Main Street was the Harkness Livery, established in 1867. This was a lucrative business for many years. Livery stables were busy places. One could rent a horse and carriage for a trip out of town or a stall to leave their horse while doing business. The livery also had a "hack," which met every train to transport passengers to hotels or private residences. Liveries went out of business after the auto replaced the horse. Later, this building was used a Ford dealership and other businesses.

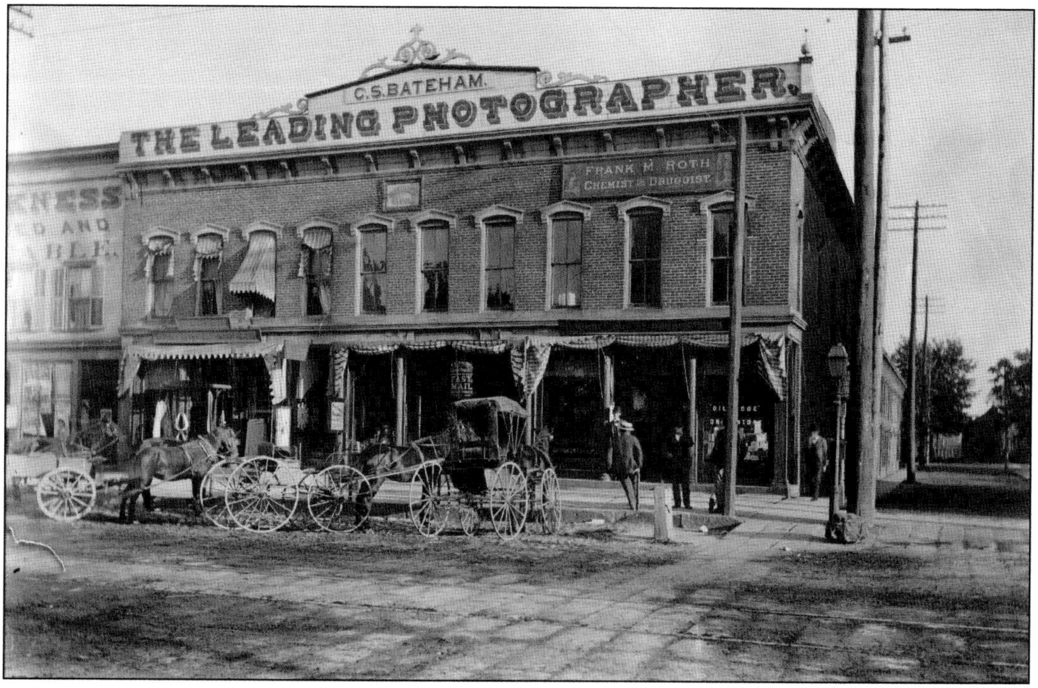

Seen here on East Main Street is the location of C.S. Bateham, "The Leading Photographer." As early as 1880, photography was an important technology.

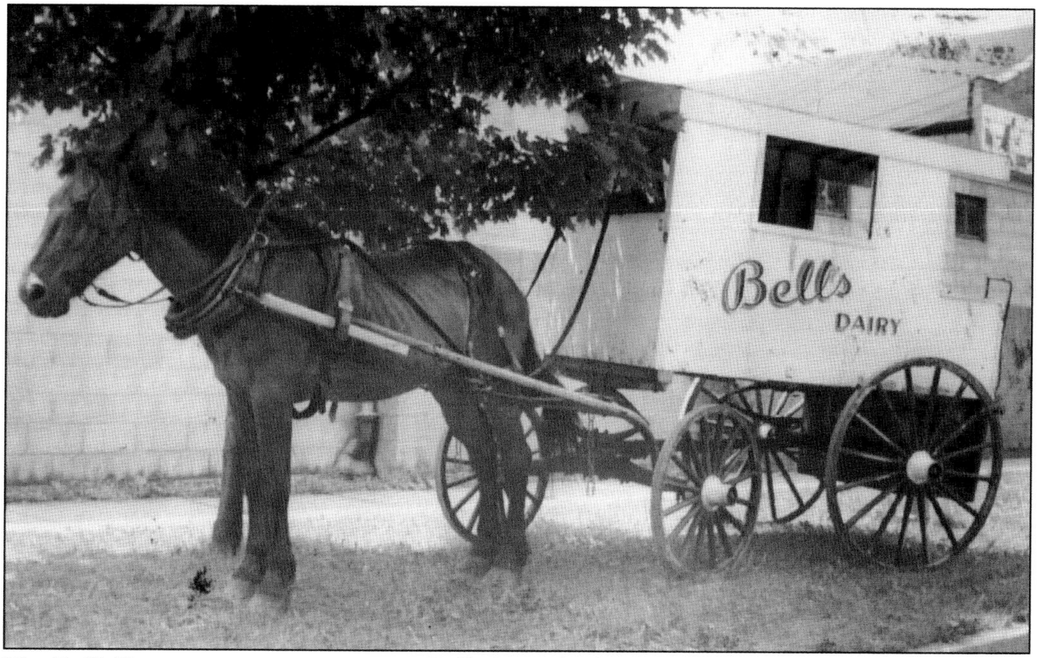

The Bell's Dairy wagon comes to town. Bell's Dairy had its start at Five Points south of Norwalk by Ralph Leonard Bell. Between 1930 and 1933, the family-owned dairy business expanded, and the old school building at 300 East Main Street was purchased by Bell. He sold the business in 1943 to former employee Gilbert Weisenberger. About this time, the "s" was dropped, and Bell Dairy began.

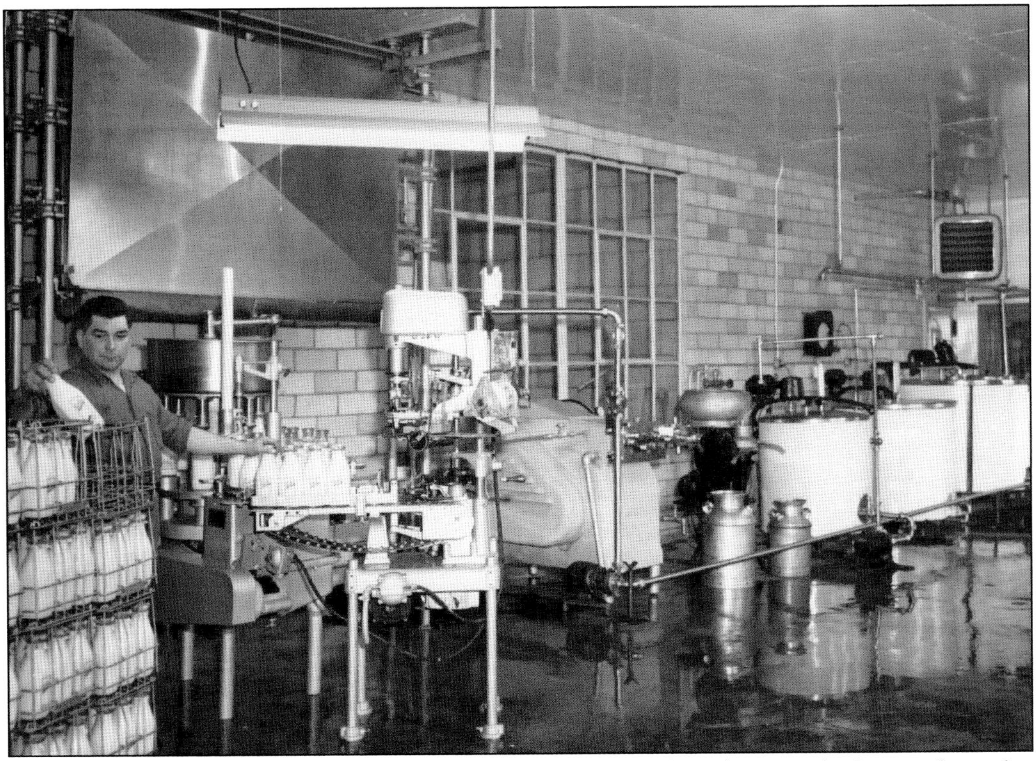

Bell Dairy moved to North Prospect Street around 1950. This photograph shows a busy day producing the familiar bottles. The worker is unidentified.

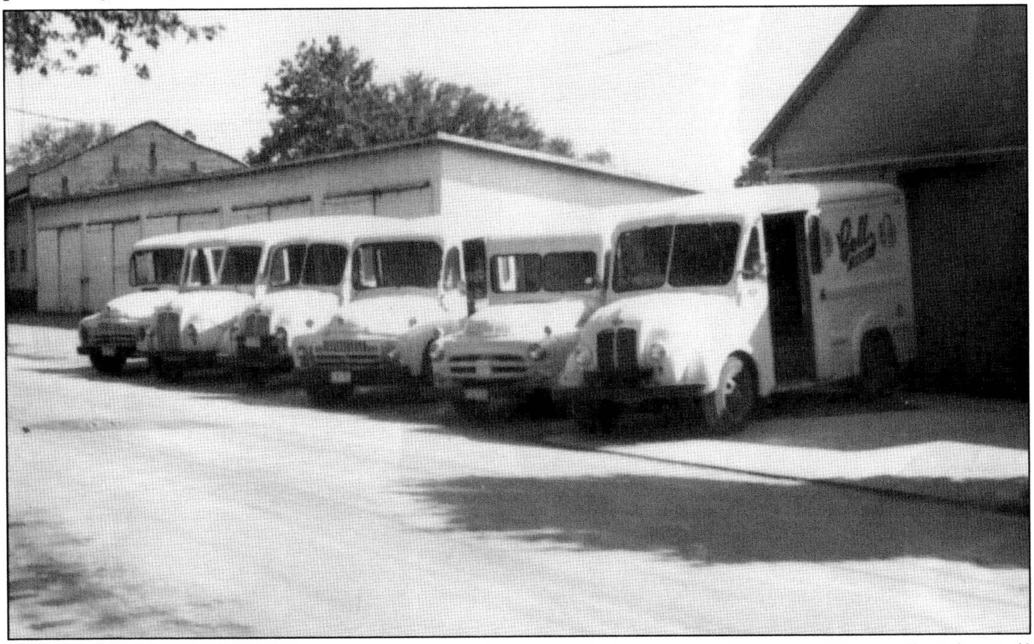

A fleet of Bell Dairy trucks stand ready to make home deliveries to the city of Norwalk. The Bell Dairy went out of business in 1966, but is remembered by many for its delicious dairy treats made from Bell Dairy milk, ice cream, and cheese.

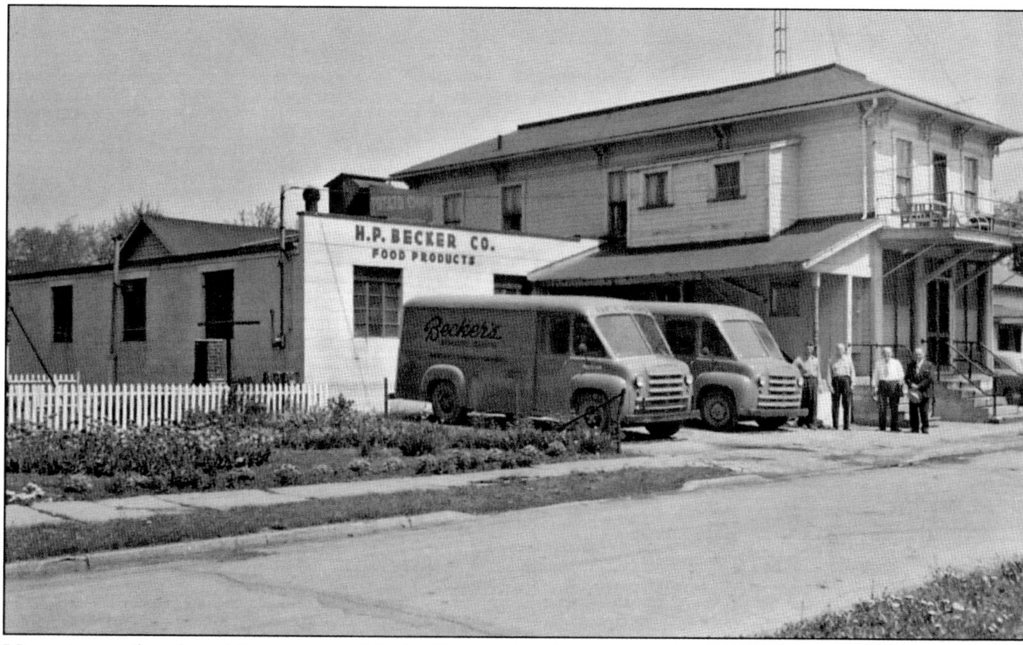


Here is another local favorite at 3 Rule Street. Becker potato chips, in the familiar red canister, were a delicious snack that was a local and regional favorite. This picture was taken in 1951 after an addition to the building. The delivery trucks were familiar in the region until the 1970s, when the company ceased production.

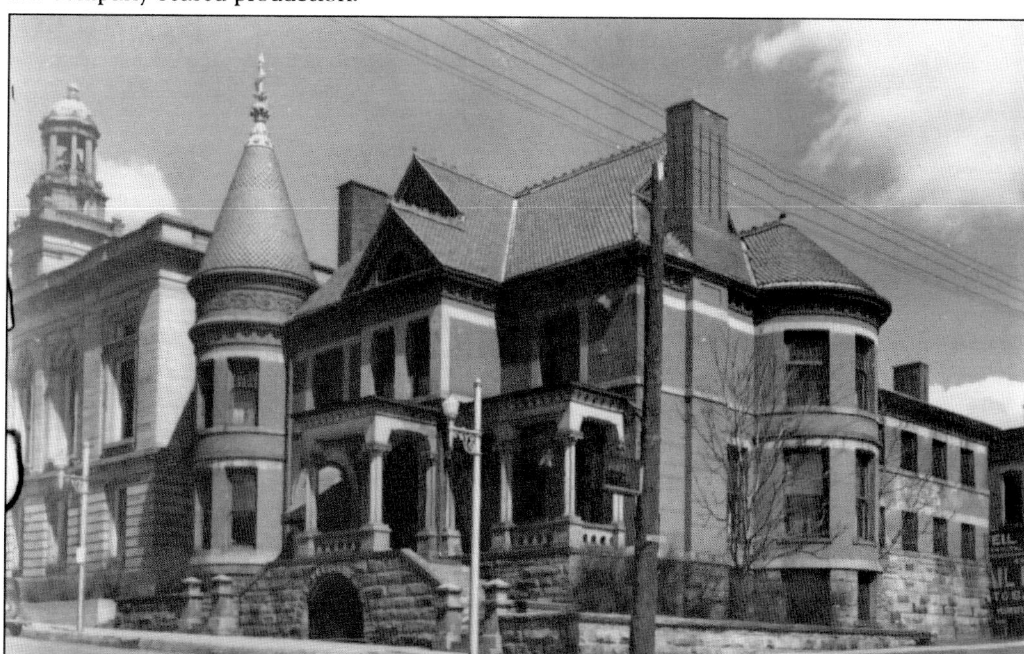

Here is a familiar view of the Huron County Courthouse and Jail heading up Benedict Avenue to Main Street.

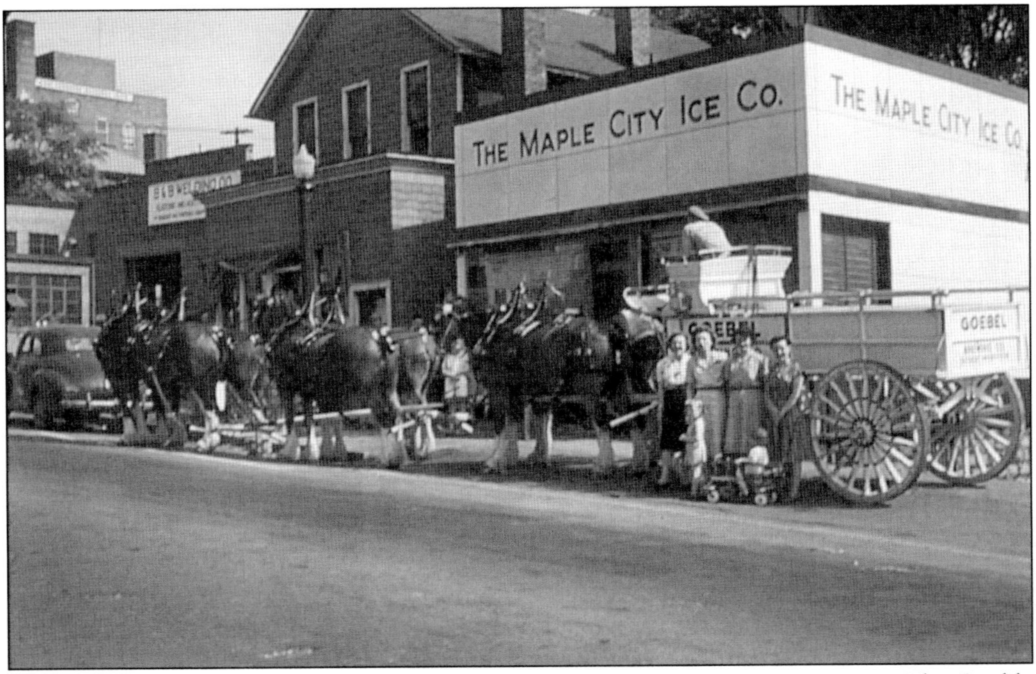


Just below Seminary Street on Benedict Avenue was the Maple City Ice Company. The Goeble beer wagon is in town from Detroit, Michigan, with some Clydesdale horses for a parade. The unidentified ladies seem to be having a good time.

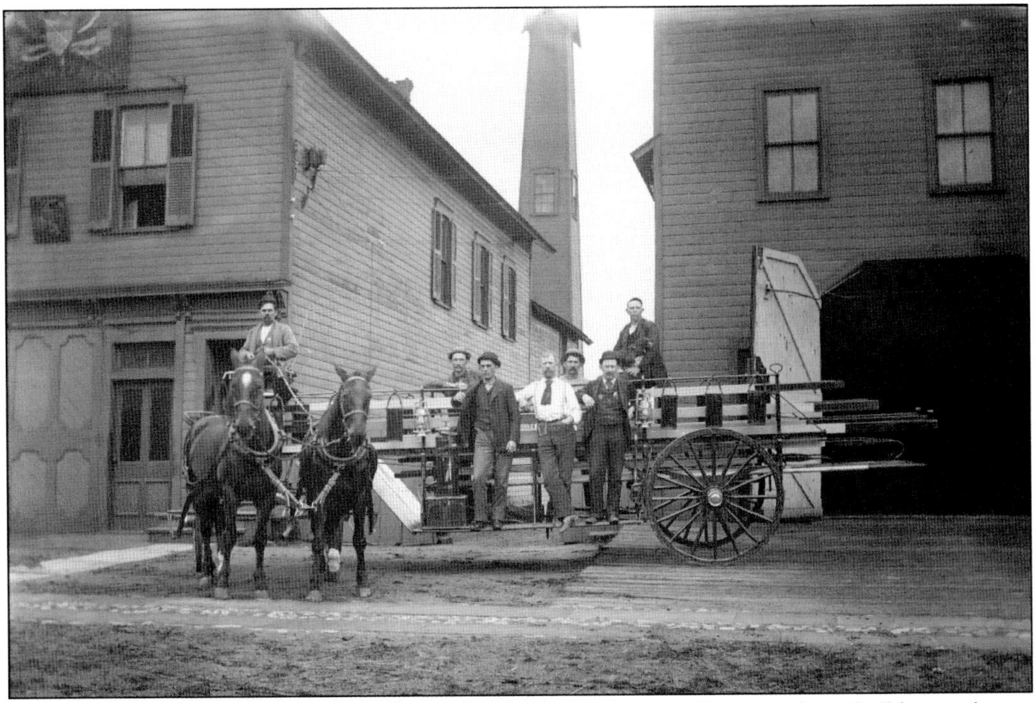

Norwalk's early fire department was located at 36 East Seminary Street and used all horse-drawn equipment. Clement "Fritz" Cramer was the driver and caretaker for many years, and he and his family lived upstairs in the fire station.

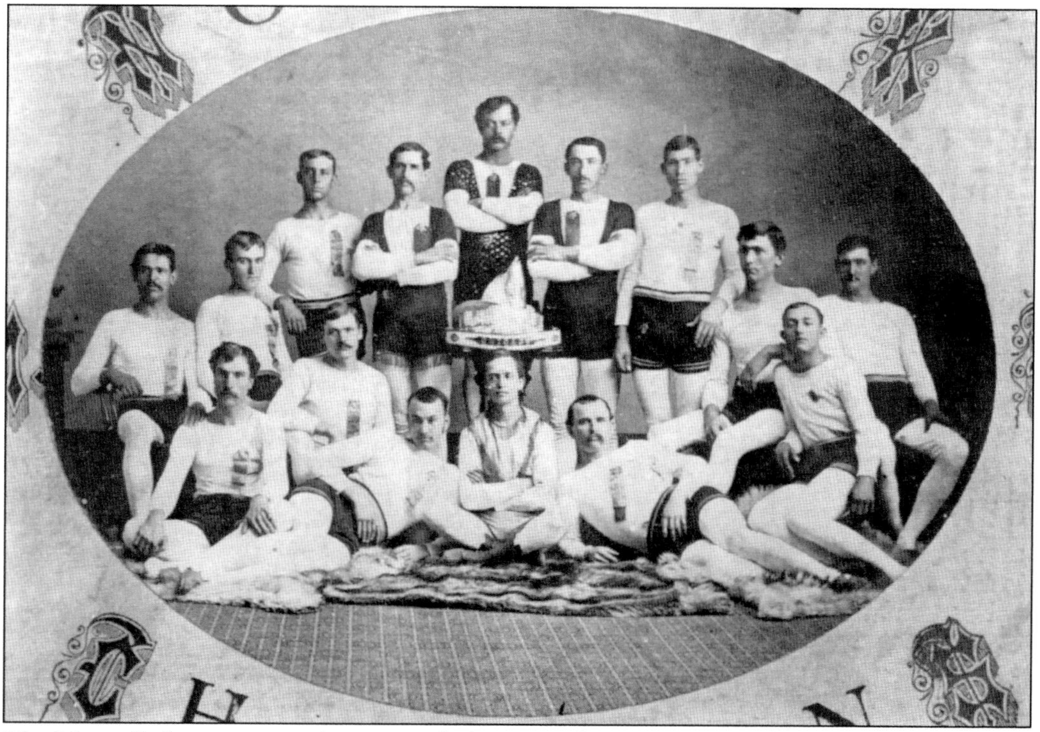

The Norwalk firemen won the national championship in 1878 at a fireman's tournament in Chicago by beating Monmouth, Illinois, in the various contests. This picture shows the men with their trophies, which included a silver helmet and belt.

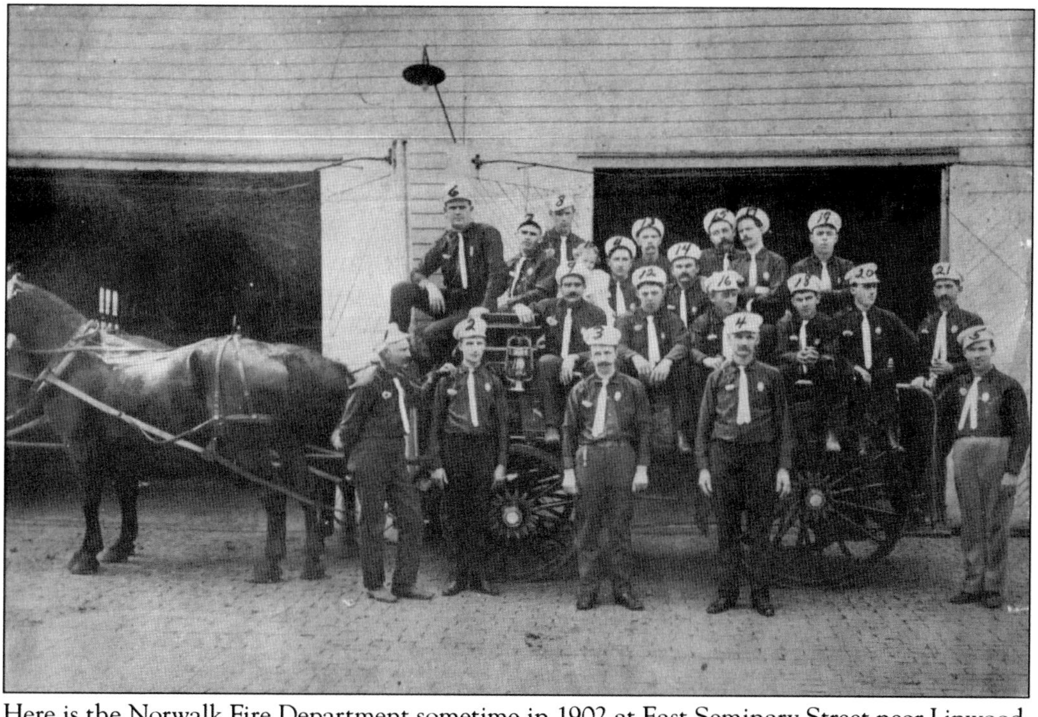

Here is the Norwalk Fire Department sometime in 1902 at East Seminary Street near Linwood.

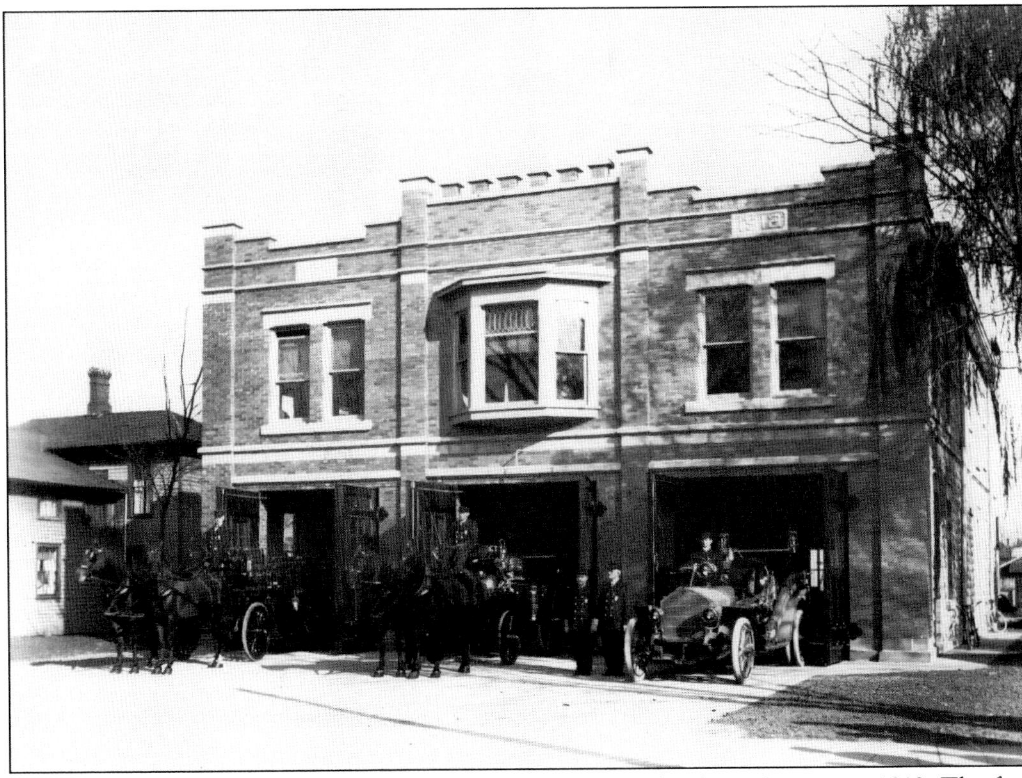

The fire department moved to the current fire station on Whittlesey Avenue in 1912. The first motor driven fire truck was a 1913 LaFrance engine.

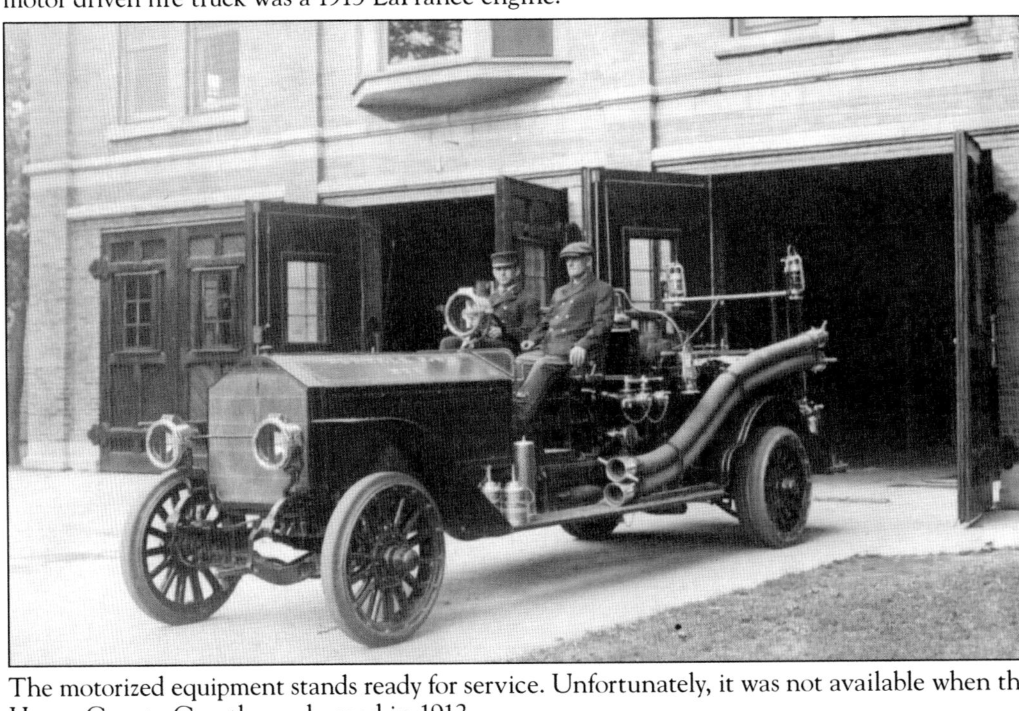

The motorized equipment stands ready for service. Unfortunately, it was not available when the Huron County Courthouse burned in 1912.

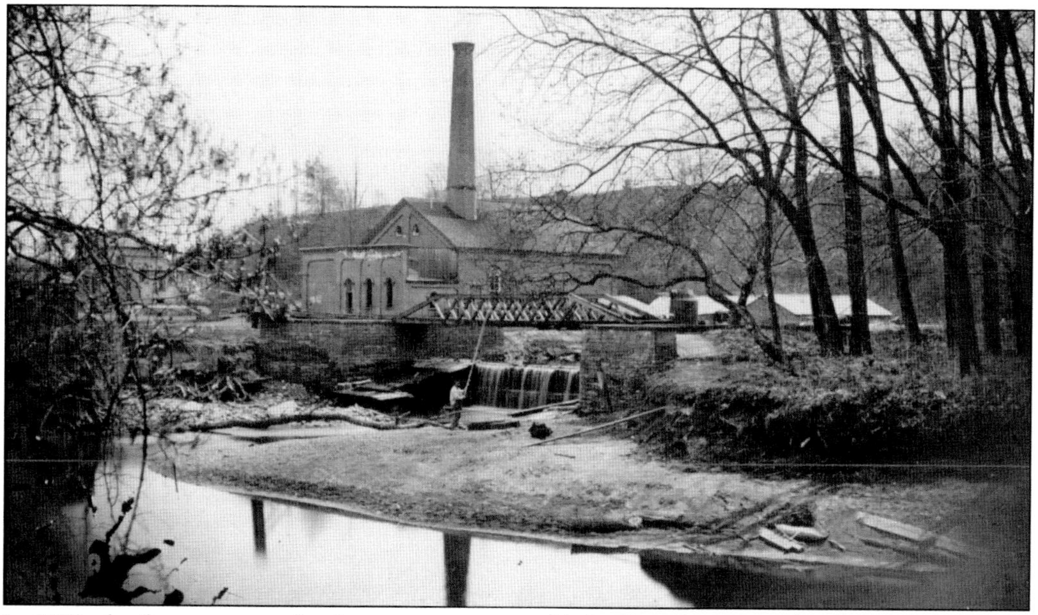

In 1870, the first water works department was established on the west side of the city, now US Route 61. Clean drinking water was important for the success of the city. Dry spells would prove problematic for the facility as well as increased population, which led to upgrades. The caretaker's house is still standing and remains a private residence.

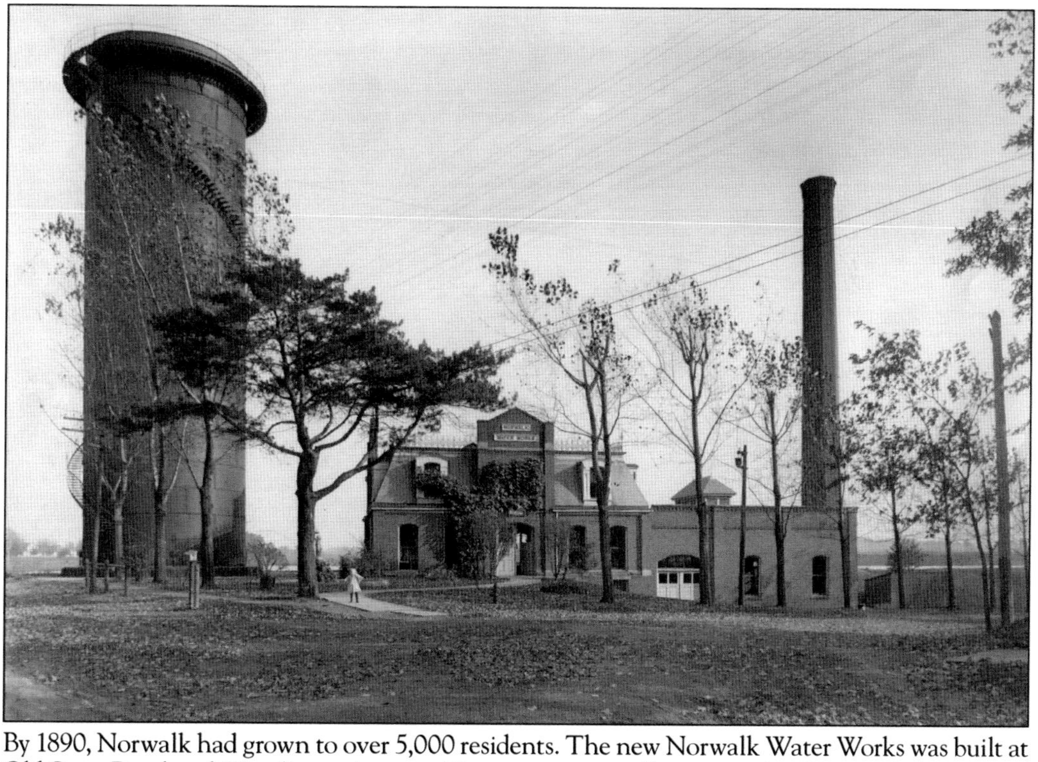

By 1890, Norwalk had grown to over 5,000 residents. The new Norwalk Water Works was built at Old State Road and Woodlawn Avenue. The reservoir is still in use today. It provided improved pressure and a constant water supply. Its water tower was modern for its time.

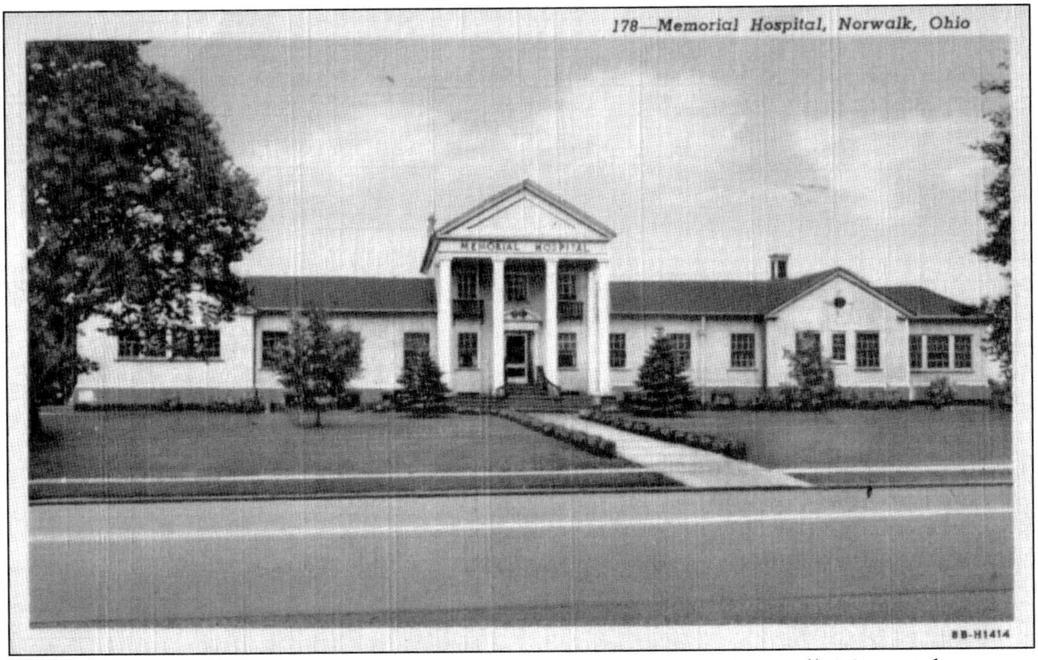


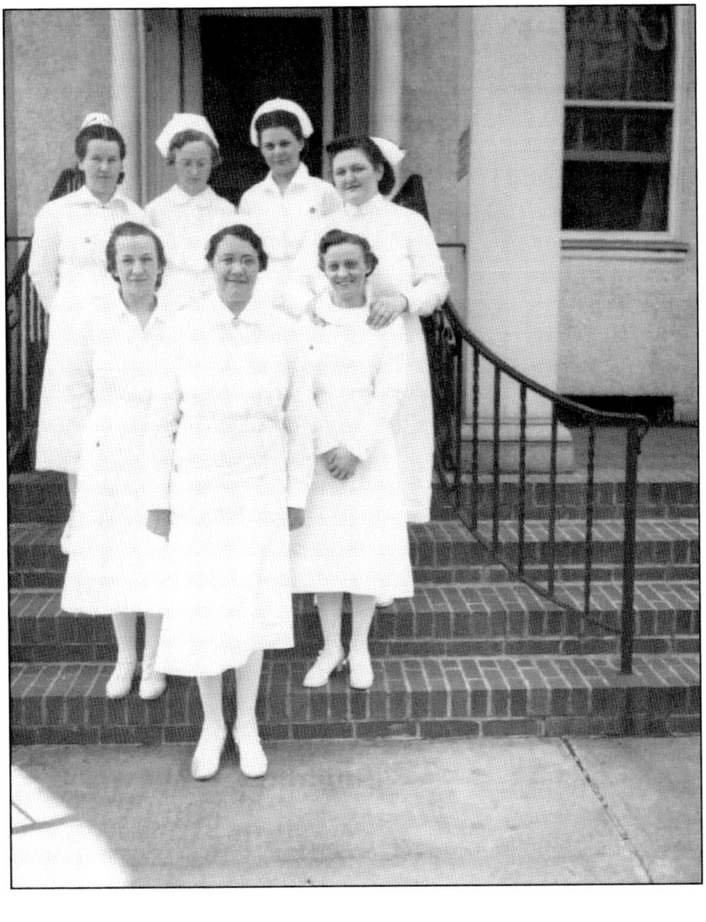

Norwalk Memorial Hospital at 269 West Main Street opened as a 38-bed hospital in 1917. It continued to operate until it was replaced by the newly built hospital on Benedict Avenue in 1957. It then was converted into a nursing home run by the Hospital Association until 1958. The building was then sold to a private individual.

Here, the nursing staff of Norwalk Memorial Hospital take time out of a busy day to pose for a picture around the 1940s. From left to right are (first row) Madeline Shug, Florence Specht, and Grace Miracle; (second row) Sophia Smith, Angela Nolan, Irene Chapin, and Theresa Felter.

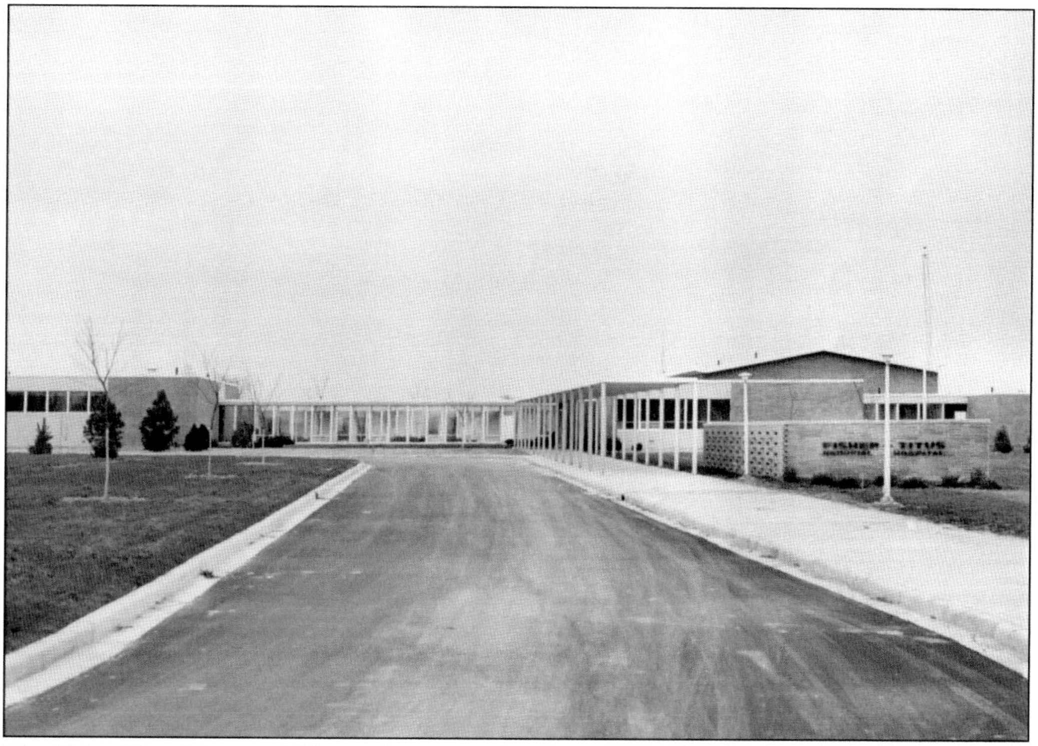

The Fisher-Titus Memorial Hospital was completed in 1957 and has grown into a modern high-rise medical center today.

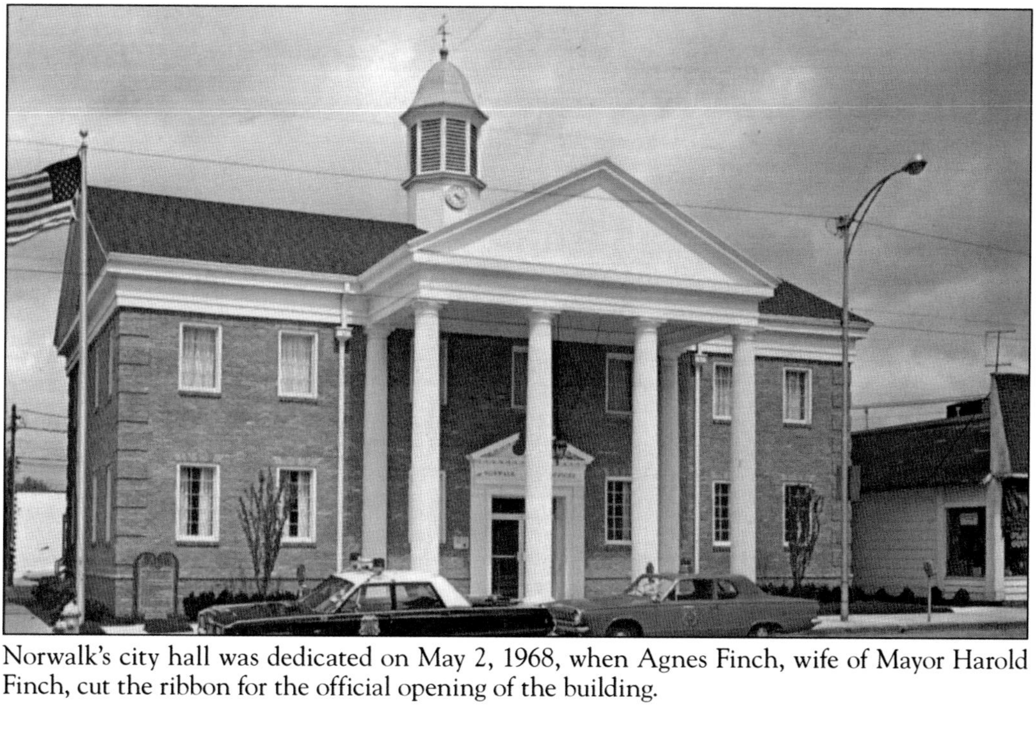

Norwalk's city hall was dedicated on May 2, 1968, when Agnes Finch, wife of Mayor Harold Finch, cut the ribbon for the official opening of the building.

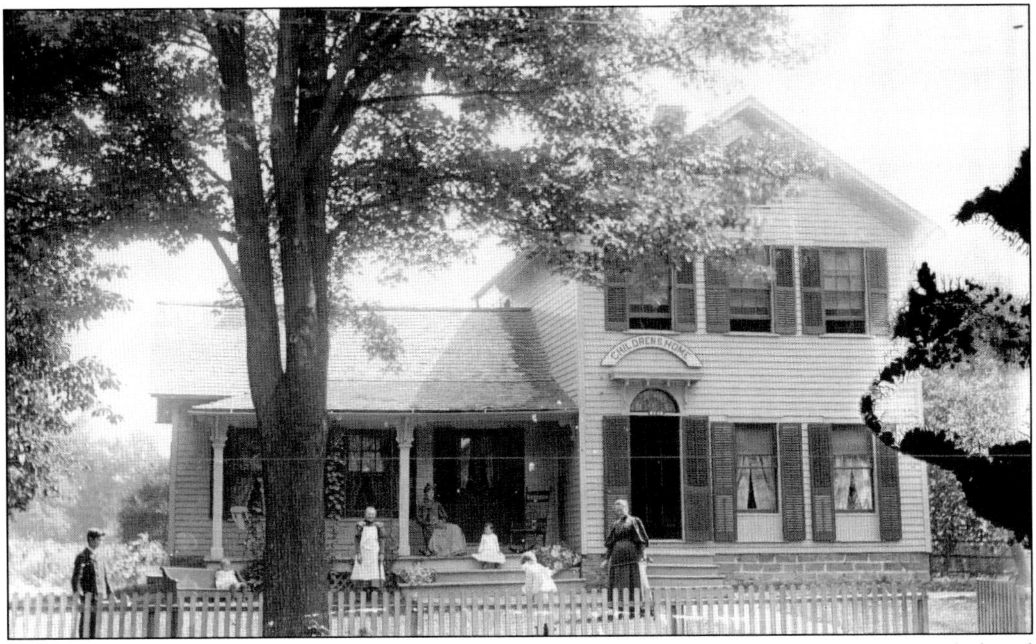


The original Children's Home at 143 Benedict Avenue opened on January 10, 1883, and closed in 1913 to be replaced by a larger facility. There seems to be a game of croquet taking place.

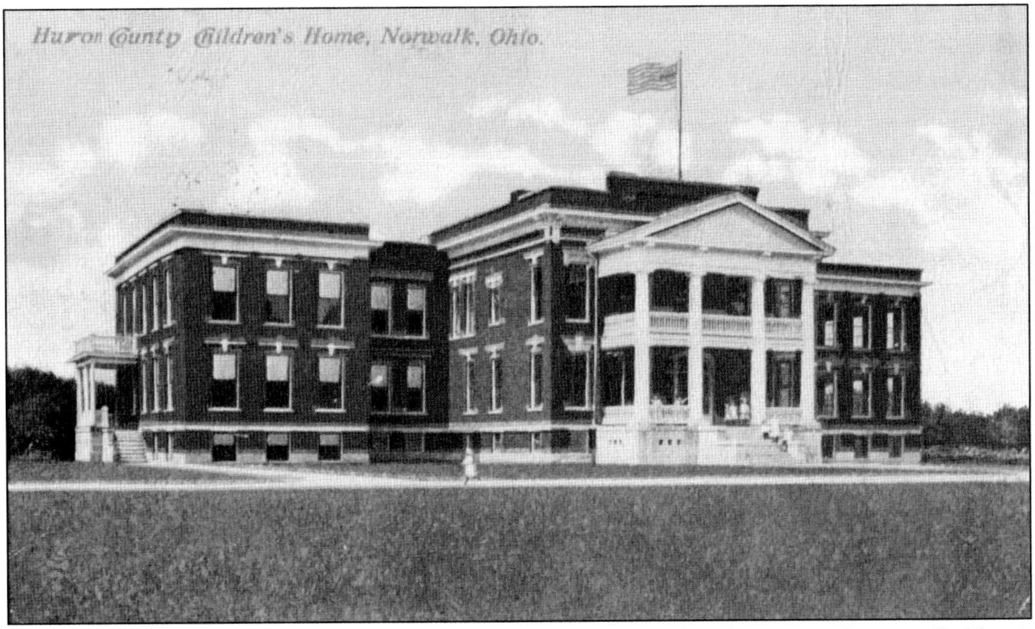


This building at 190 Benedict Avenue was built in 1913. It served as the Huron County Children's Home, a refuge for children whose families had split up, fell on hard times, or were orphaned. The boys lived in the south wing, the girls in the north wing, and the younger children in the west wing of the building. The caring staff would attend to them until they were adopted or reunited with their families.

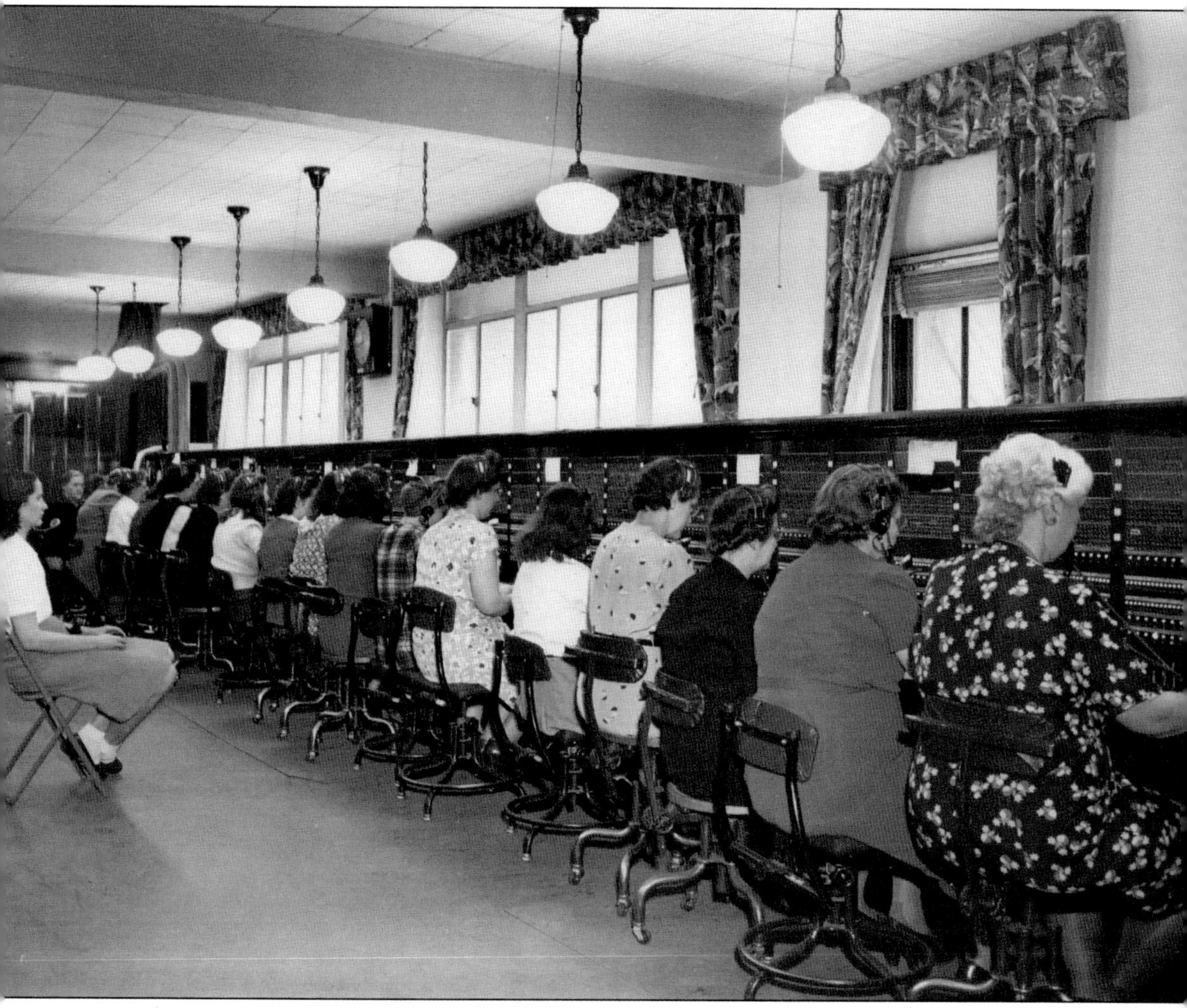

Here is the Norwalk Bell Telephone office. They had no computers to work with. The switchboard operators would manually connect the callers.

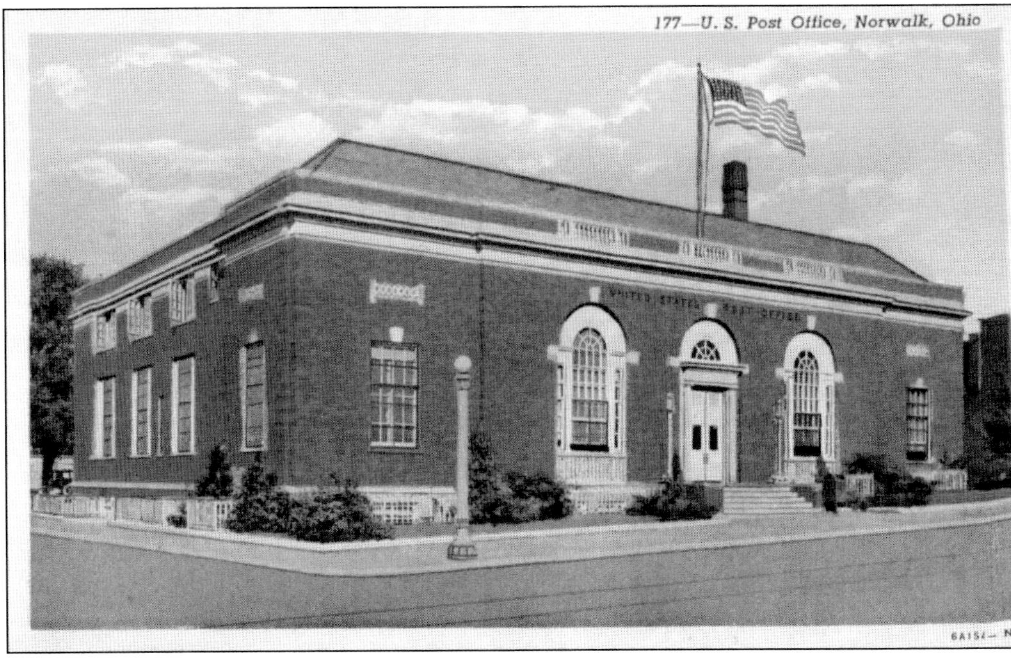


Seen here is the current US Post Office on Whittlesey Avenue across the street from the old location. The building was dedicated in 1932.

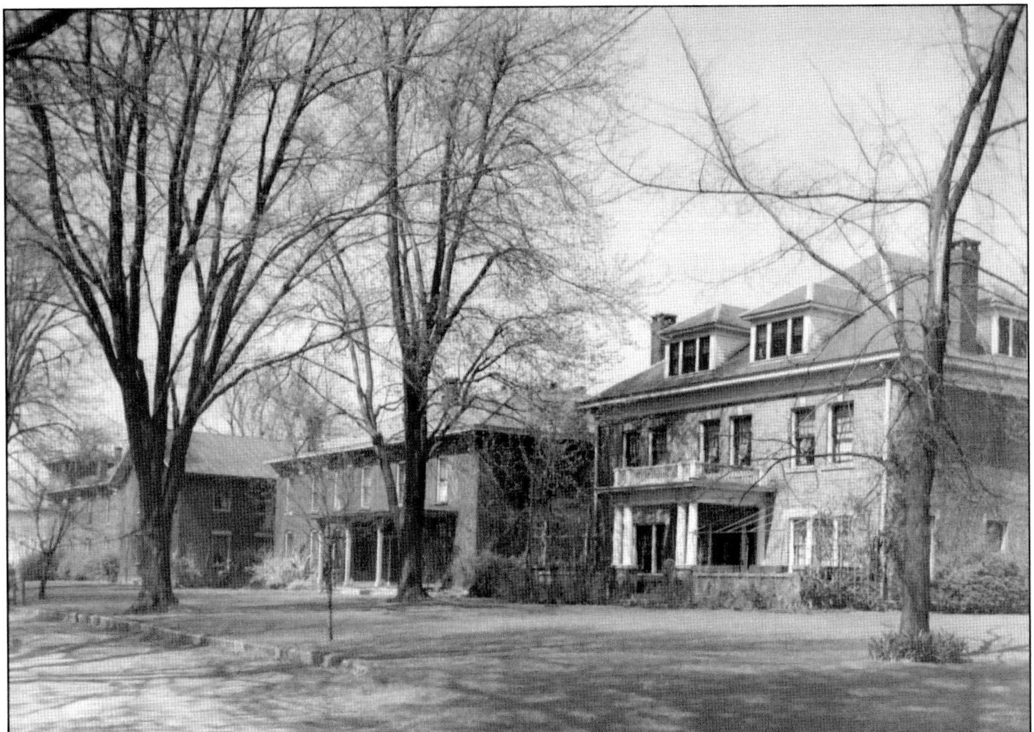

The Shady Lane Complex was Norwalk's "poor house." In the age before government retirement pensions, this was sometimes the last option for those in need.

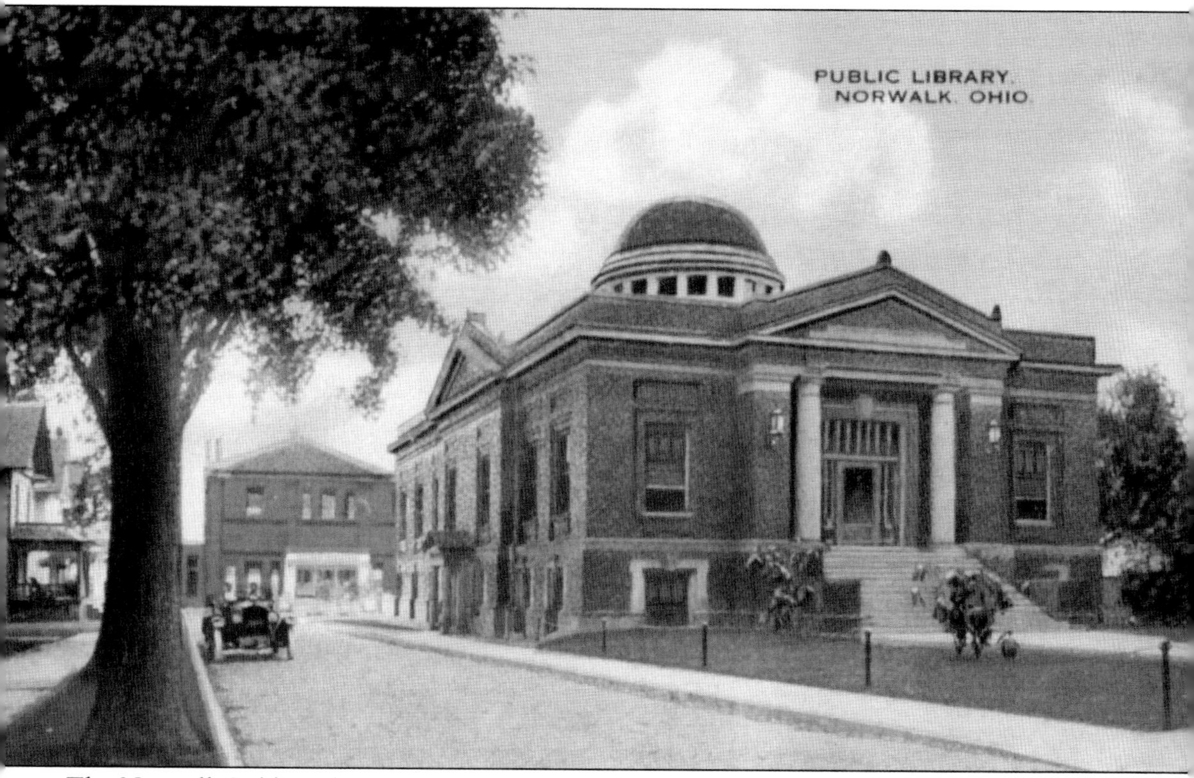

The Norwalk Public Library was a Carnegie endowed building with Neoclassical features including a dome. It was completed on May 10, 1905, and is still in use today. It once housed the Firelands Museum.

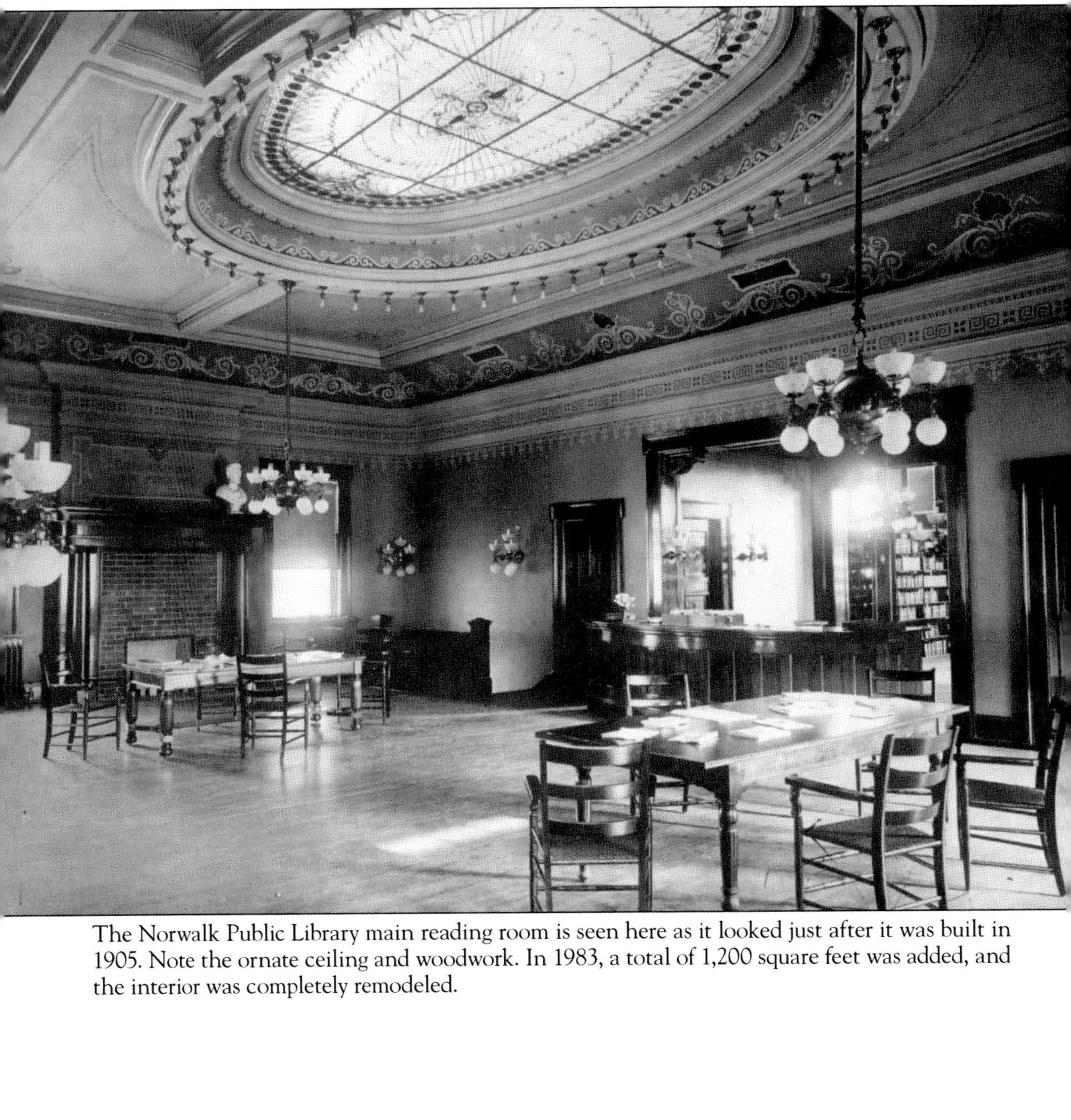

The Norwalk Public Library main reading room is seen here as it looked just after it was built in 1905. Note the ornate ceiling and woodwork. In 1983, a total of 1,200 square feet was added, and the interior was completely remodeled.

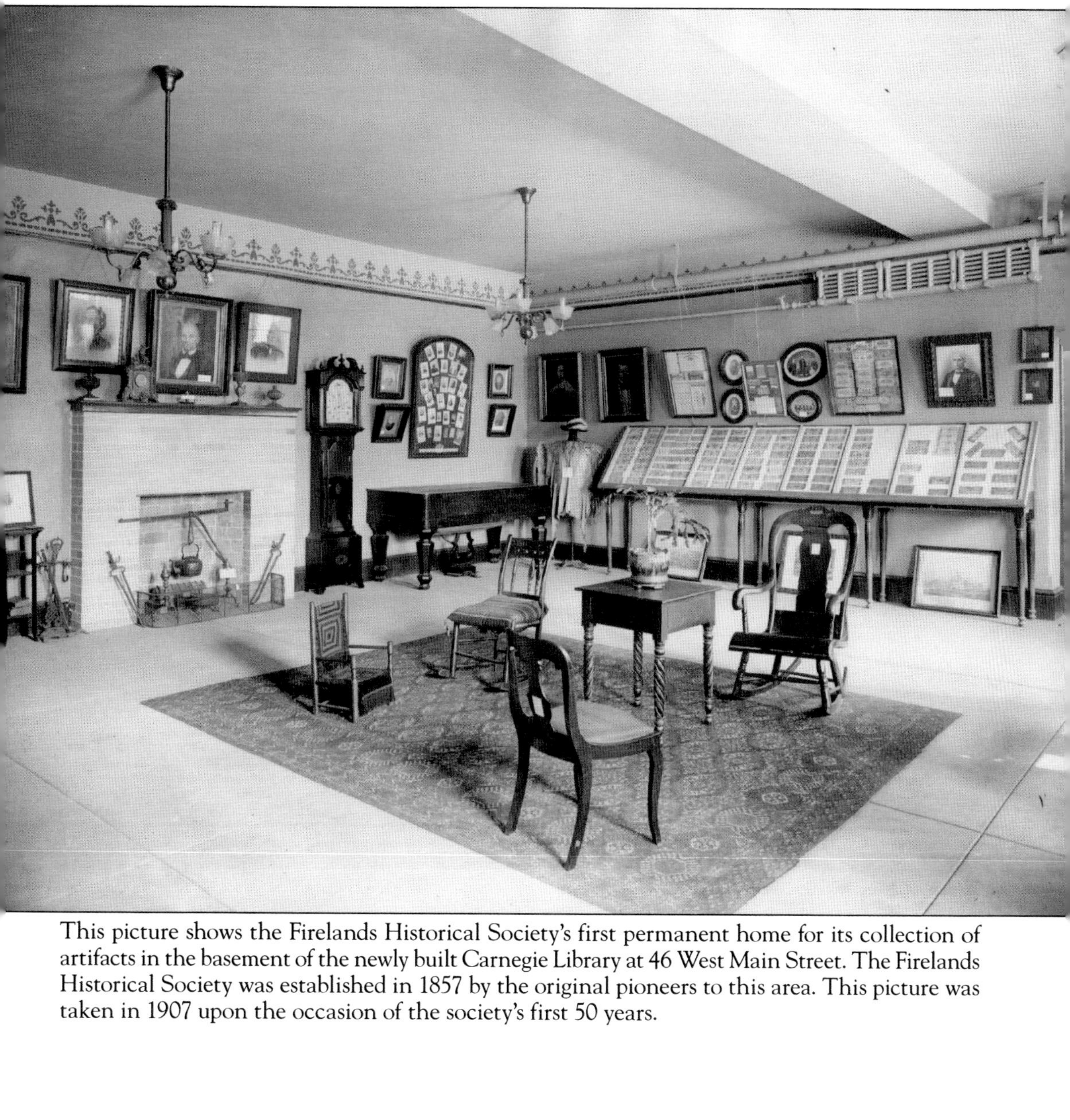

This picture shows the Firelands Historical Society's first permanent home for its collection of artifacts in the basement of the newly built Carnegie Library at 46 West Main Street. The Firelands Historical Society was established in 1857 by the original pioneers to this area. This picture was taken in 1907 upon the occasion of the society's first 50 years.

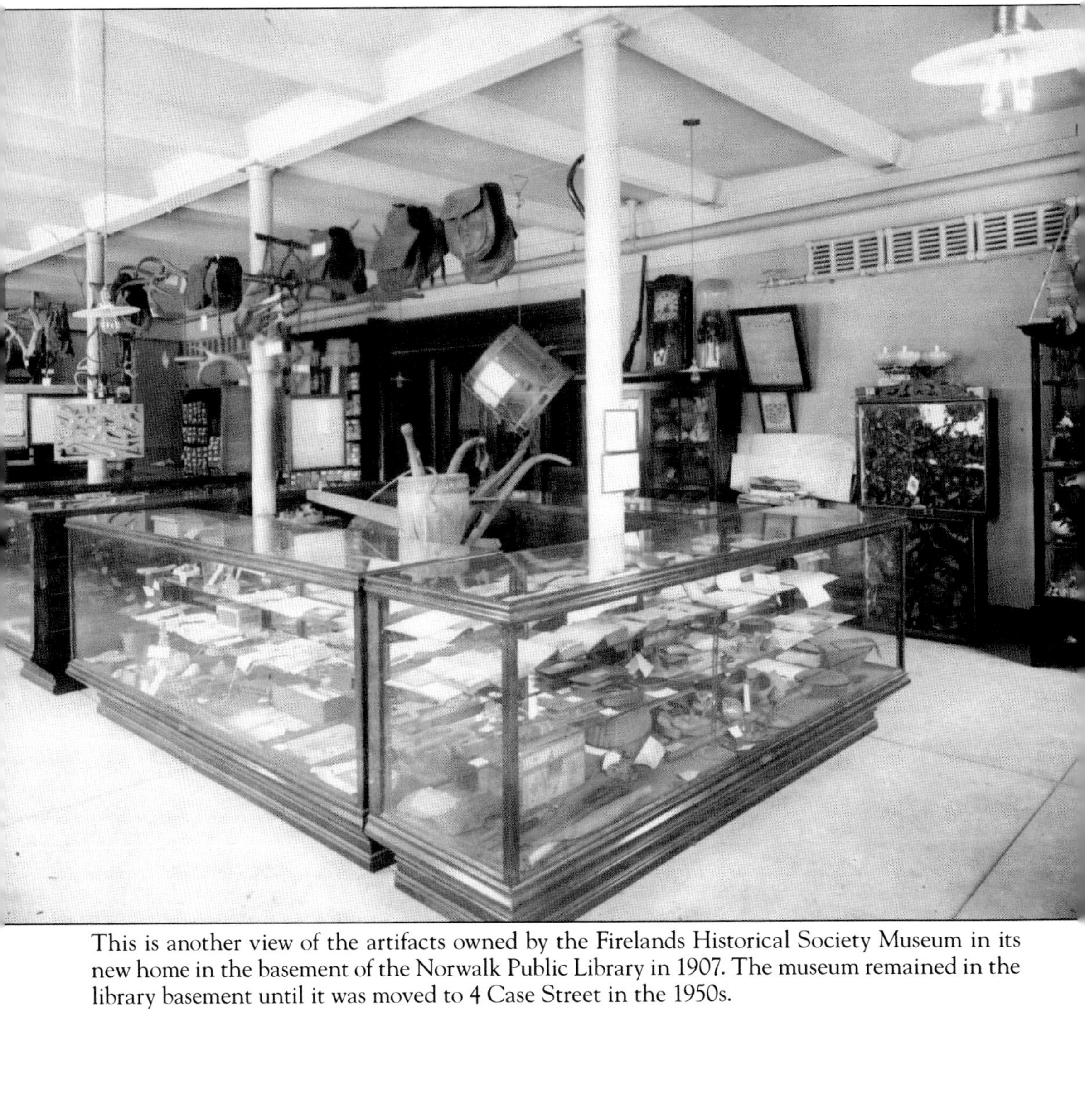

This is another view of the artifacts owned by the Firelands Historical Society Museum in its new home in the basement of the Norwalk Public Library in 1907. The museum remained in the library basement until it was moved to 4 Case Street in the 1950s.

# *Five*

# Manufacturing and Industries

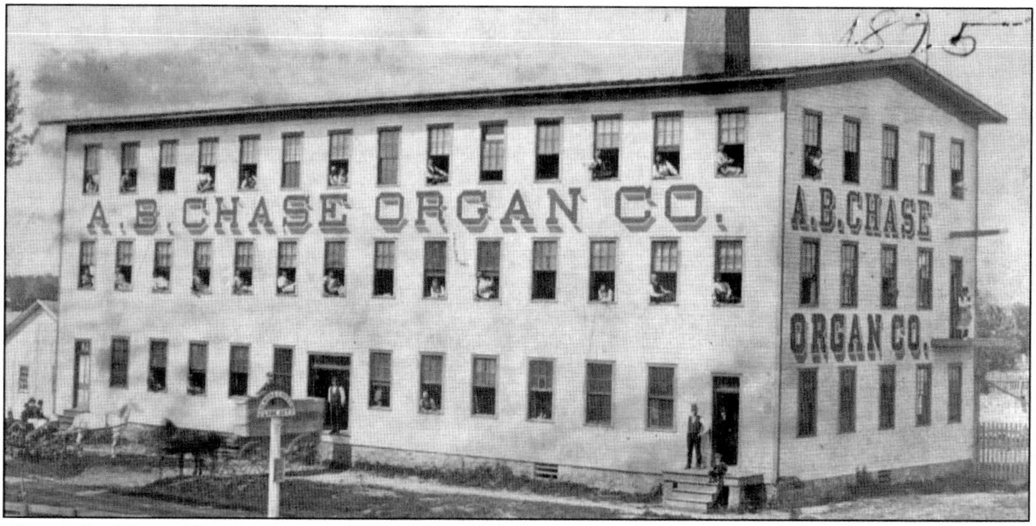


The A.B. Chase Organ Company was founded by Capt. Alvin B. Chase in 1875 in this wooden building on Newton Street, which was previously owned by Norwalk Barrel Company. At first, the company only made reed organs. A total of 2,000 organs had been made when on August 28, 1880, the factory was completely destroyed by fire.

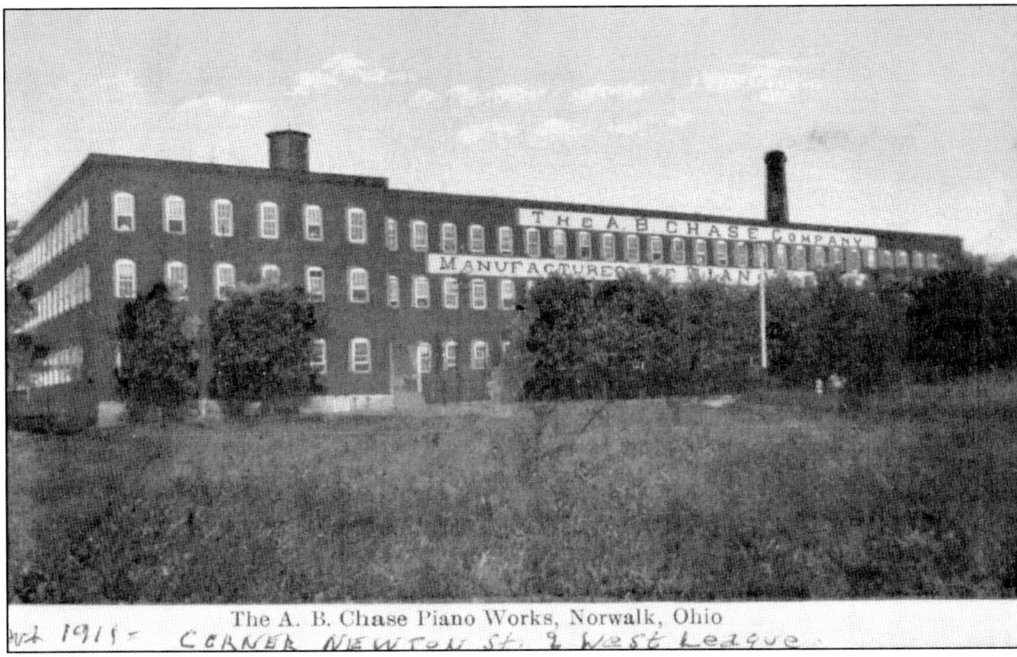


After the fire, a new larger brick building was immediately erected in the same location at the corner of Newton and League Streets. The company started making pianos in 1885. They were nationally known for their superior workmanship. By 1892, they employed 225 men and were selling 25 different piano styles and 70 different organ styles. The last organ was made in about 1905, after which the company concentrated on making pianos. The company weathered several financial hard times and finally sold to a company that made pianos under the name of New York–Norwalk. The company closed in about 1930, having operated in Norwalk for more than 50 years. The building was purchased in the late 1930s by the Norwalk Upholstering Company, later called Norwalk Furniture. It occupied the building until the early 1970s, before moving to a new building on Route 18 east of downtown Norwalk.

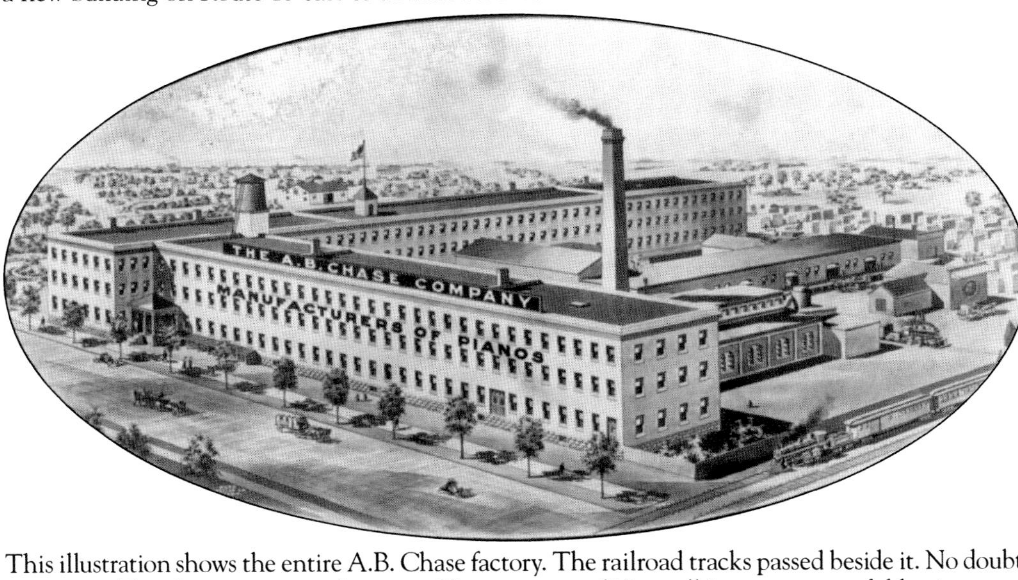


This illustration shows the entire A.B. Chase factory. The railroad tracks passed beside it. No doubt, trains would pick up organs and pianos. This was one of Norwalk's most successful businesses.

This advertisement shows that no Victorian parlor was complete without a Chase organ. Before the phonograph, the only source of music in the home was the piano, and piano lessons were often given to the lady of the home.

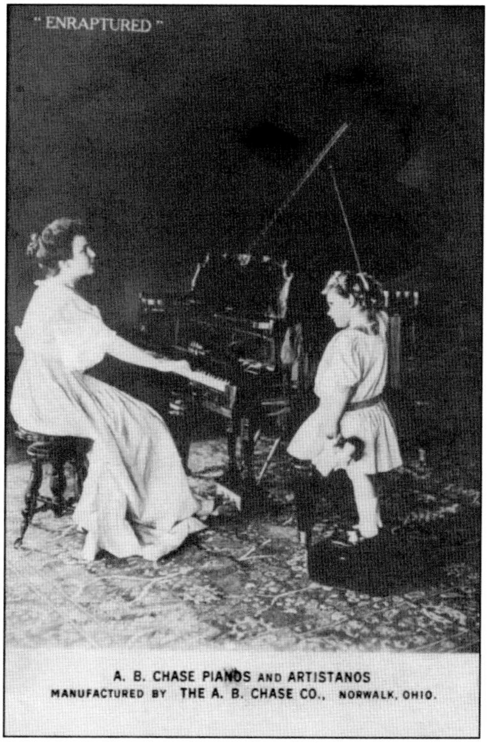


Here are some of the employees of the A.B. Chase piano factory busy at work around the early 1900s. These men were skilled craftsmen, not mere assembly line workers.

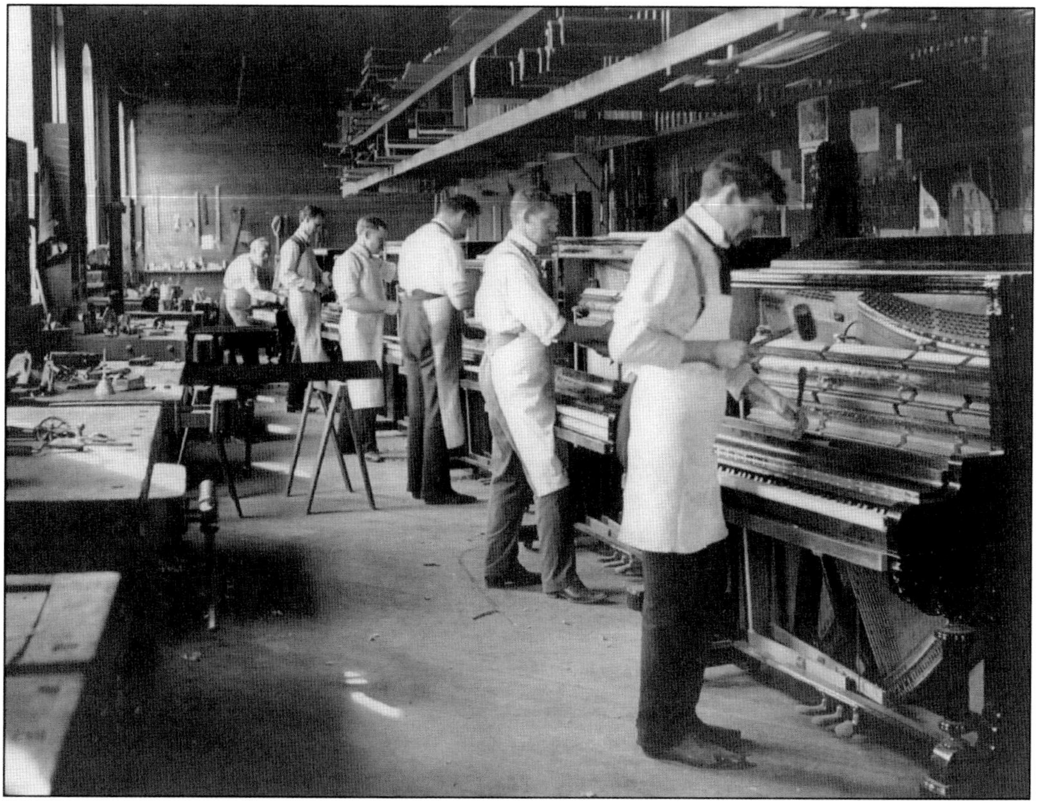

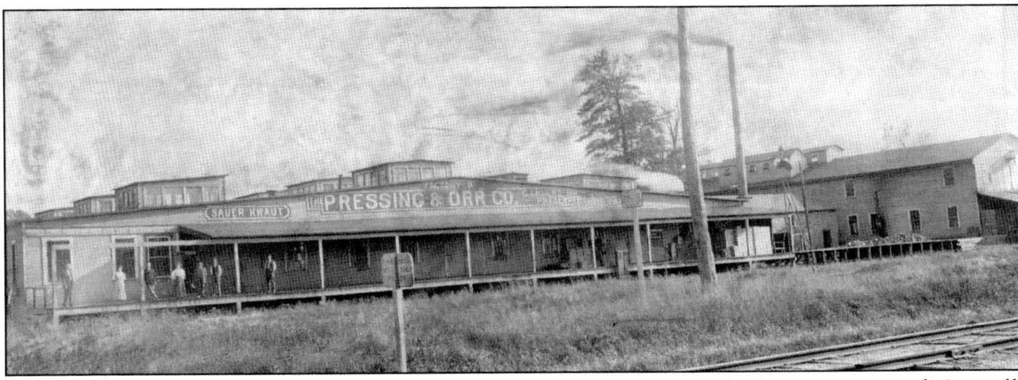


The Pressing & Orr canning factory opened in Norwalk in 1902, with the agreement of Norwalk-area farmers to plant 200 acres of cucumbers and 100 acres of tomatoes and corn. The factory was continued by the Pressing family for a while after the death of the founder, William Pressing, in 1919. The facility at 71 North West Street was eventually sold to the Stokely-Van Camp company and continued to be a canning factory through the mid-1980s.

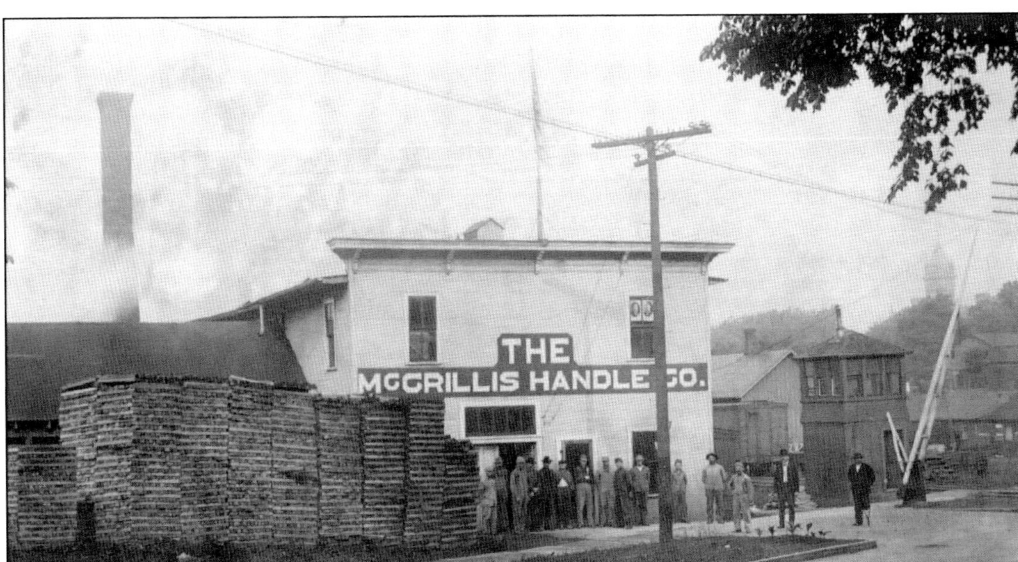


The McCrillis Handle Company came to Norwalk in 1896 after its factory burned in Milan, Ohio. The factory was built at 46 Woodlawn Avenue near the railroad tracks. They made wooden handles and various novelty items, such as cribbage boards. The tower of Norwalk High School can be seen on the right.

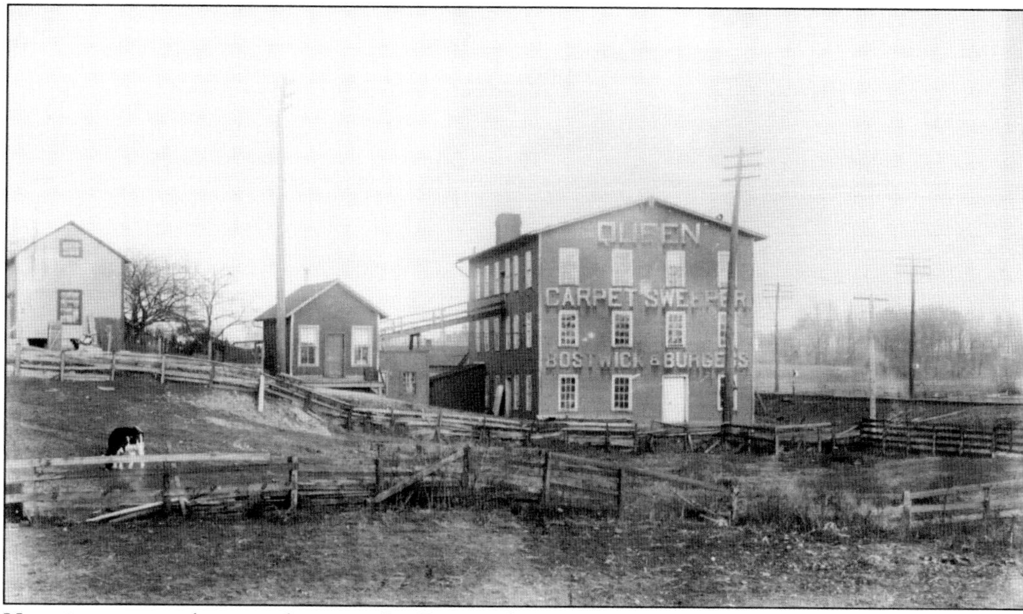


Here is a pastoral scene showing the Bostwick & Burgess Queen Carpet Sweeper factory on Water Street at the end of South Prospect Street. This early industrial structure looks more like a farm with the cow and pasture.

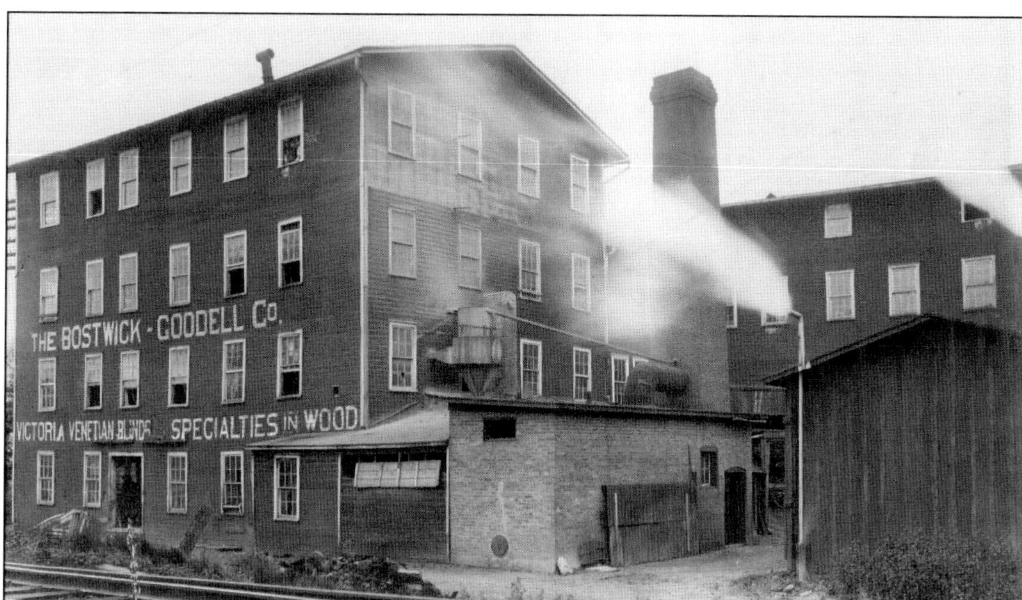


Bostwick & Burgess, started in 1880, manufactured wooden carpet sweepers. In 1889, they made a musical instrument called the calliope similar to an organ and, in 1893, a wooden Columbus Clock in honor of the 500th anniversary of Christopher Columbus discovering America. Charles W. Burgess eventually sold his interest, and the firm became Bostwick and Goodell, which manufactured Venetian window blinds.

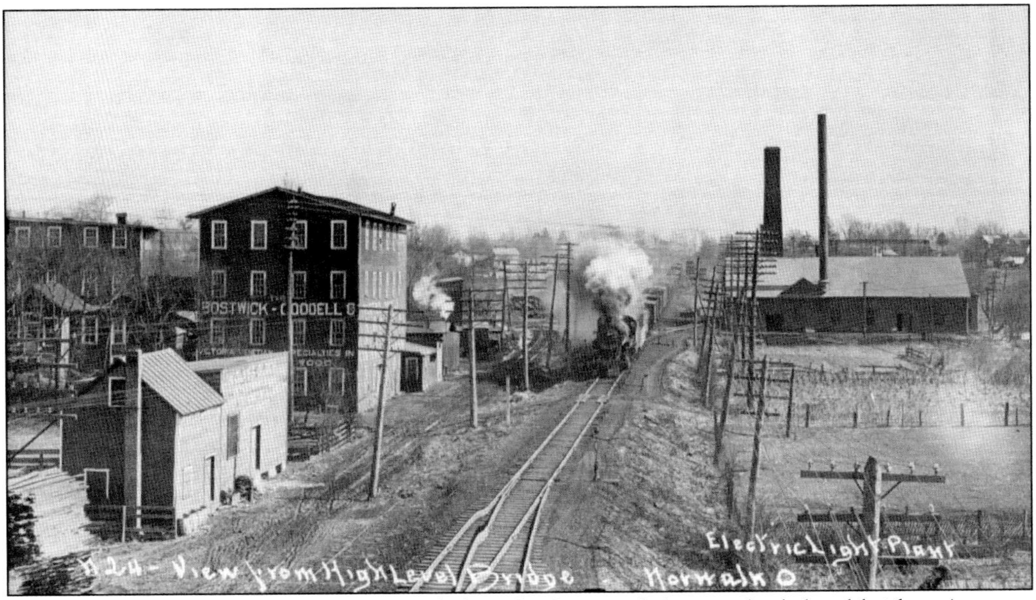

Norwalk's early industrial park was just below the Linwood Avenue high level bridge. A steam train is pictured rolling into town. The Electric Light Plant dates the picture to around 1900. The power lines are leading uptown, and Water Street is still a dirt road.

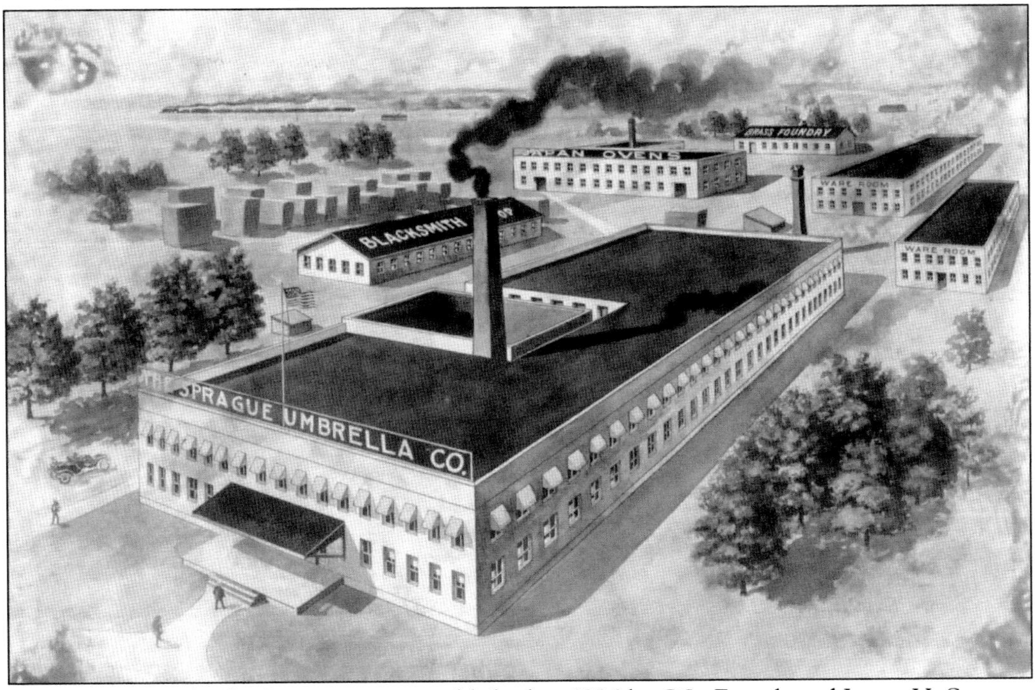

The Sprague Umbrella Company was established in 1886 by C.L. French and James H. Sprague and later taken over by Sprague. By 1897, they were making 100 umbrellas a day, and employed 150 people including 12 salesmen. They made all types of umbrellas, such as buggy canopies, lawn, black ones for hearses, and small ones for children. In August 1898, the factory was destroyed by fire. It was rebuilt, and after the coming of the automobile, the factory became the Sprague Auto-Top Company. It was torn down after World War II.

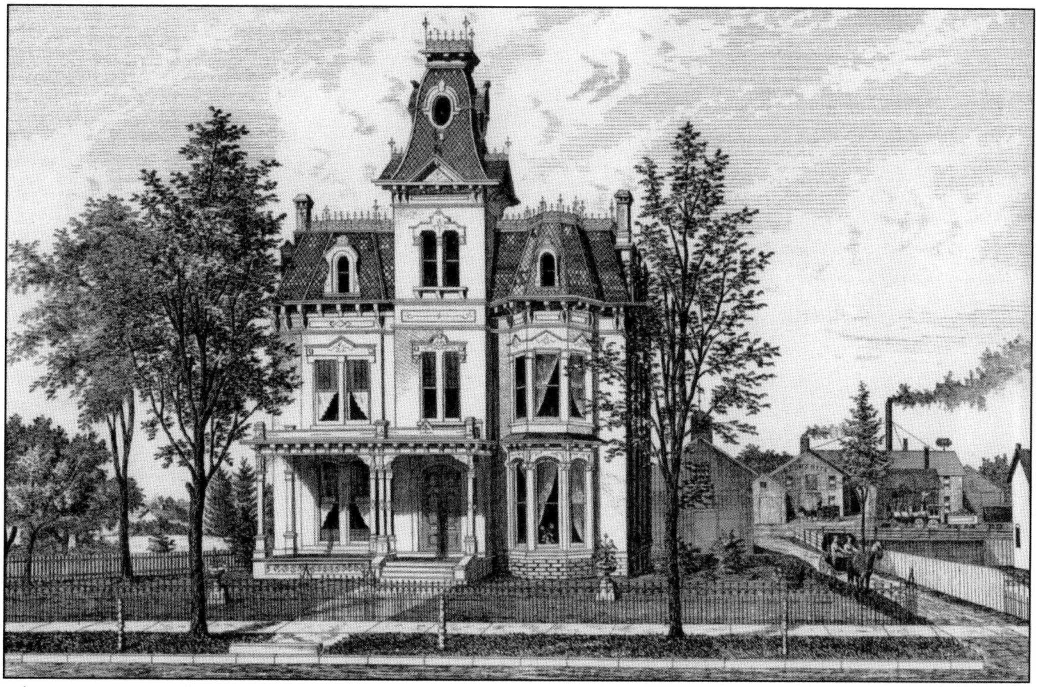

This engraving illustrates the local ingenuity of a clever Norwalk Victorian-era entrepreneur. It is a wonderful example of Third Empire–style home standing at 119 East Main Street. There was a small factory behind the home. Bernard Cortrite was born in New York, and after attempting farming, he was hired as a salesman for a machinery manufacturer. He was encouraged to move to Ohio and engage in Fanning Mill production. He was quite successful, producing over 1,000 a year. The only evidence of his "micro empire" is this home that is still standing, and a Fanning Mill in the Firelands Museum.

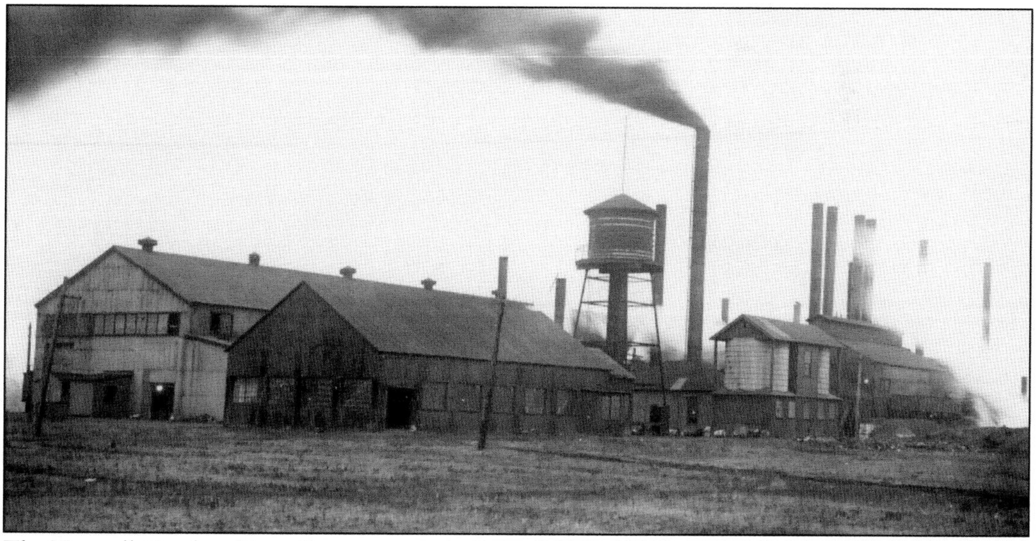

The Norwalk Steel and Iron Company was built in 1901. In 1907, it merged with William Kavanaugh Manufacturing Company and became American Steel and Iron. A month later it went into receivership, causing bank failures and other financial problems until 1910 when the plant was leased to Crucible Steel Company of America and operated at a modest output until 1929.

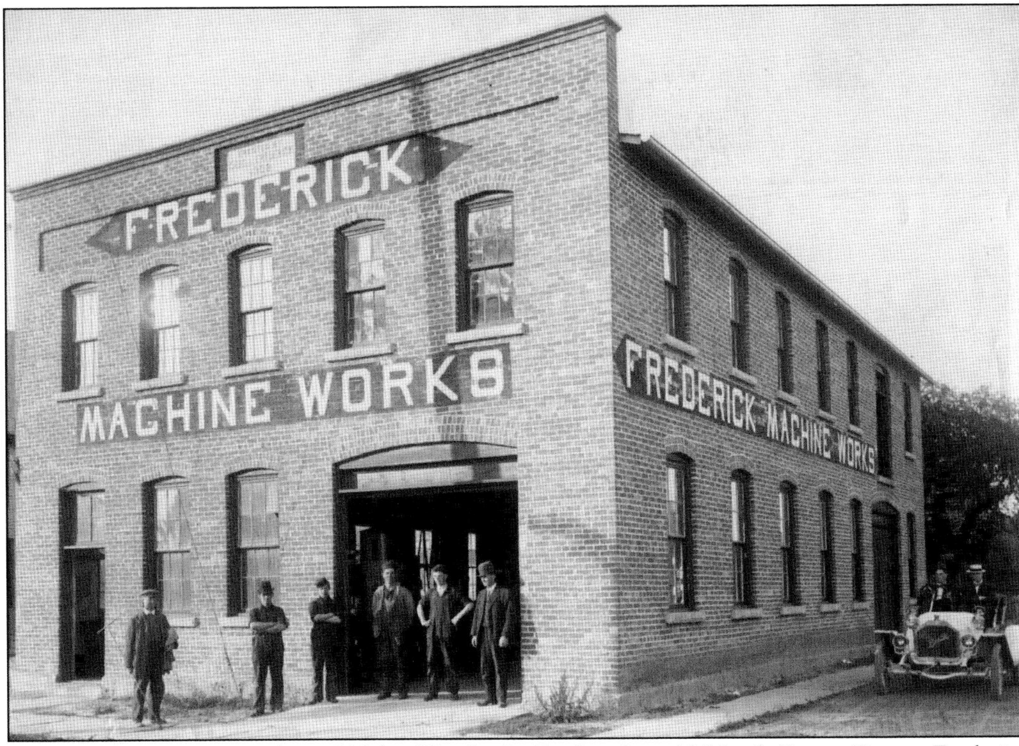


This building was erected in 1908 by Charles L. Frederick at 46 North Foster Street. Frederick Machine Works restored parts or made new ones for many farmers and area industries. They also made children's wagons, lawn tractors, cedar chests, wooden toys, and other items. The building is now the maintenance garage for St. Paul Catholic Church.

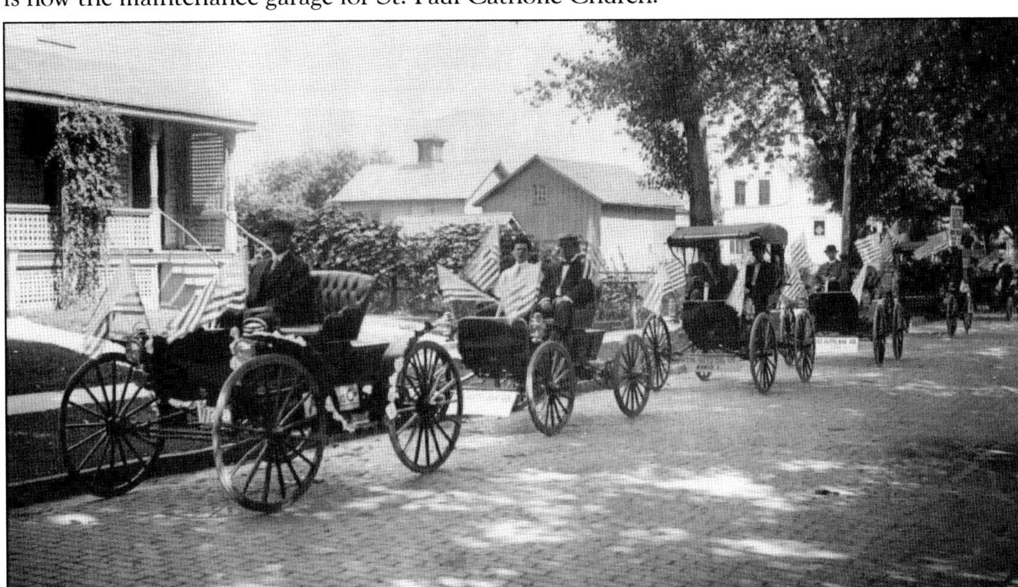

The Norwalk Auto Bug Company was formed in 1909. This horseless carriage had a brief, but important, chapter in the city's history. This is the 1909 centennial parade with the Norwalk Auto Bug joining the festivities.

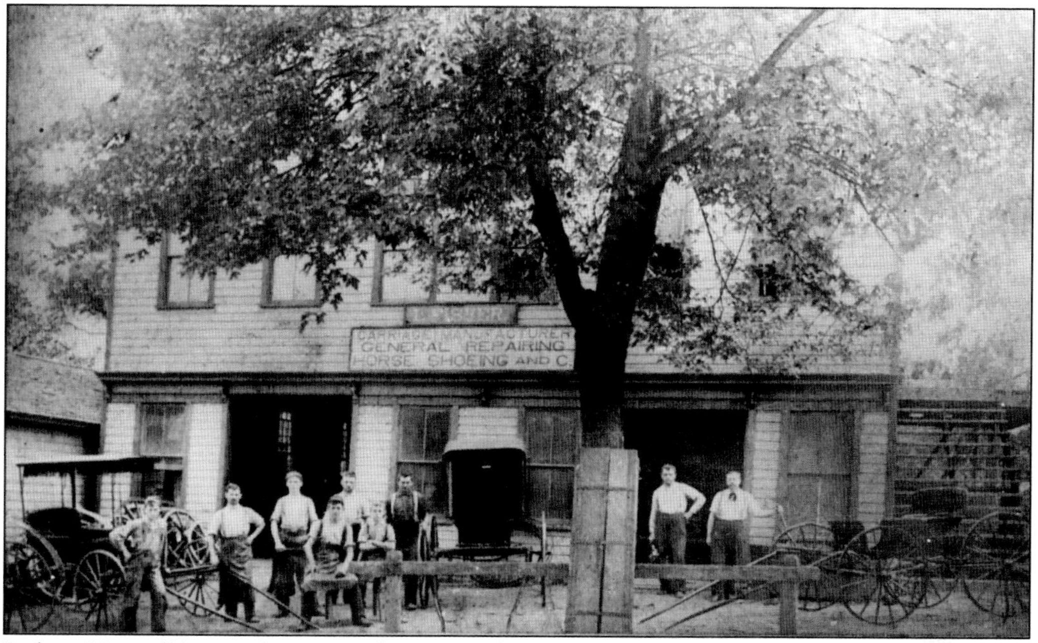


Perhaps Norwalk's most famous residents were the Fisher family. The Fisher Carriage Company was started in 1880 by Lawrence Fisher. He moved here from Peru, Ohio, just south of Norwalk. He had a family of 11 children; seven sons are pictured above at their humble workshop on Benedict Avenue. The sons would move to Detroit, taking with them the skills they learned in Norwalk. The "covered automobile" would revolutionize the industry, creating all-weather vehicles. The Fisher stamp became universally recognized as a symbol of safety and comfort. The Fisher Building in Detroit became the world headquarters for General Motors.

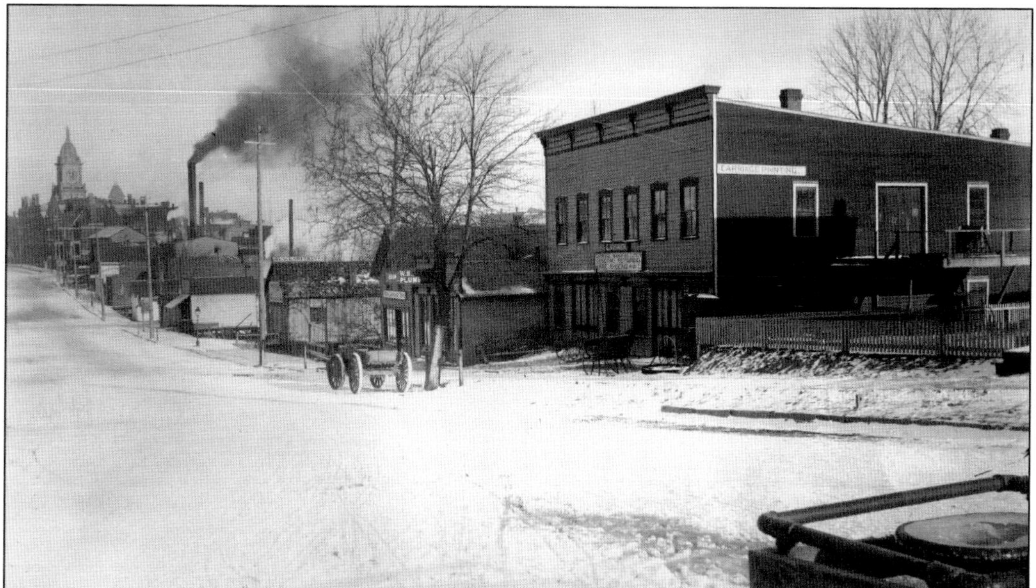

This is a c. 1890 view of Benedict Avenue with the Fisher Carriage Company perched on the hill. The top of the Huron County Courthouse and Gardiner Building look over the booming industrial park on a frigid winter day.

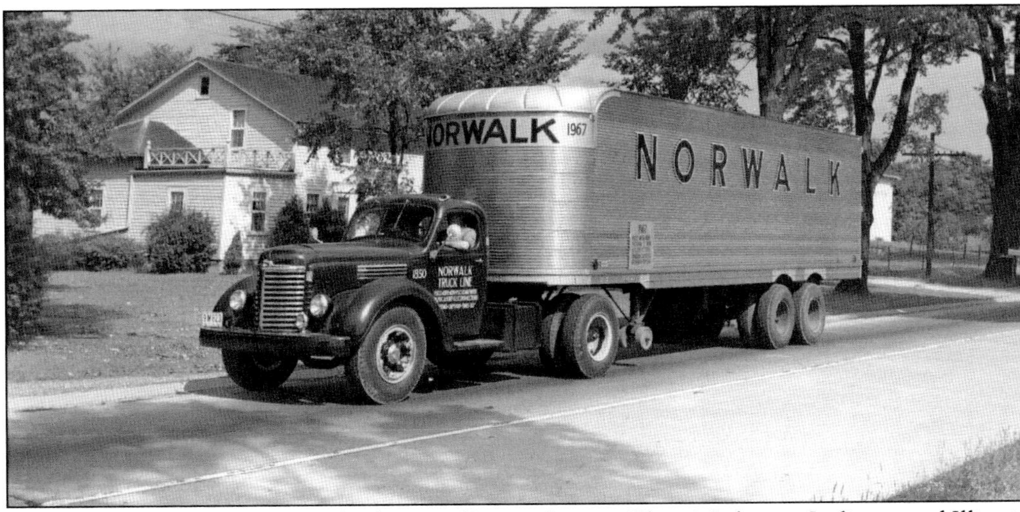


This was a familiar sight on the highways of Pennsylvania, Ohio, Michigan, Indiana, and Illinois. The Norwalk Trucking Line flourished in the 1930s during the Great Depression, as trucks became the most economical way to transport goods. The highway systems were still small compared to today's interstates. Indeed, US Route 20, which ran coast to coast, passed though Main Street. By the 1950s, the Norwalk Truck Line was one of the biggest haulers in the country. The Norwalk High School sports teams became the Norwalk Truckers in 1948.

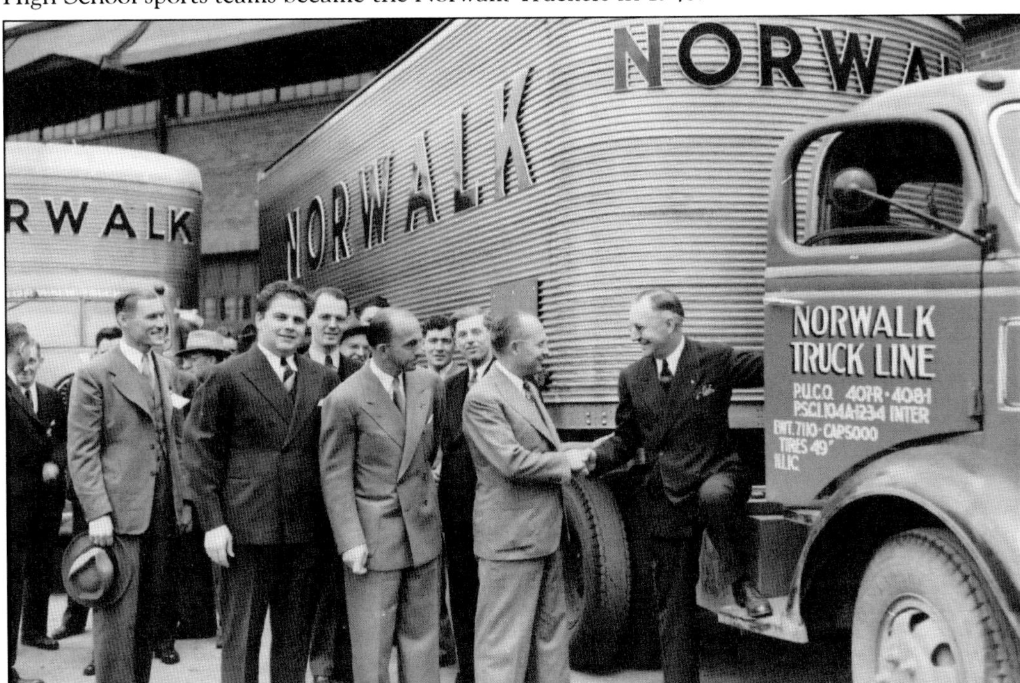


In 1912, John Ernsthausen and Rolla Fader started a small truck company, which evolved into the Norwalk Truck Line. It became the largest independently owned trucking company in the United States. After many successful years, it was sold in 1968 and moved to Colorado. Profits from the company's success eventually funded the Ernsthausen Foundation, which continues to benefit Norwalk today.

# *Six*

# Schools and Churches

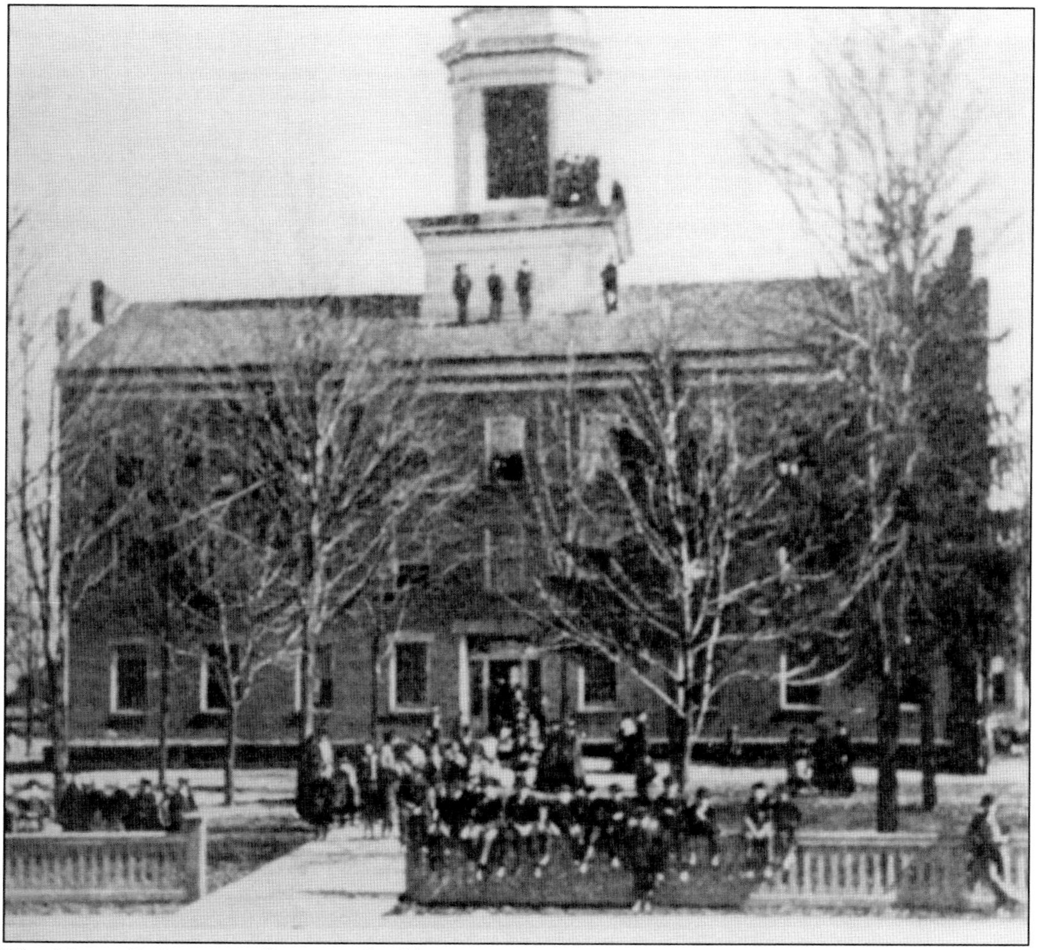

The Norwalk Seminary/Institute building was constructed on Main Street in 1837–1838 by the Methodists, who conducted a seminary there until about 1846. Male and female classes were separate. Several prominent people attended this school, including future president of the United States Rutherford B. Hayes. The building was sold to the Baptist Church, which also used it as a school under the name of the Norwalk Institute. There was no graded high school system at that time, so schools like this were established to enable students to prepare for college. In 1855, the property was sold to the Norwalk Village School District. It became the Norwalk High School, with the first graduation taking place in 1861, and continued to be used until the new Central High School was built in 1884.

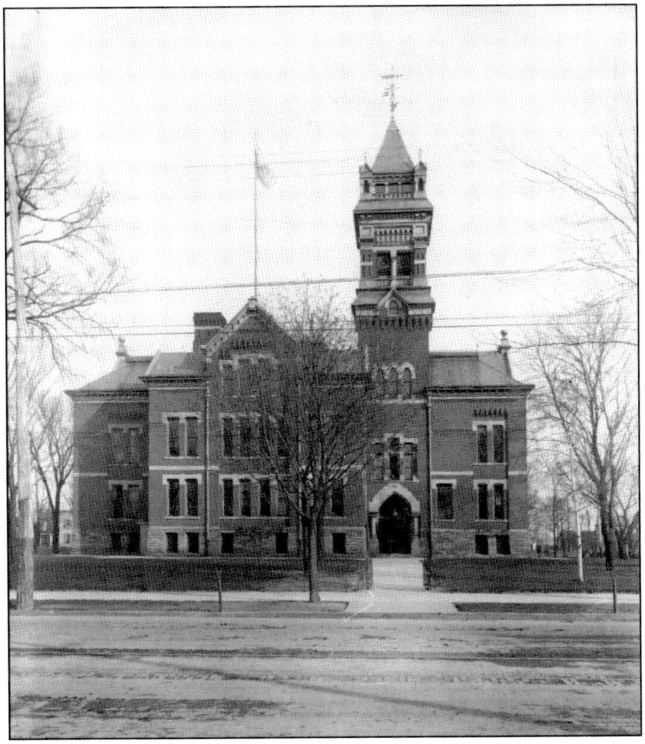

Norwalk Central High School was built in 1884 on the same location as the Norwalk Institute. Its elegant Victorian bell tower immediately became part of the early skyline. Educational buildings at the time were more about style than practicality, and over the years, it became structurally unstable. It was used as a high school until the Community High School (Cole Building) was built in 1919. It then was used as a grade school with grades first through sixth on the first floor and seventh and eighth on the second floor. The third floor was unsafe to use. The building was demolished in 1939 to make way for the new Norwalk High School.

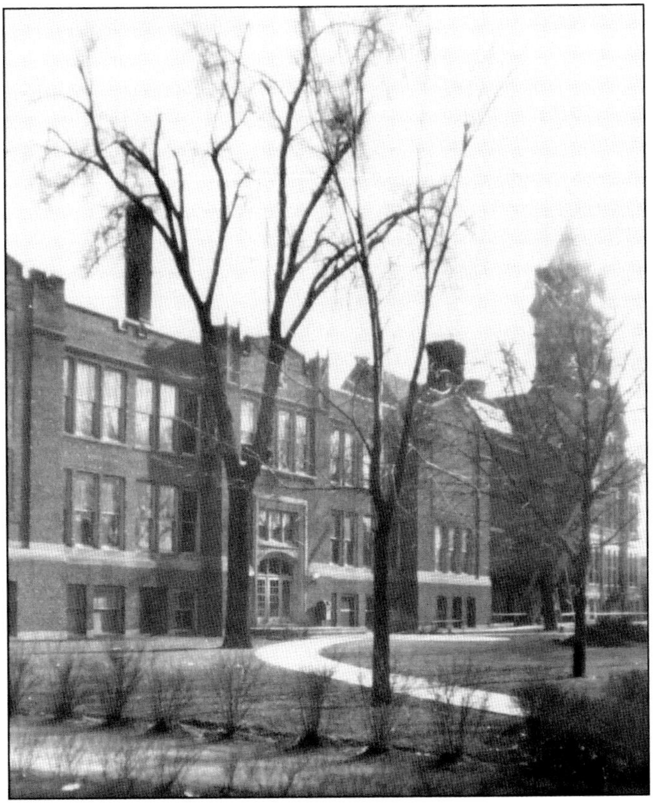

The Community High School was constructed in 1919 just to the south of the older Central High School building. The tower of the older building can be seen at right in this picture. The structure was renamed the Cole Building in honor of the longtime principal James Cole in 1938. After the Norwalk High School was erected in 1940, the building then became the Junior High and was also used for elementary grades.

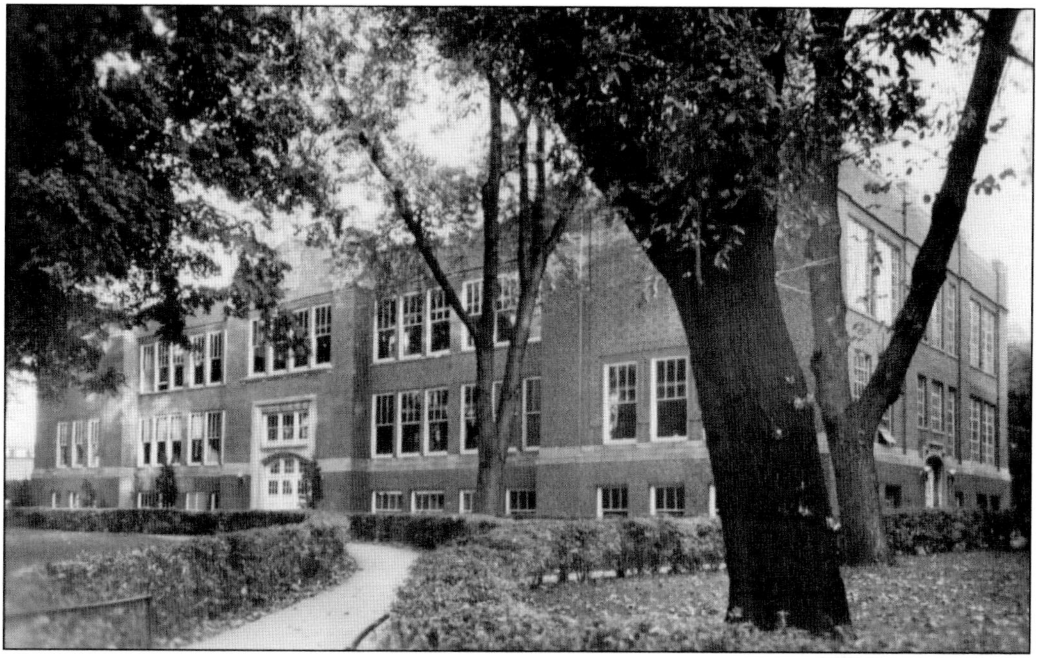

The Cole Building was demolished in 2002, and the area is now a playground for the Main Street School children.

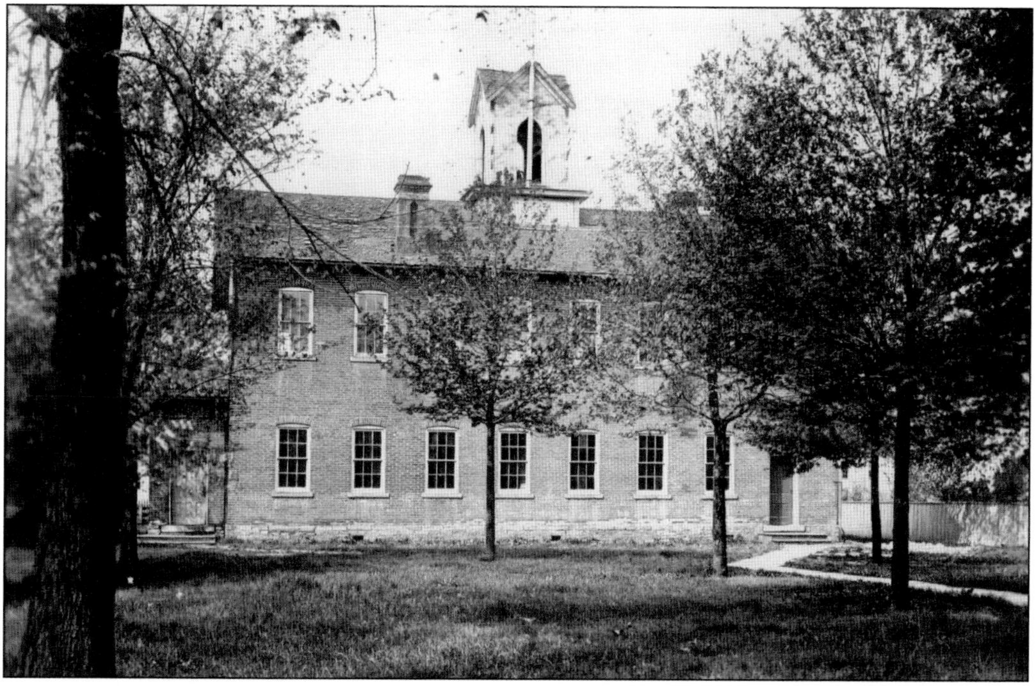

This Hester Street building was erected by the German Catholics of Norwalk for their church and school in 1868. Due to many conflicts, the building was only used by the Catholics for eight years and then sold to the Norwalk School Board. In 1913, it was purchased by the Fisher Body Company of Detroit to make tops for automobiles. By 1939, they made the carpets for all General Motors cars except the Cadillac. The company closed in 1963.

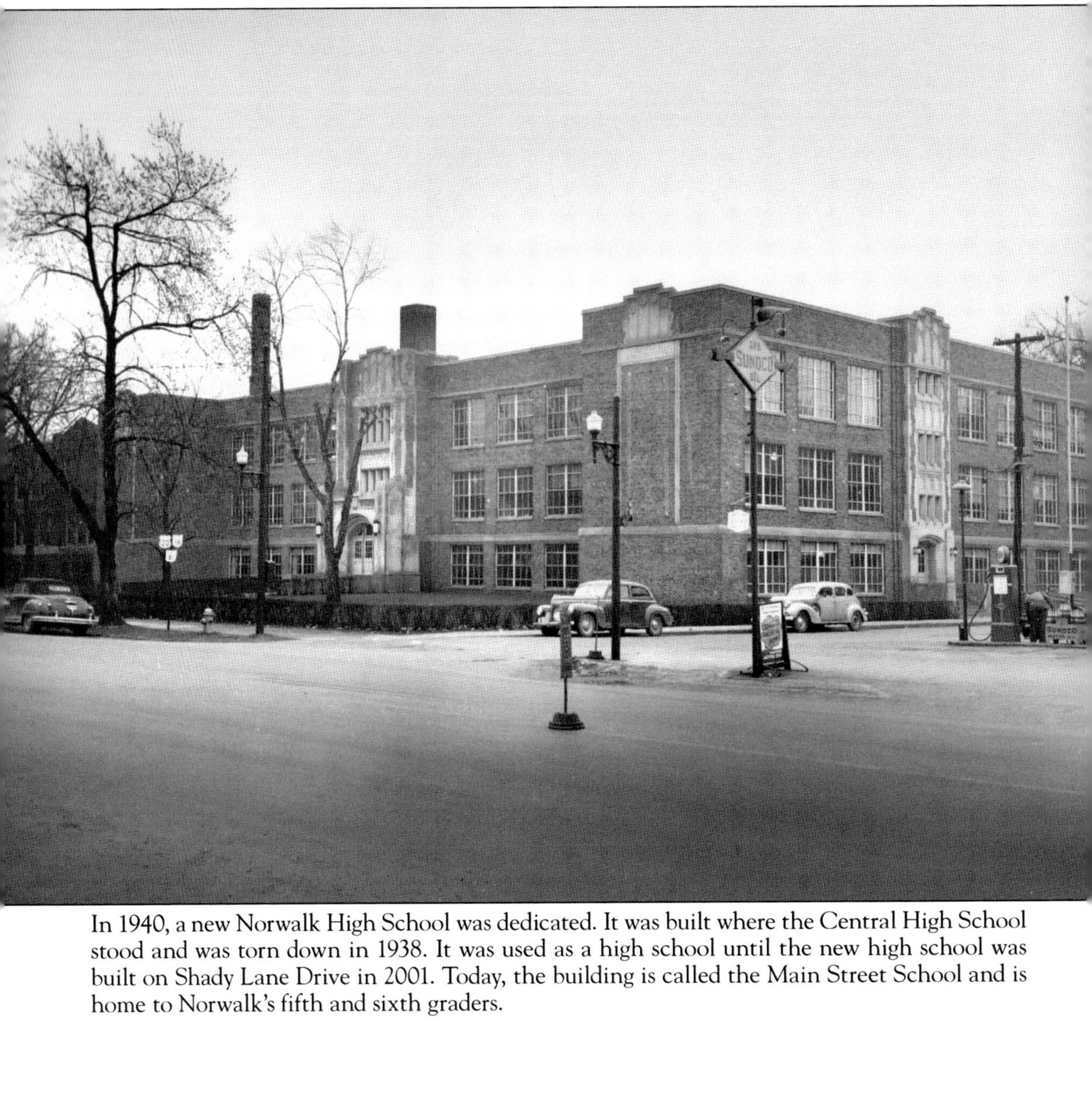


In 1940, a new Norwalk High School was dedicated. It was built where the Central High School stood and was torn down in 1938. It was used as a high school until the new high school was built on Shady Lane Drive in 2001. Today, the building is called the Main Street School and is home to Norwalk's fifth and sixth graders.

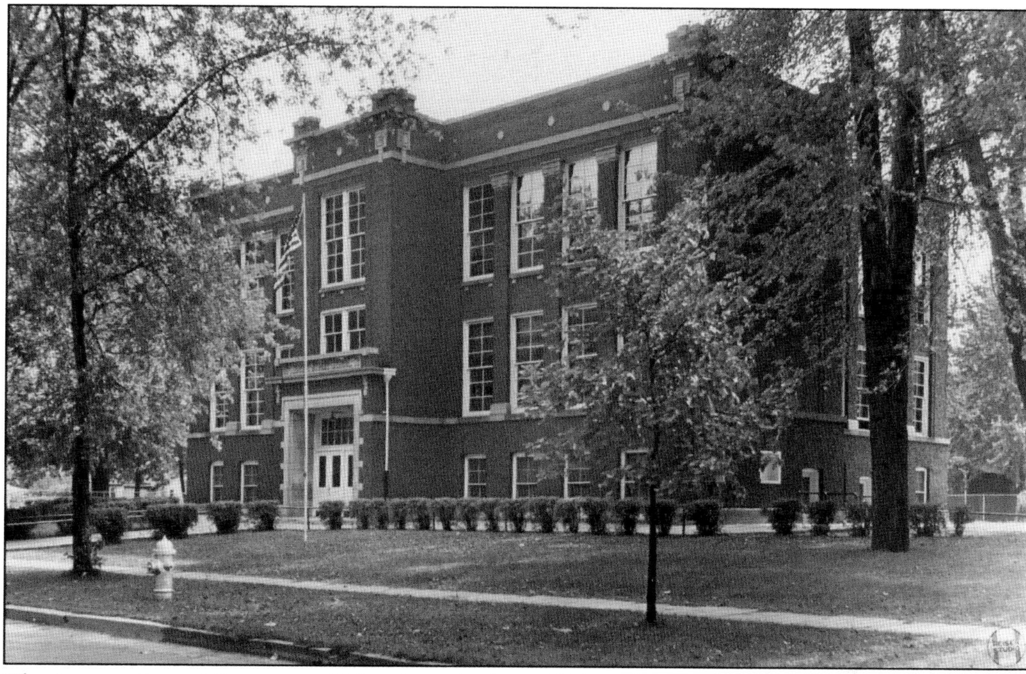

The League Street Elementary School was built in 1913, replacing an earlier property constructed in 1872. It currently serves Norwalk's fourth grade students. It is the oldest functioning school in town. This facility was for children from the northern neighborhoods.

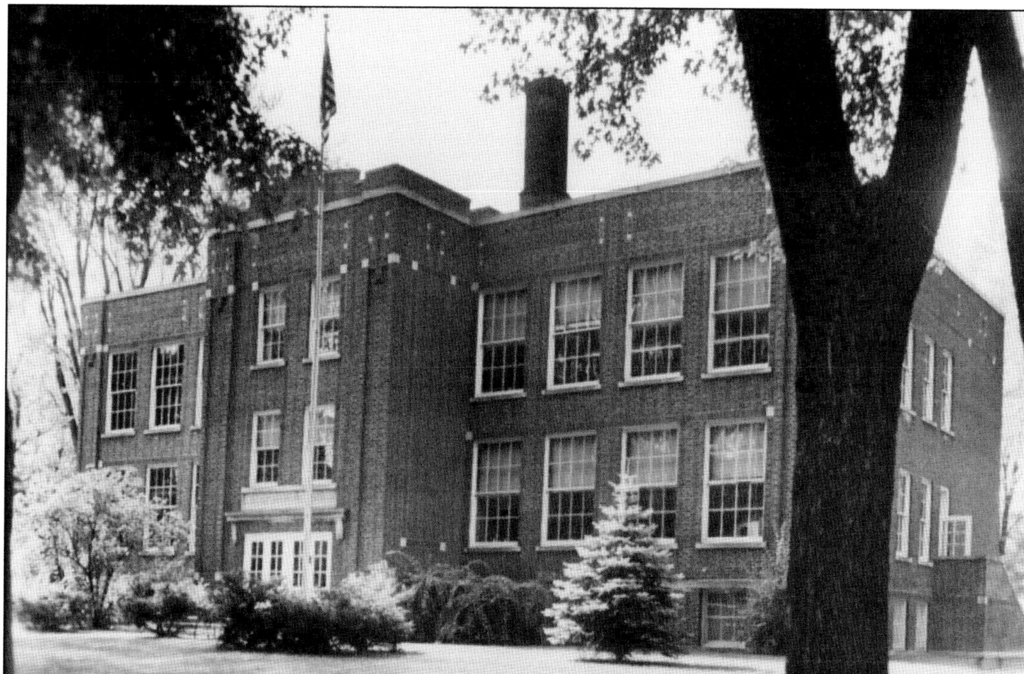

The Benedict School was built in 1917 and replaced an earlier building built in 1872. It was used as an elementary school until it closed in 1953. It is now used for board of education offices. This school served children from the southern neighborhoods.

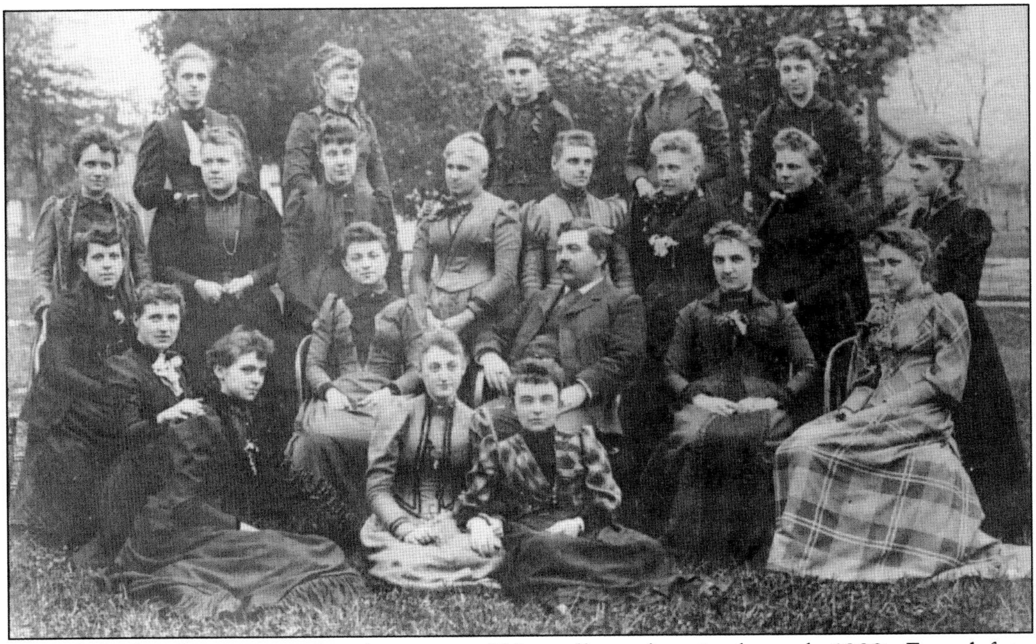

Supt. A.D. Beachy is pictured with a group of Norwalk teachers in the early 1900s. From left to right are (first row) Flora Simpson, Stella Wood, Fannie Kennan, and Mary Knapp; (second row) Fran Husted, Nellie Hughes, Superintendent Beachy, Miss Baker, and Minnie Stoughton; (third row) Grace Evans, Pheobe Smith, Florence Kellogg, Mrs. King, Alice Cook, Aurelia Greene, Edith Baker, and Sara Knapp; (fourth row) Fannie States, Lucy Roberts, Clara Johnson, Jessie Husted, and Lulu Webb.

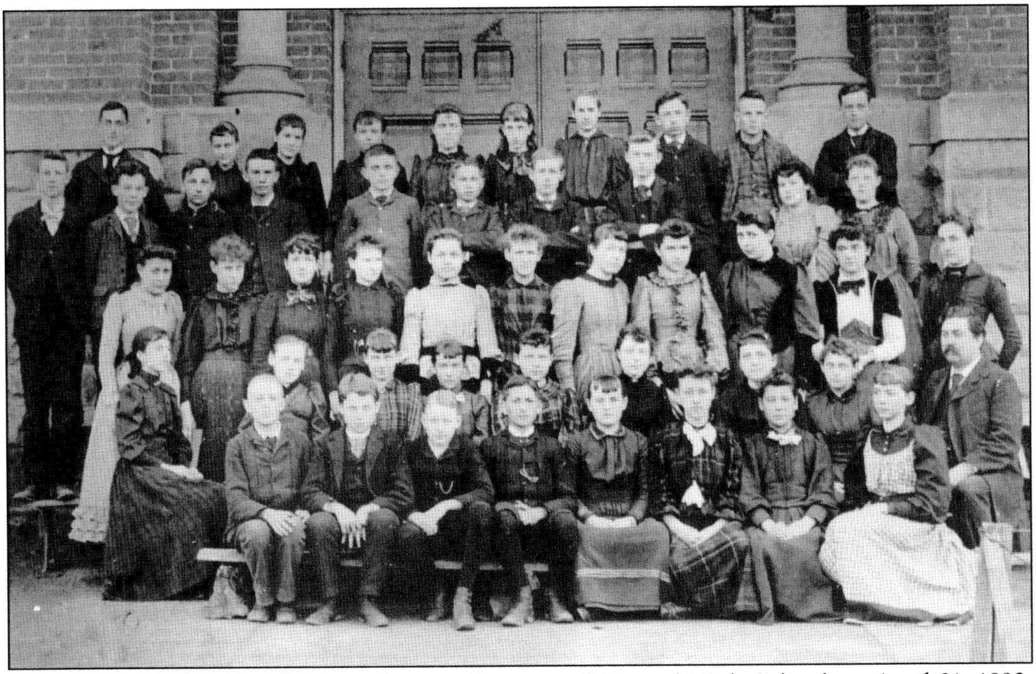

This appears to be the collective class on the steps of Central High School on April 21, 1892, with Superintendent Beachy.

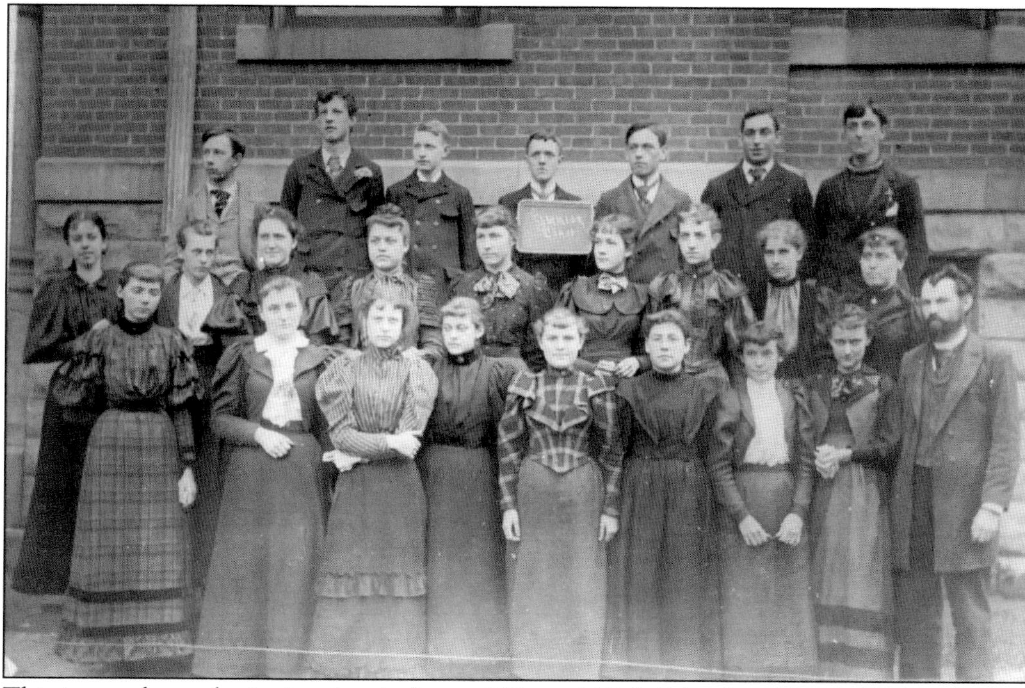

This image shows the junior class in front of Central High School on May 4, 1884, with their teacher, Professor W.P. Thurston.

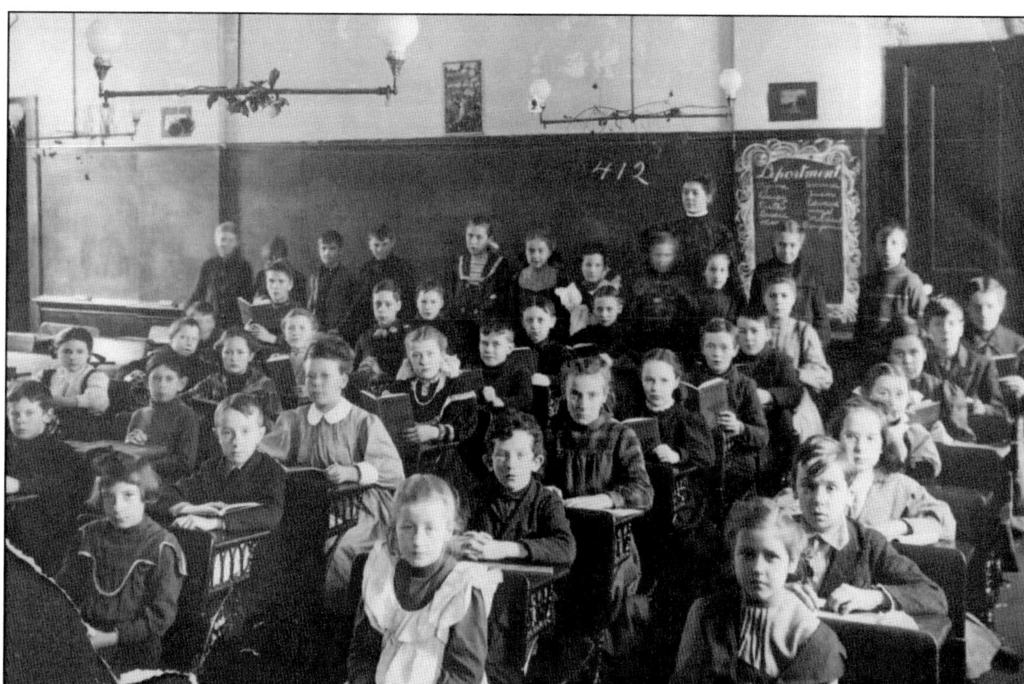

Here is an attentive looking class in 1900 with Miss Reeder. Note the gas lights overhead.

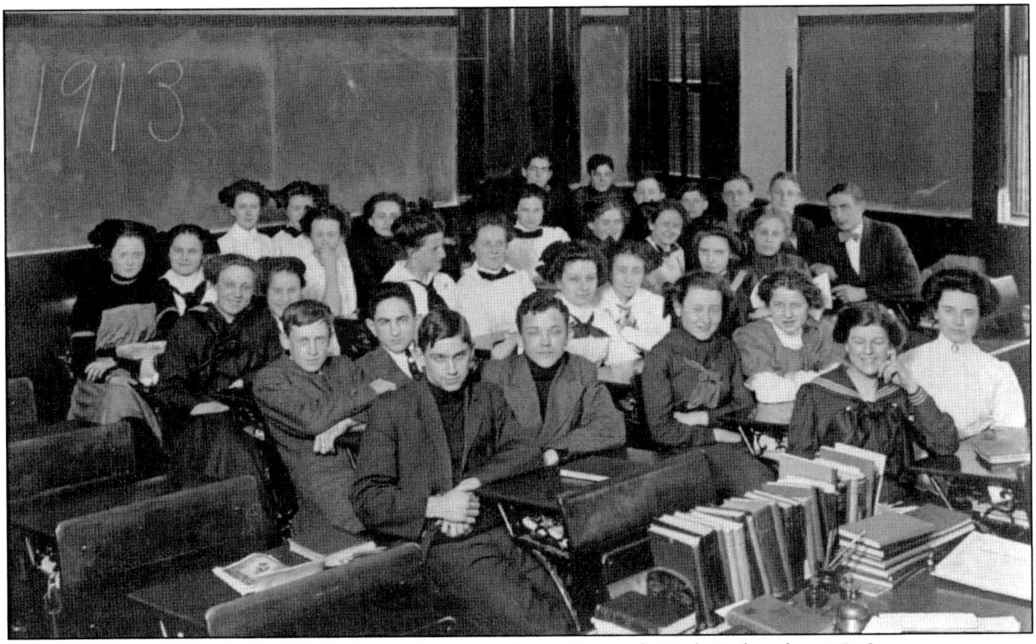


The blackboard dates this classroom photograph at Central High School to 1913.

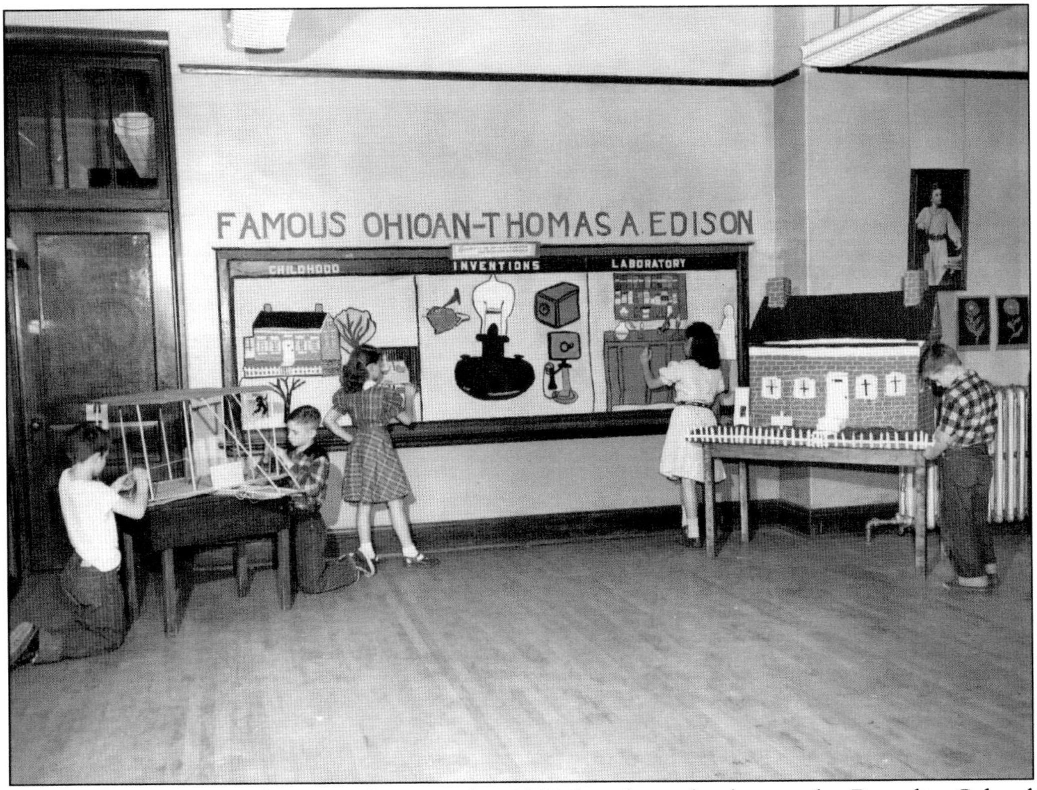


In honor of Thomas Edison, students in this 1952 fourth grade class at the Benedict School work on a project celebrating his achievements, including a model of his birthplace in nearby Milan, Ohio.

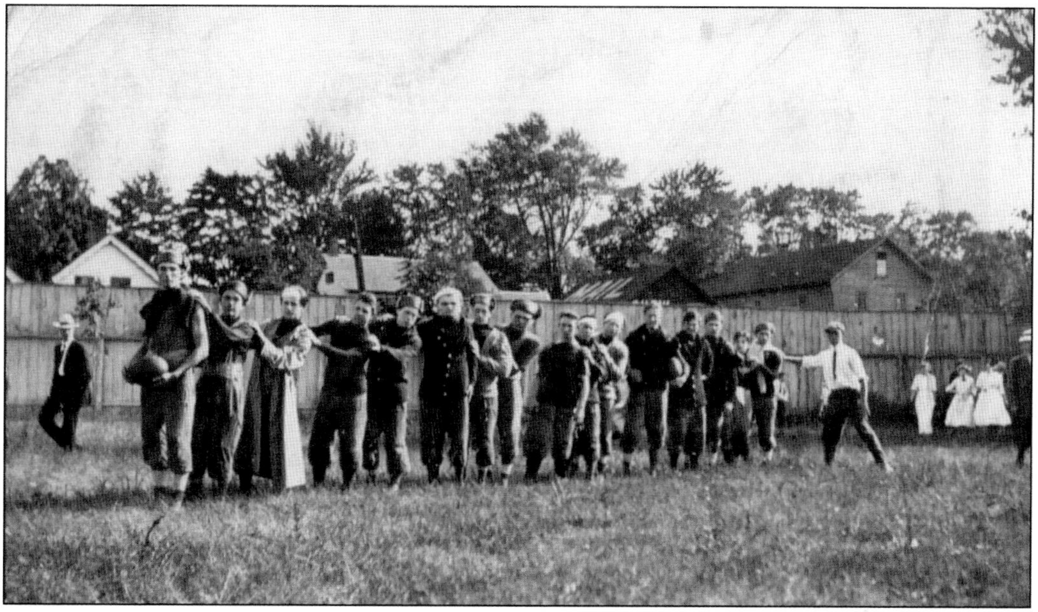

This Central High School football team appears to be lining up for practice. Perhaps this practice took place at the new Whitney Field acquired in 1909.

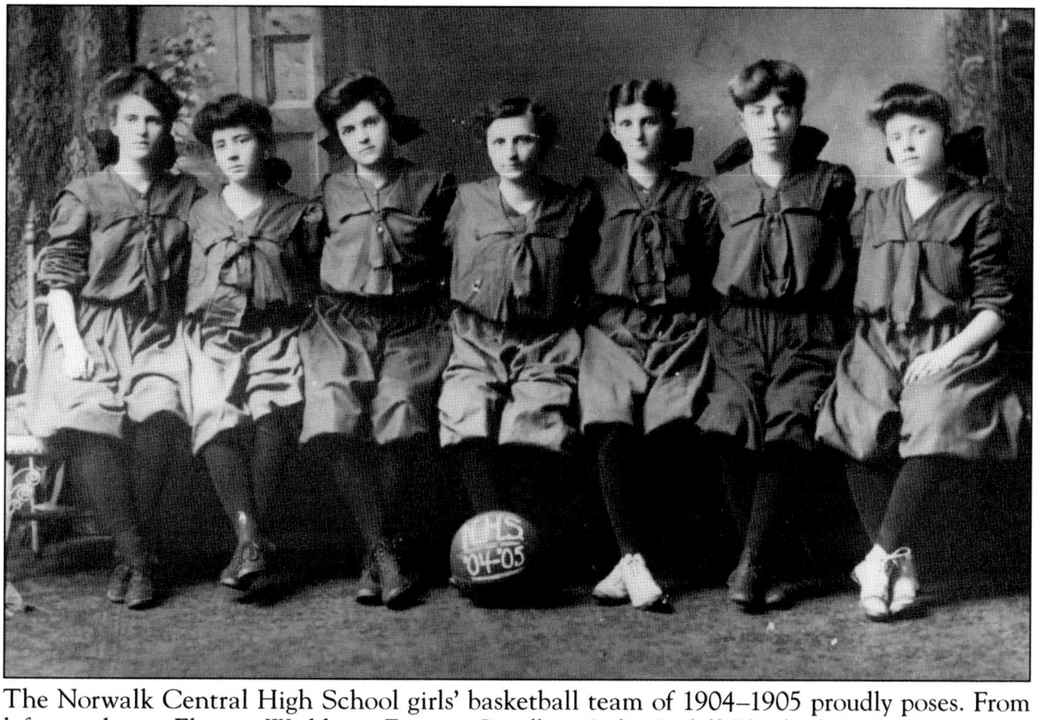


The Norwalk Central High School girls' basketball team of 1904–1905 proudly poses. From left to right are Eleanor Wickham, Frances Goodhue, Lelia Sutliff, Elizabeth Roth, Grace Kies, Charlotte Butler, and Grace Wickham.

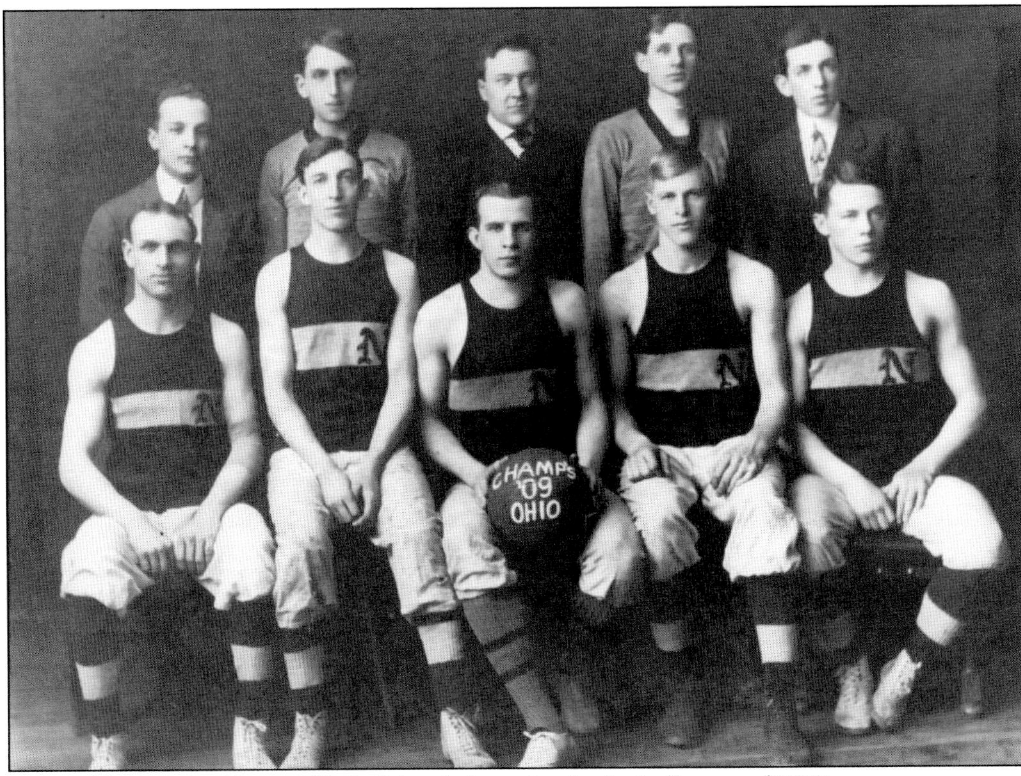


Pictured here is the Central High School champion basketball team of 1909.

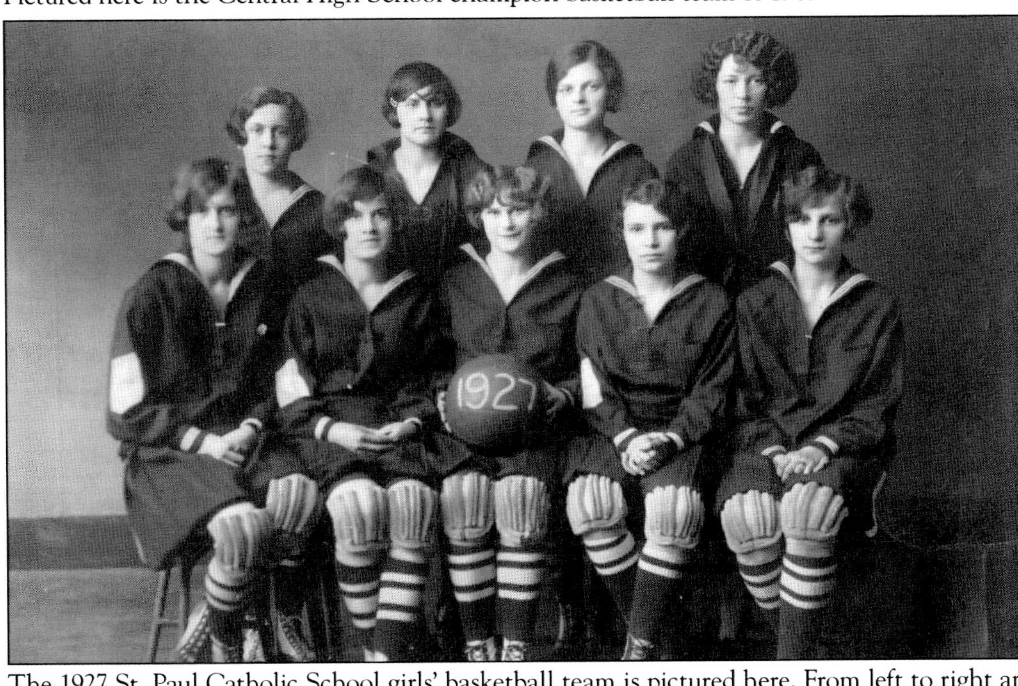


The 1927 St. Paul Catholic School girls' basketball team is pictured here. From left to right are (first row) Myrtle Myers, Mary Hug, Hazel Smith, Rose Stoll, and Elizabeth Rossman; (second row) Laura Myers, Marian Schaffer, Mildred Camp, and coach G. Conrad.

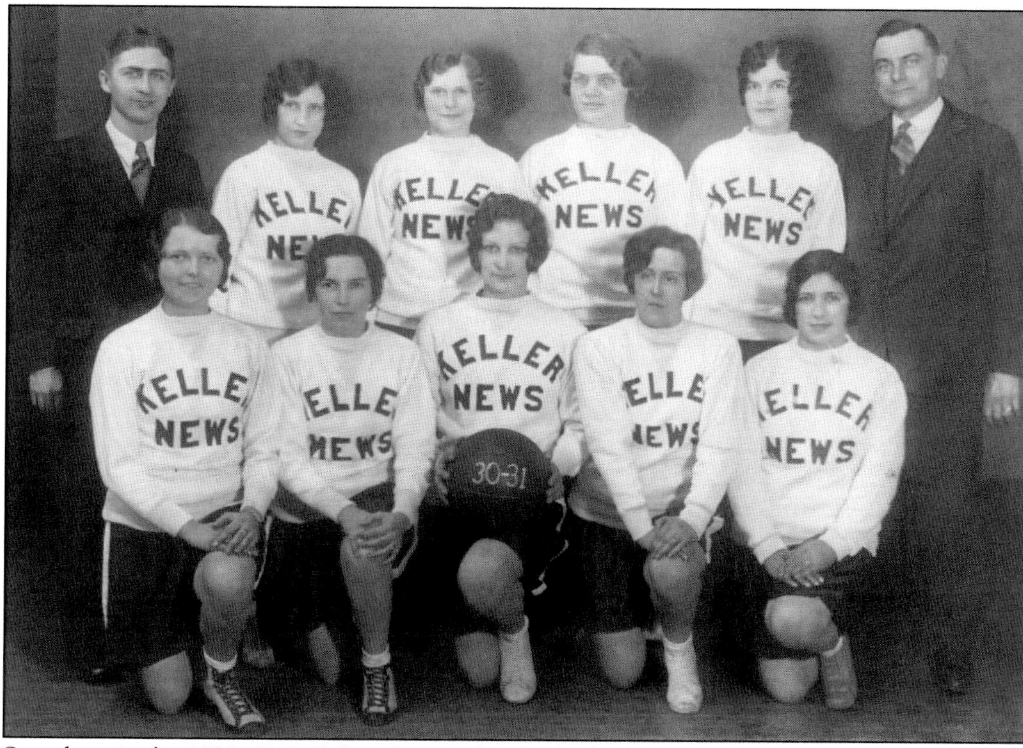


Seen here is the 1930–1931 Keller News ladies' basketball team. Keller's newsstand, sponsor of the team, was located at 86 Milan Avenue.

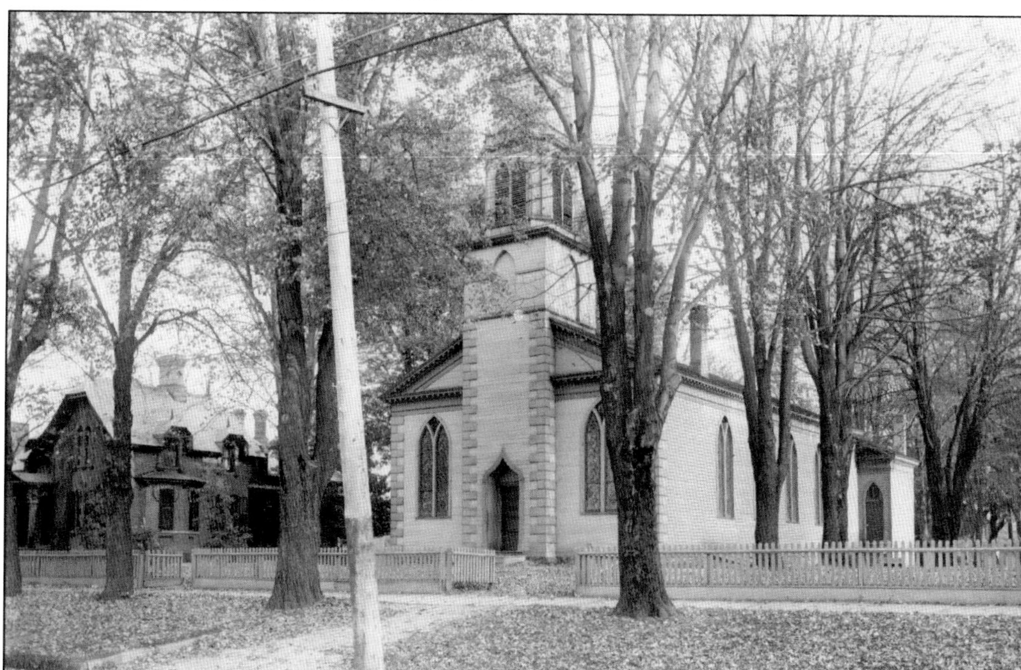

The first Episcopal church was built in 1836 and enlarged in 1853. In 1909, it was moved to the back of the lot and used for many years as a parish hall. It was destroyed by fire in 1976.

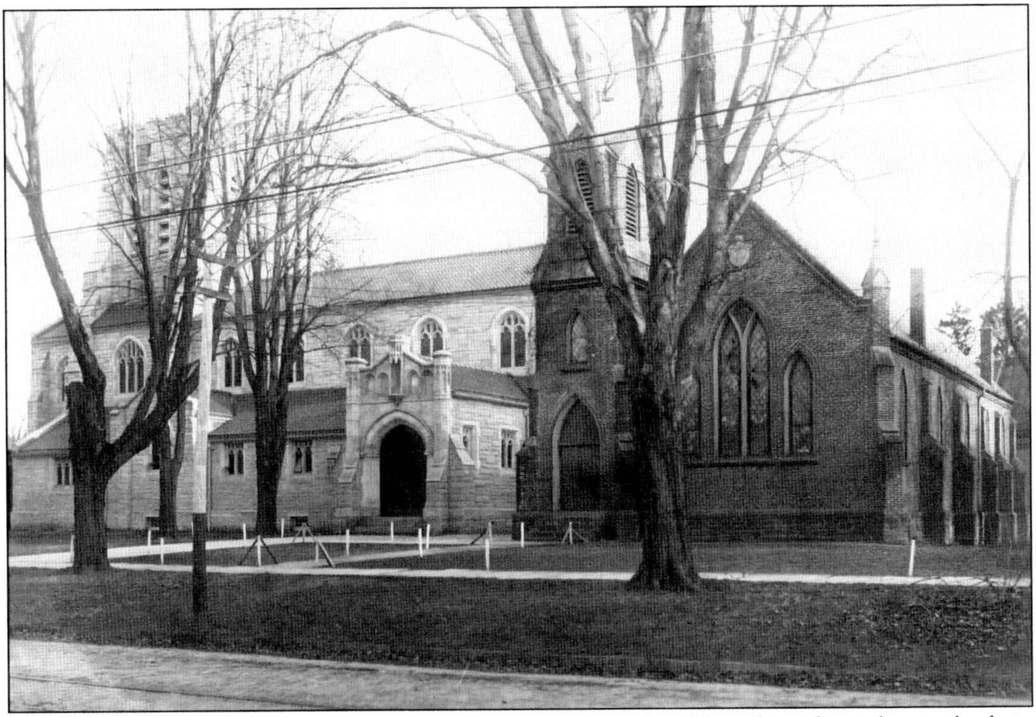

The current Episcopal church was built in 1909. The Benedict Chapel on the right was built in 1863 with a large donation from Platt Benedict.

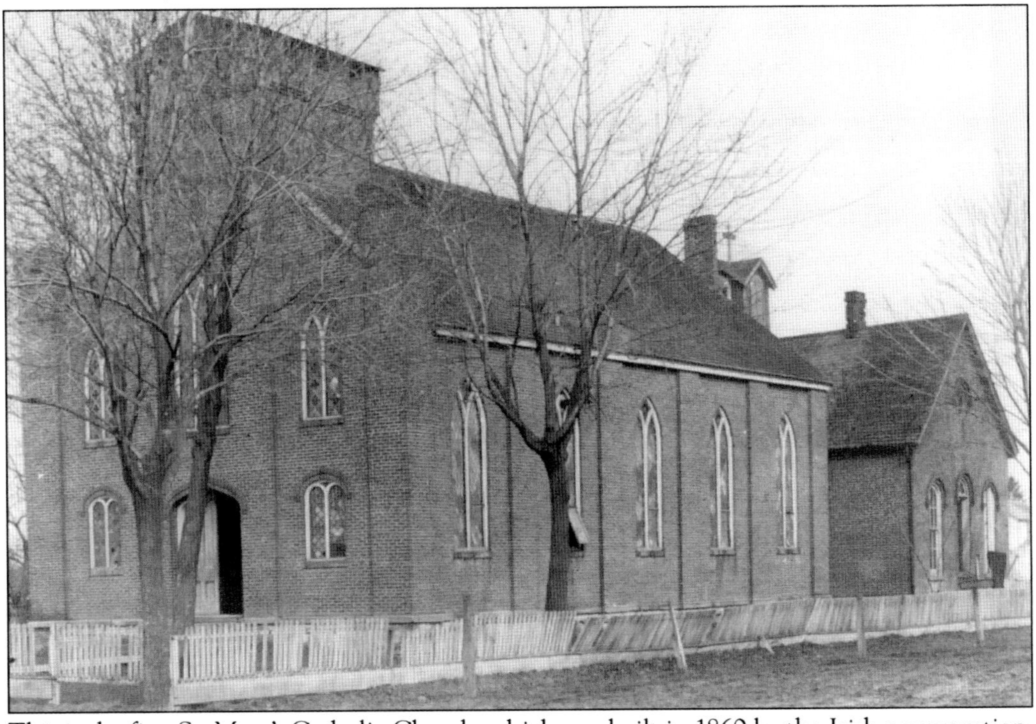

This is the first St. Mary's Catholic Church, which was built in 1860 by the Irish congregation. It was located at the corner of Milan Avenue and St. Mary's Street.

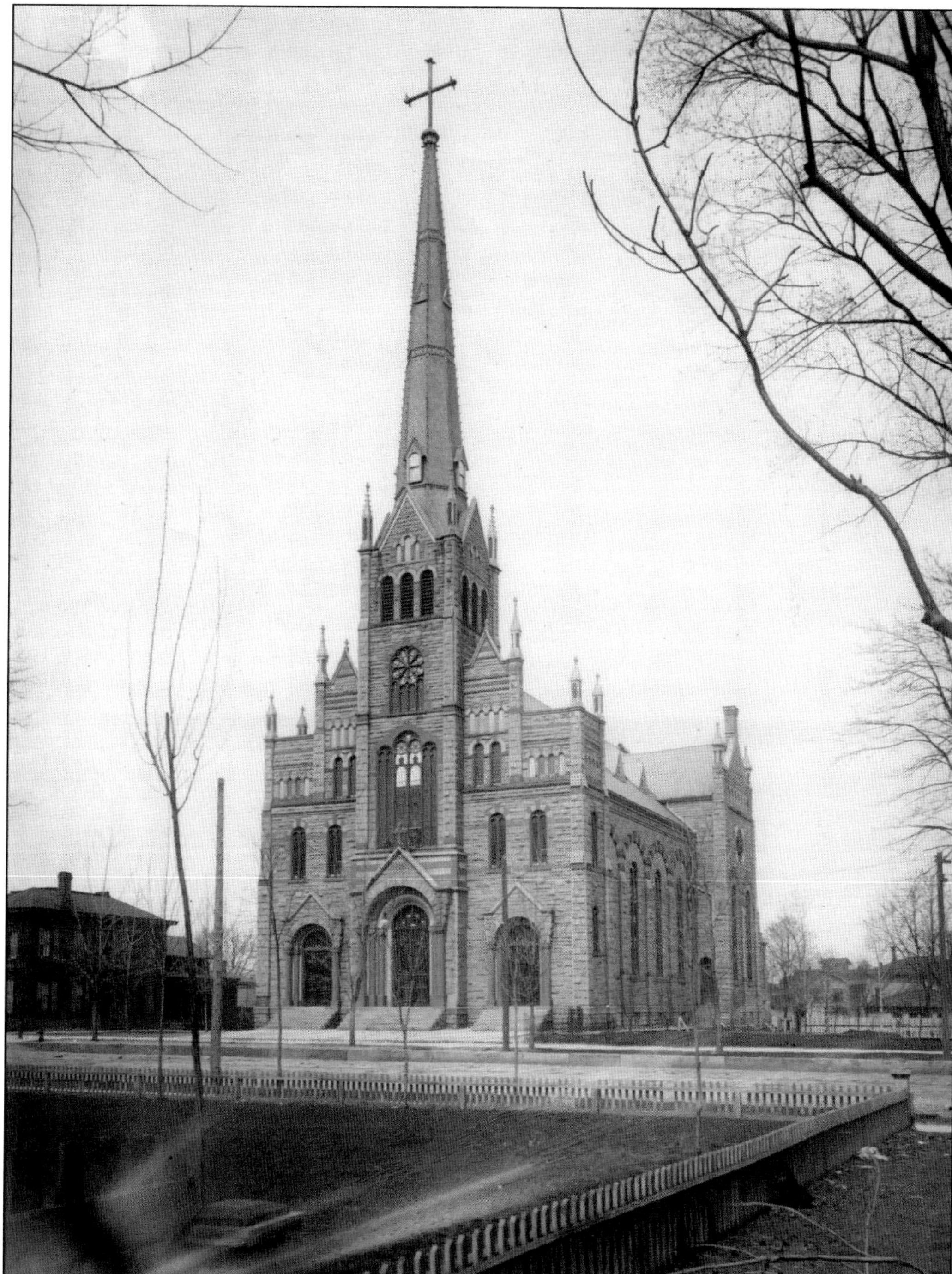

The new St. Paul's Catholic Church was built at 91 East Main Street in 1890 and dedicated in 1893. The spire soared high in the skyline but was later removed.

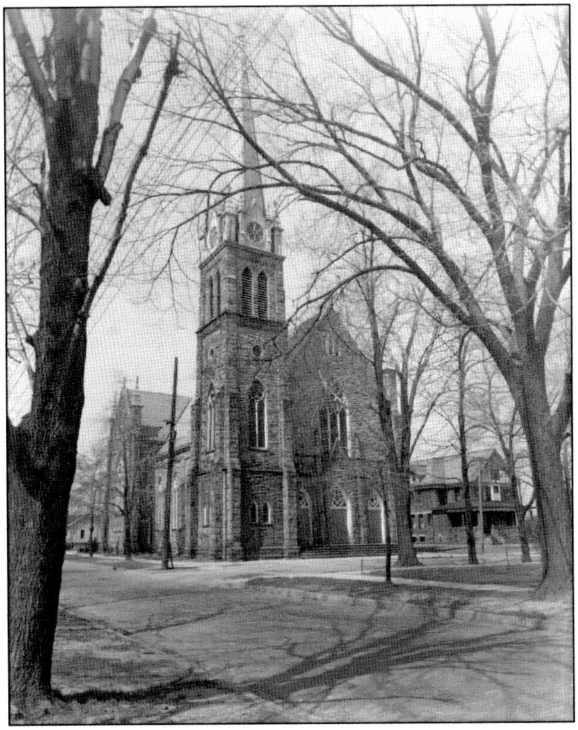

Norwalk has a second Catholic church. This is St. Mary's Mother of the Redeemer Church at 38 West League Street, dedicated in 1889. Its spire was removed as well. This church was for the Irish immigrants.

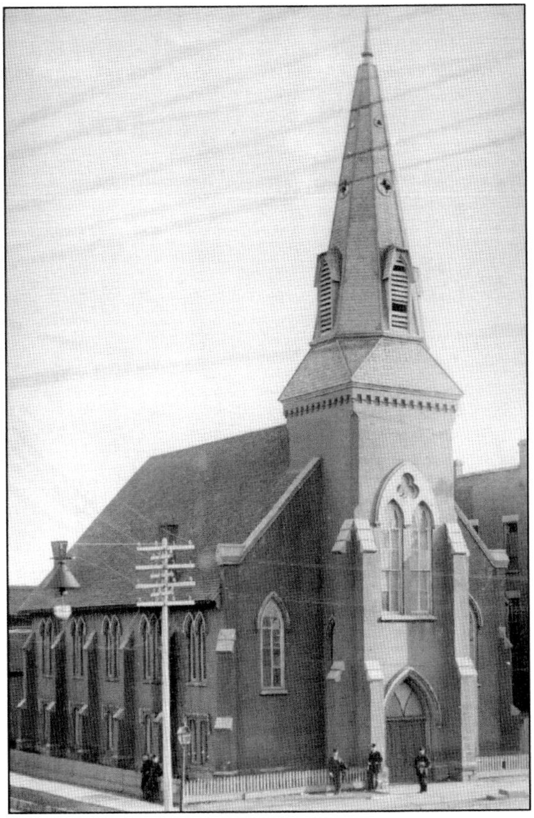

This Methodist church stood on West Main Street and Benedict Avenue from 1854 until 1892, when it was razed for the Glass Block Building.

In 1897, the First United Methodist Church members built a new church on the corner of West Main and State Streets. It was built in the Romanesque Revival style with a distinct bell tower and is still used for services today.

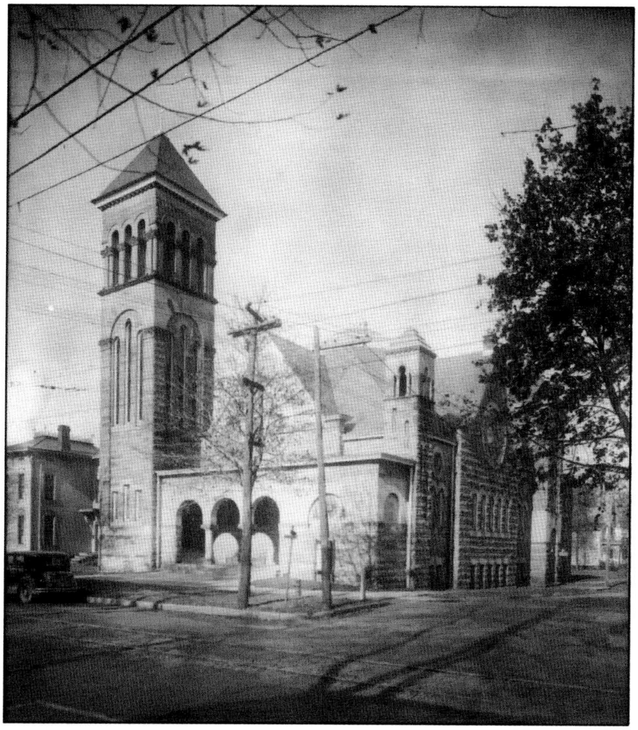

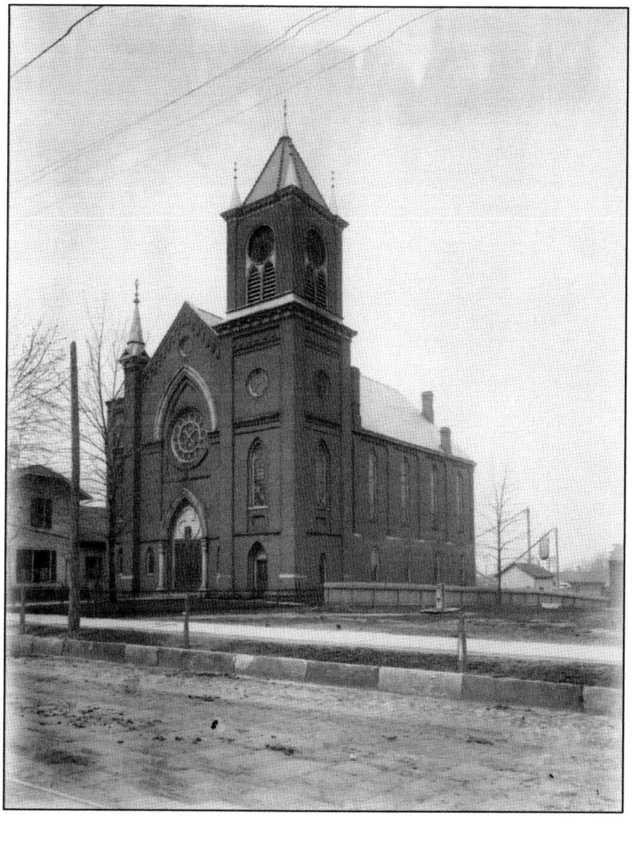

The First Baptist Church in Norwalk was formed in 1819. The first church was built in 1836 and replaced in 1879 at the same location, 67 East Main Street. Built for $14,000, it was dedicated in 1880 and continues to be used for services today.

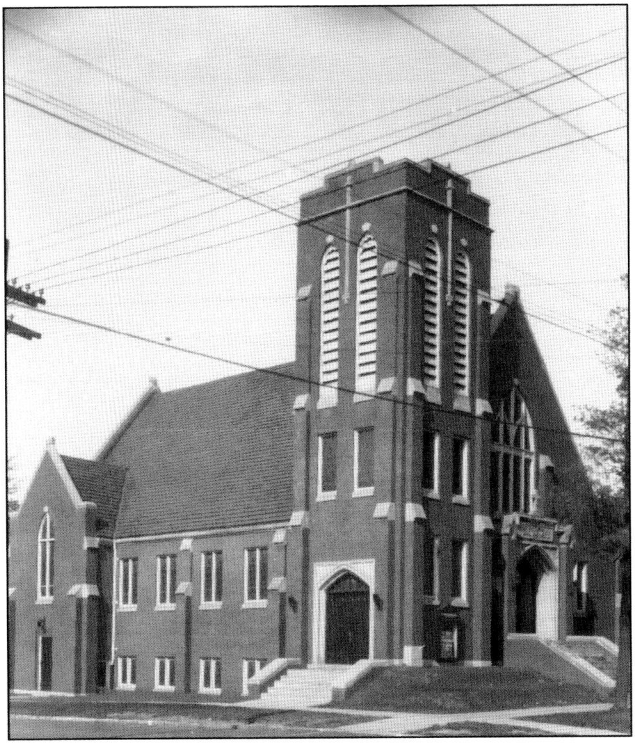

The English Lutheran church was built at 99 East Main Street at the corner of Milan Avenue. It was dedicated in 1925. In 1974, due to expanding membership, it was sold and currently sits vacant. The new church is on Executive Drive.

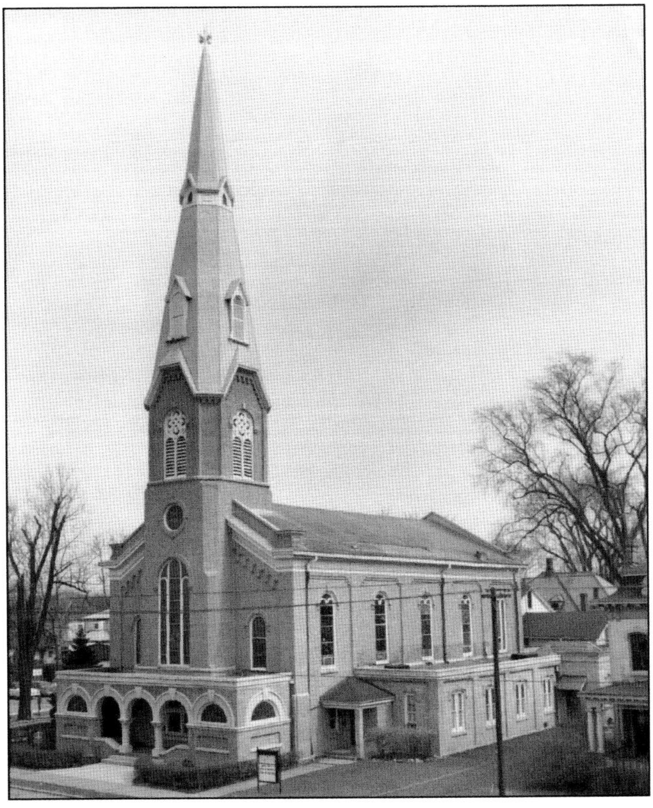

This Presbyterian church at 51 West Main Street was built in 1870. It served its congregation until 1967, when the new church on Firelands Boulevard was constructed. The church no longer stands.

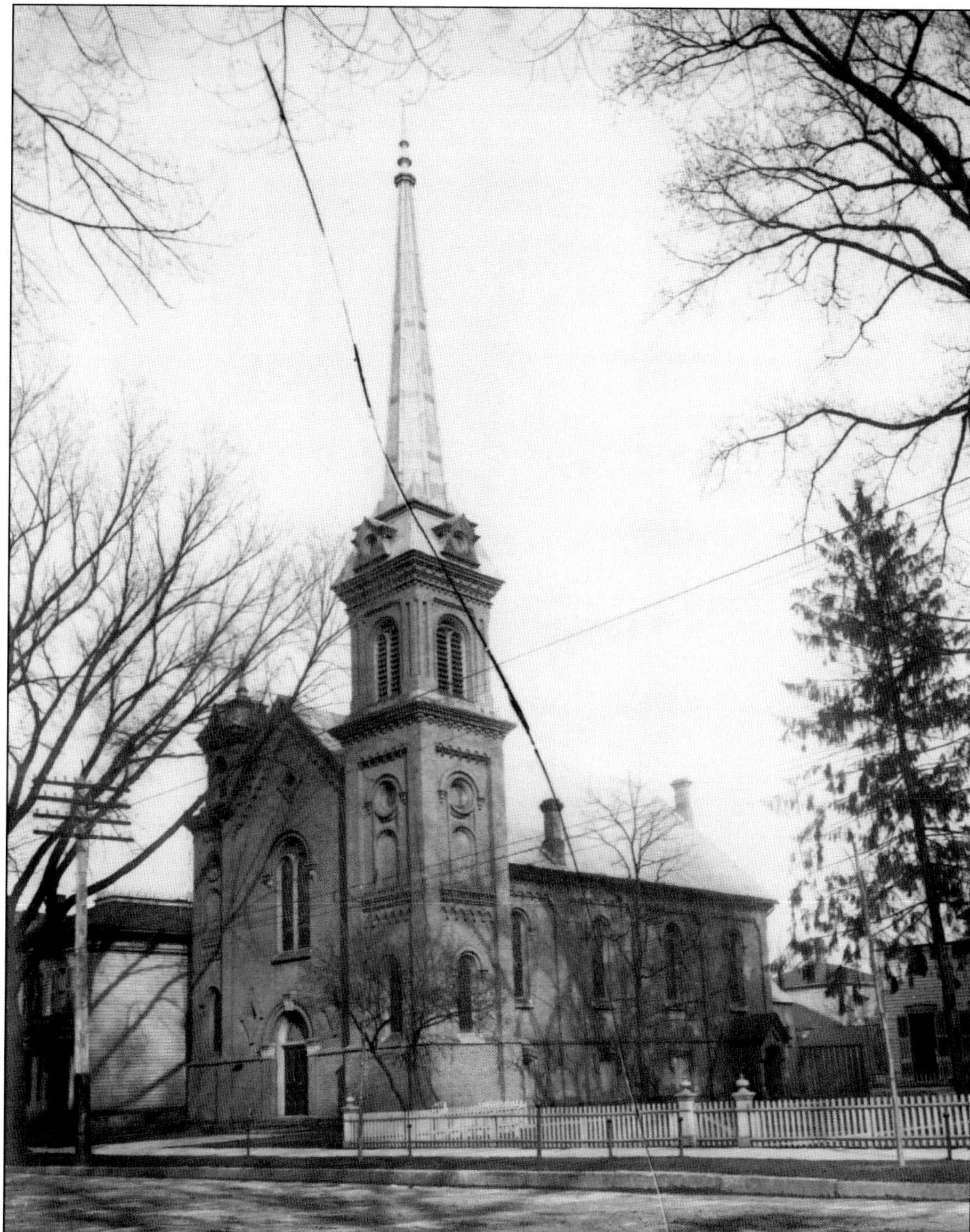

The Universalist church, which featured a Romanesque Revival style, was at 41 West Main Street. It was dedicated on December 8, 1872. It is no longer standing.

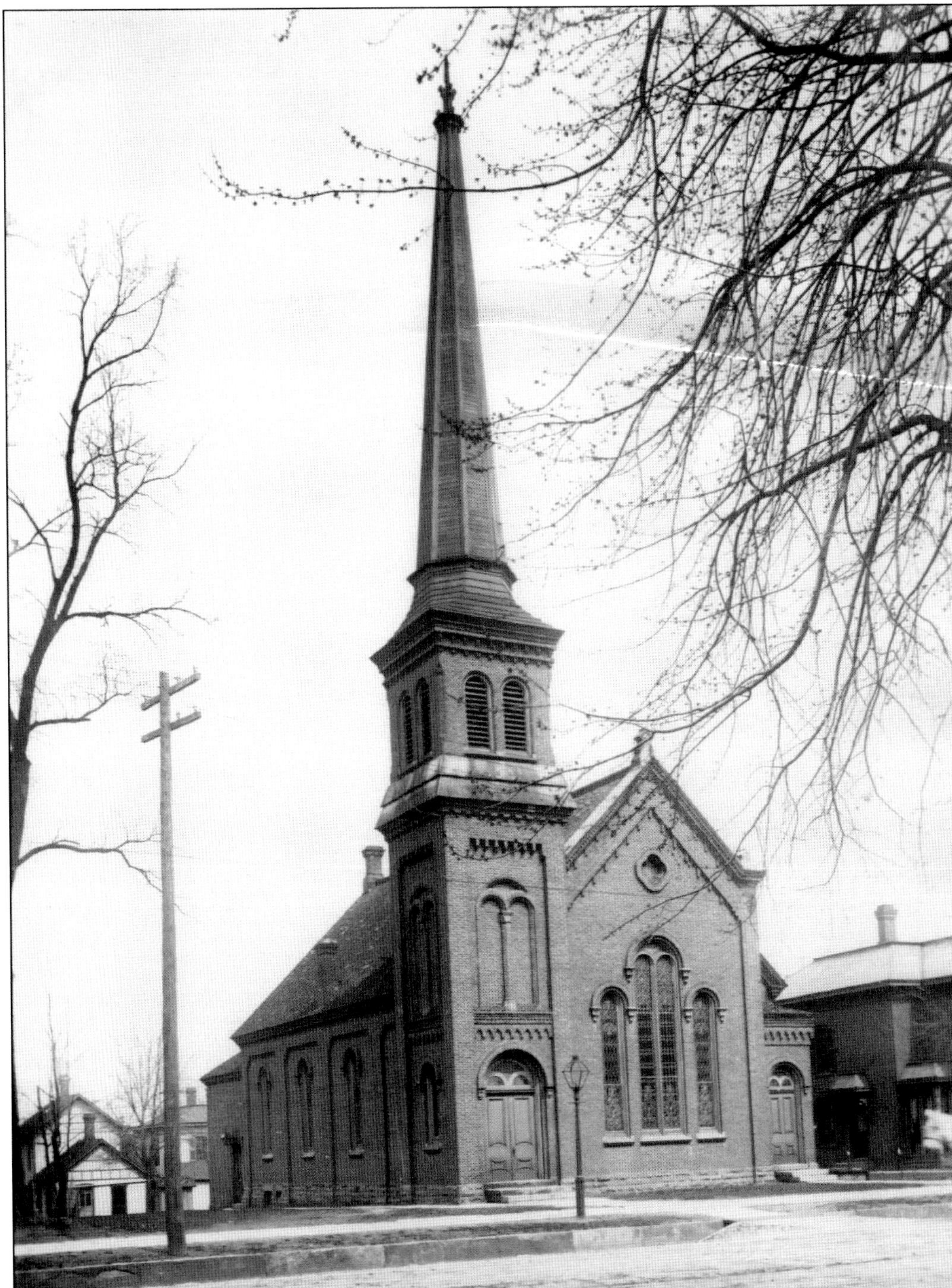

This Congregational church, located at 79 East Main Street, was built in 1871. Its congregation was active until 1929. The building was then sold and used by several businesses. In later years, it returned to being used for church services by several denominations. The exterior of the building has been altered. It is currently the Norwalk Assembly of God Church.

# *Seven*

# Historic Homes

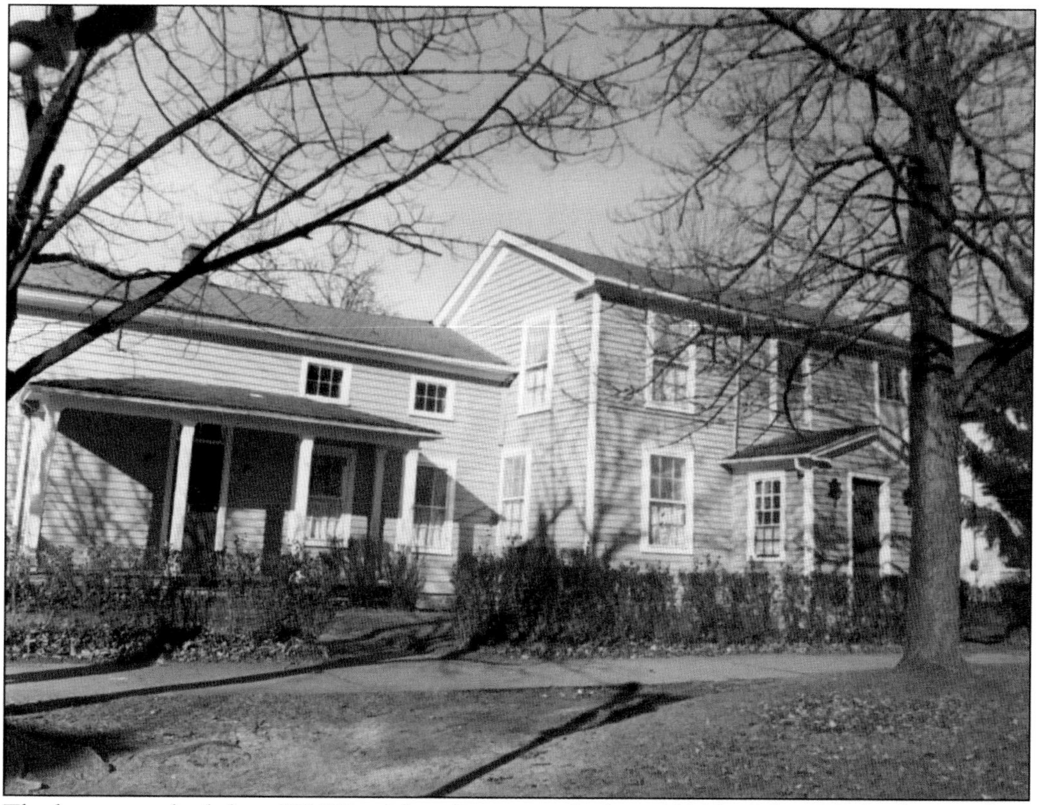

The house on the left at 108 West Main Street was built in 1826 by John Whyler for a trading post. It is the oldest house standing in the city. Native Americans who lived on a reservation in Seneca County would come to trade with Whyler. In 1835, the house was sold to the Gibbs family, and it remained in the family until 1972.

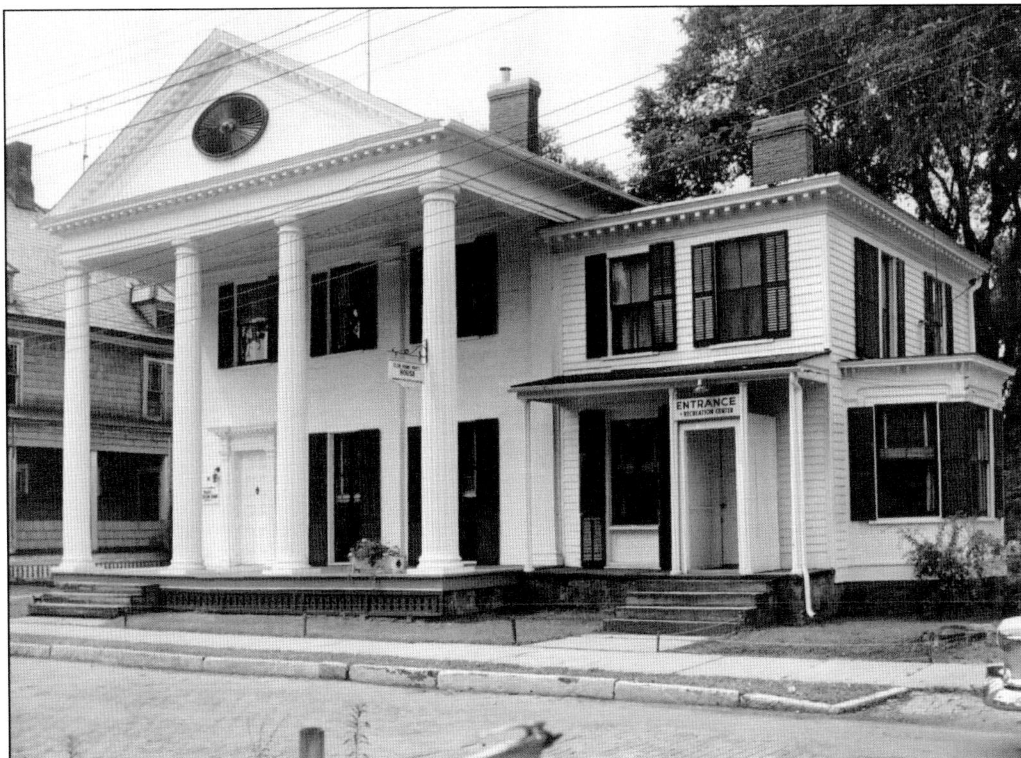


This house was built in 1834 on the southwest corner of West Main and Church Streets by Dr. William Kittredge. He later sold it to Dr. George Baker. The house was moved to the rear of the lot, and at the time of this photograph, was being used as the Norwalk Recreation Center. It is no longer standing.

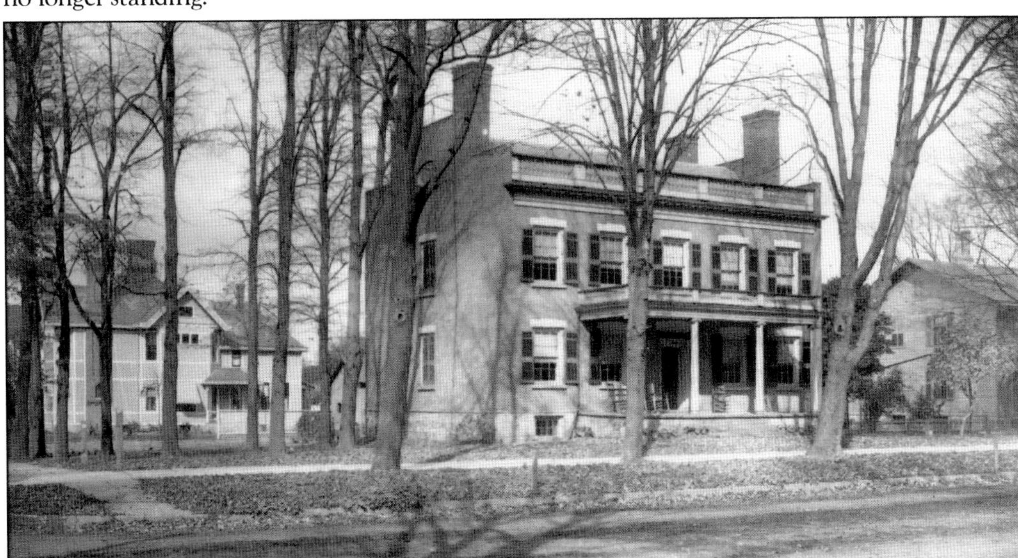

The Kimball home at 54 West Main Street is pictured here. It was built in 1832 by William Brewster for Moses Kimball, an early businessman. The house is an outstanding example of Federal architecture.

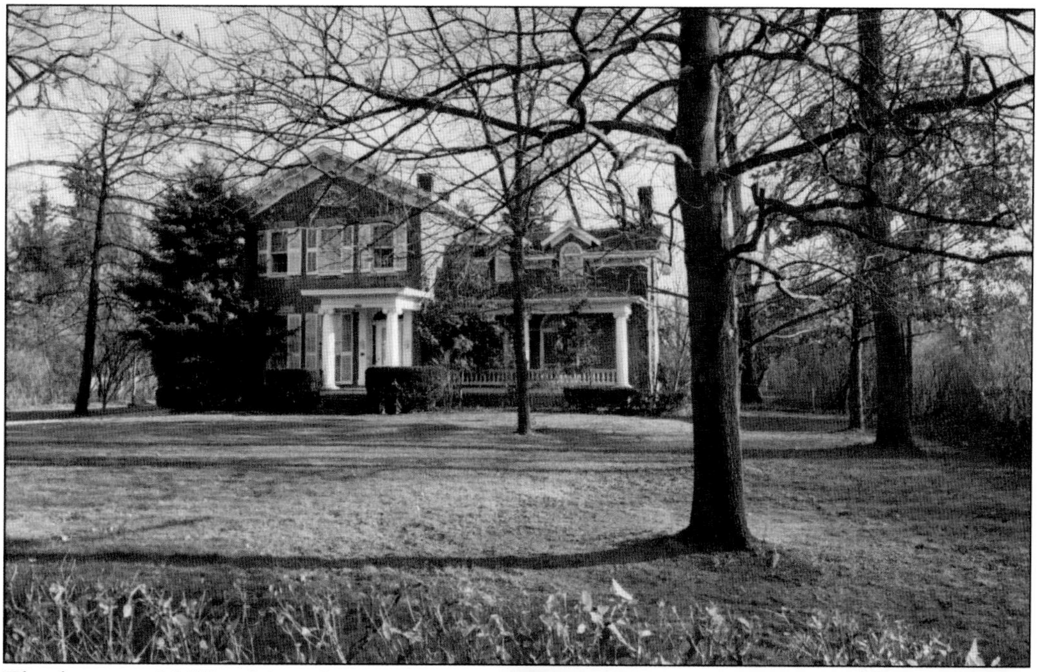

This house at 95 West Main Street was built in 1856 by John Gray, an Irishman from Chicago who wanted a narrow "city house" and bragged he was going to build the finest house this side of Chicago. An addition was constructed in 1870, followed by another one later.

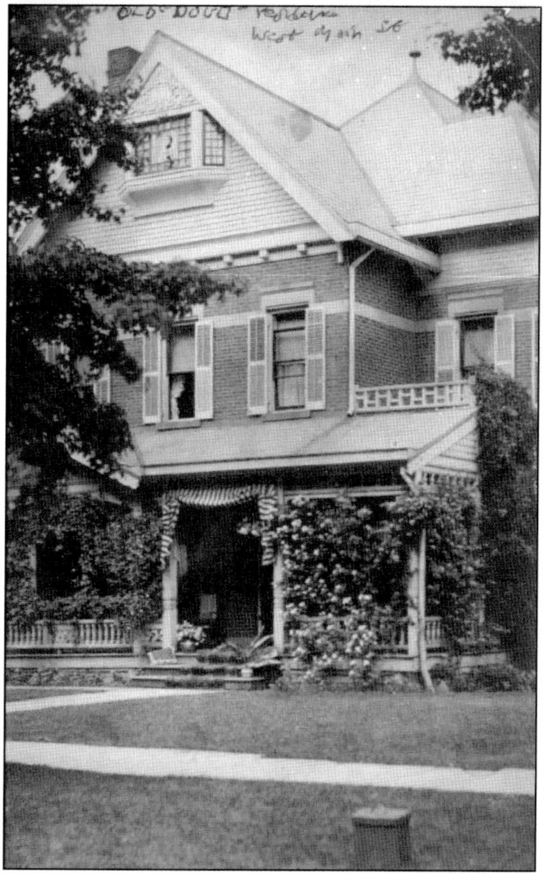

Leander L. Doud built this Queen Anne–style house at 98 West Main Street in 1882. Doud was the secretary-treasurer for the A.B. Chase Organ Company. The home still has some woodwork that was carved by A.B. Chase craftsmen. It is now the Walker Funeral Home.

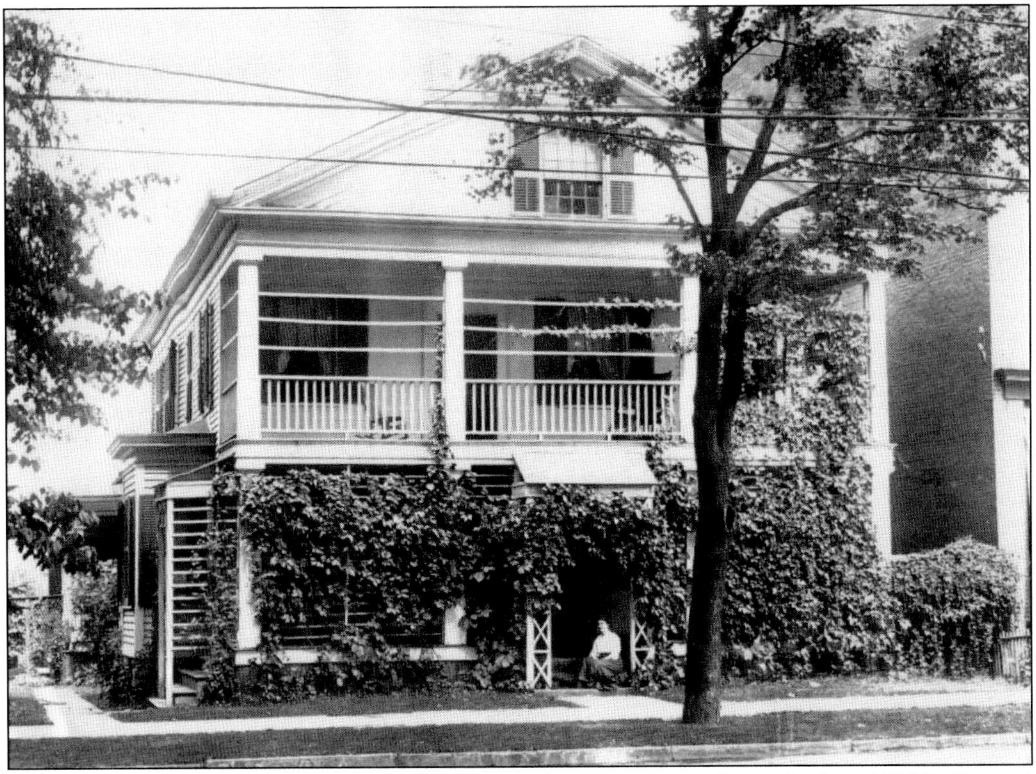

The Wickham home is seen here as it stood at 38 West Main Street. It was built in 1836 by Samuel Preston as a wedding gift for his daughter Lucy when she married Frederick Wickham. The house was moved in the 1950s to face Case Street and is now the Firelands Museum.

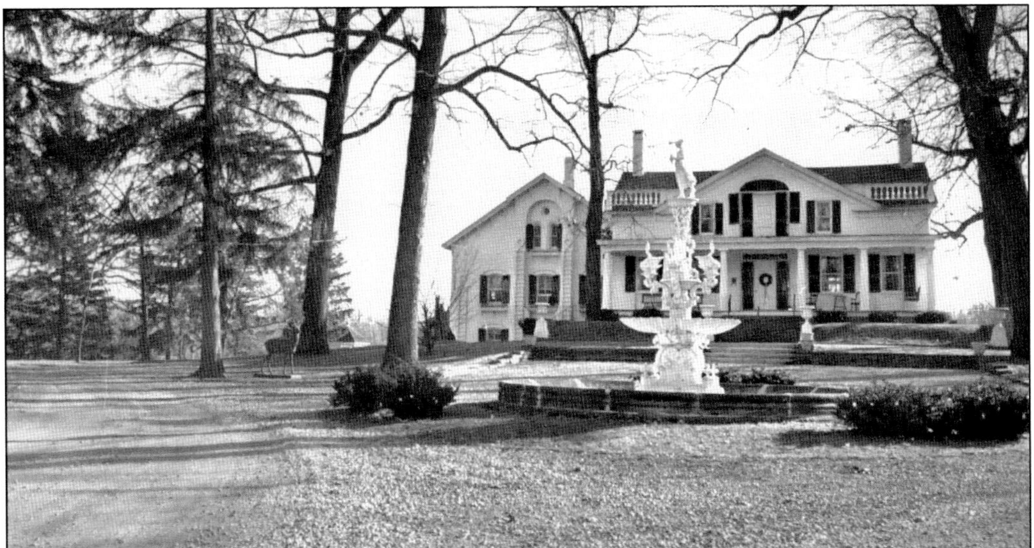

The original portion of this house (with the porch) was built in 1833 by John Vredenburgh at 133 West Main Street. John Gardiner, a banker and local railroad tycoon, purchased the property in 1848. He made many improvements and enlarged the home to about 30 rooms. The fountain in the front yard was installed in 1872. Gardiner's descendants still occupy the residence.

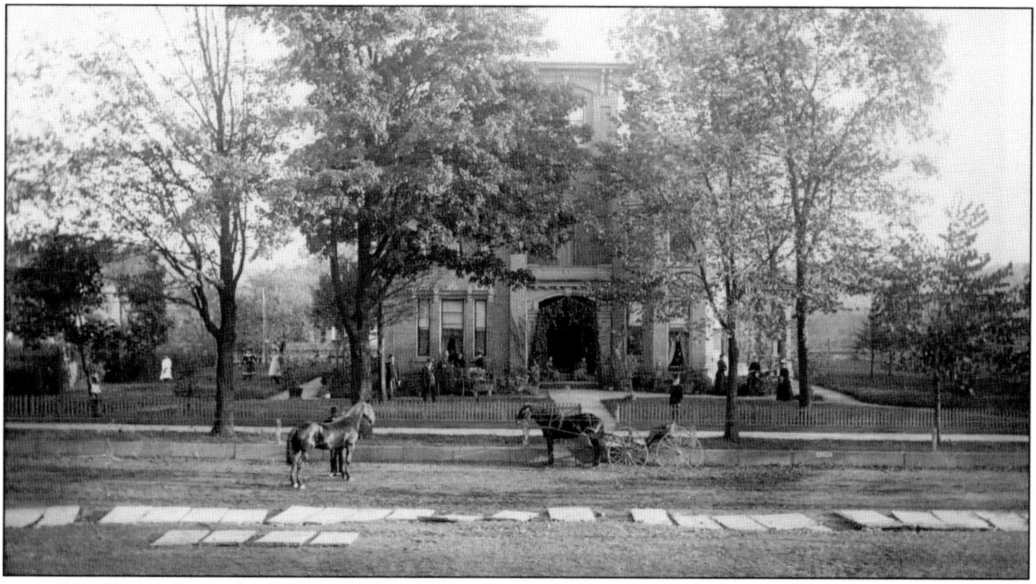

David DeForest Benedict built this house around 1885. It was one of the best houses of Italianate-style architecture in the city. It was located at 80 East Seminary Street. Benedict, a medical doctor and grandson of Platt Benedict, served as an assistant surgeon during the Civil War. After the war, he practiced medicine and operated a drugstore and made patent medicines. The home was lost in a fire.

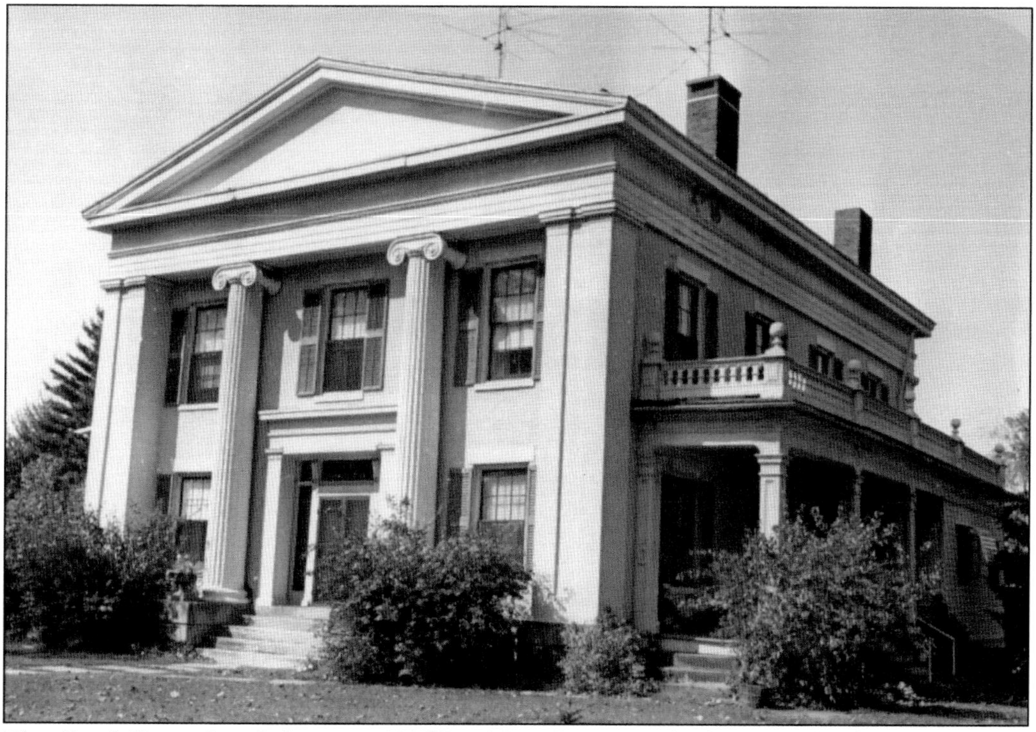

This Greek Revival–style house at 114 West Main Street was built in 1847 by the Presbyterians for use as the Female Seminary, a school for girls. The school was never a financial success. About 10 years later, it was sold to Henry Wooster, who converted it into a home for his family.

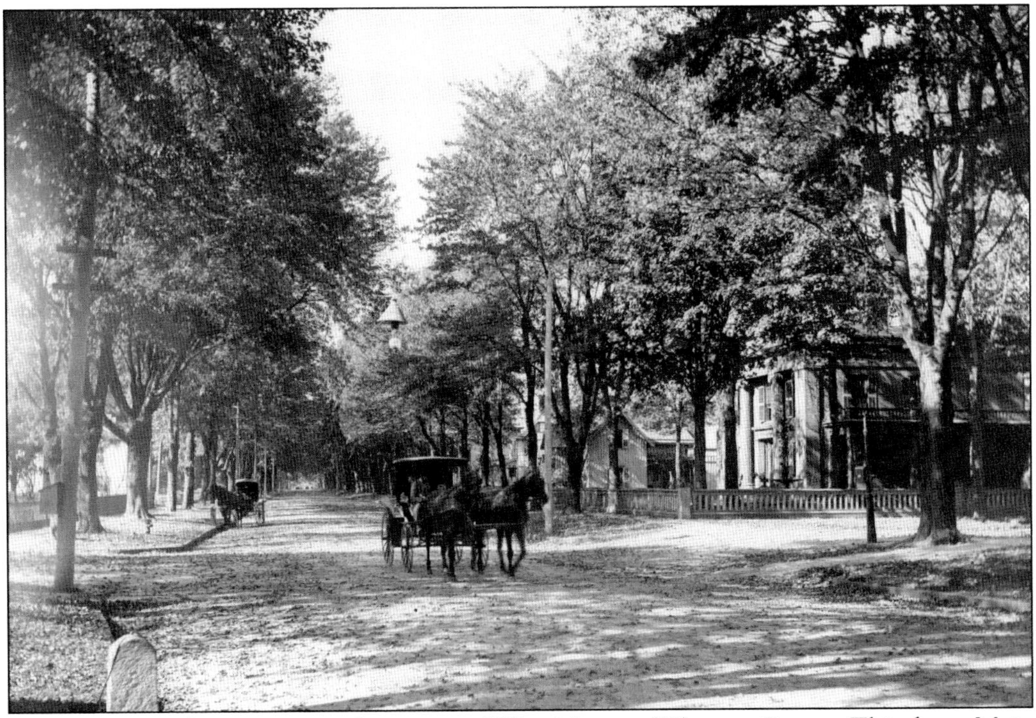

Here is the Female Seminary at the corner of West Main and Pleasant Streets. This shows Main Street unpaved, with the horse and carriage as the main mode of transportation. This picture represents a pastoral environment before the arrival of the interurban trolley.

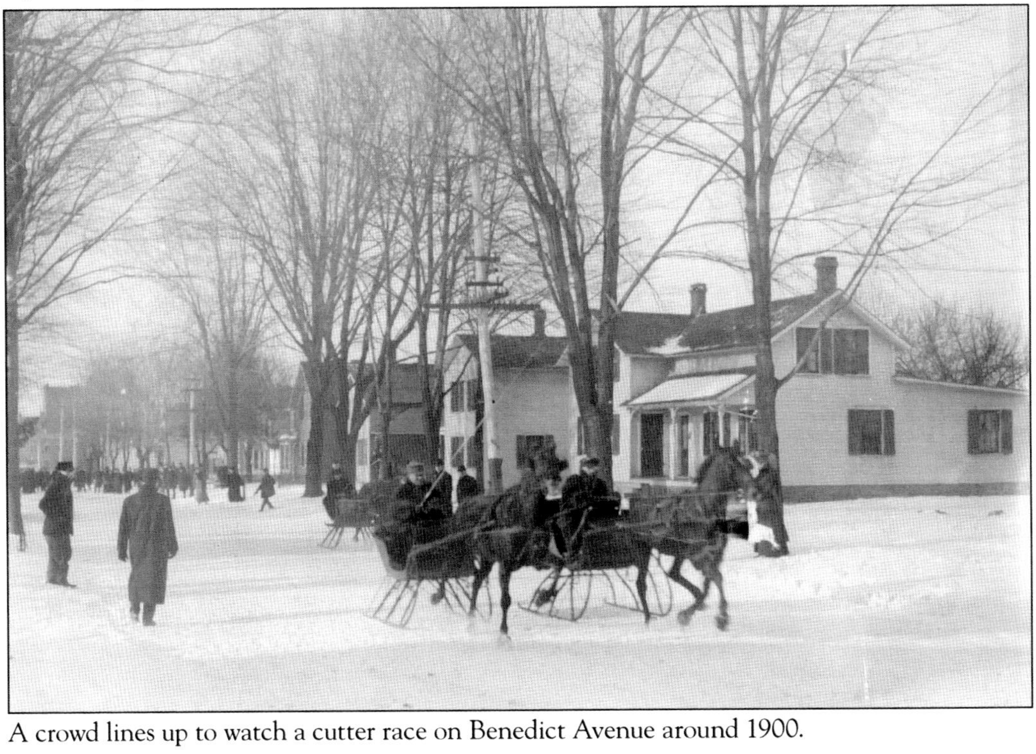

A crowd lines up to watch a cutter race on Benedict Avenue around 1900.

This is the home of Henry Wheeler Shaw, which was located on Whittlesey Avenue in the location of the present post office. He was a nationally known humorist of the 19th century and used the pseudonym Josh Billings.

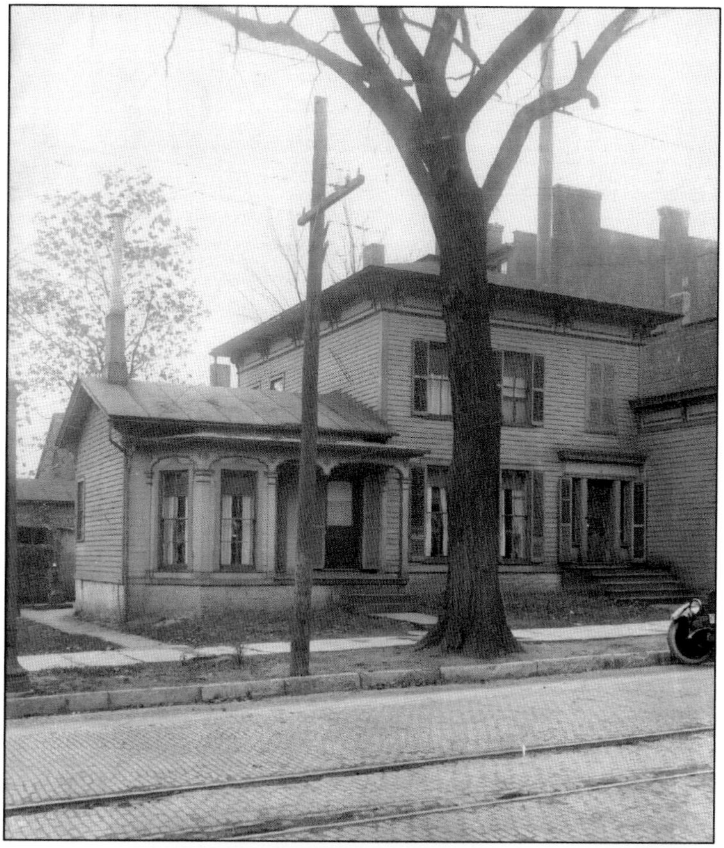

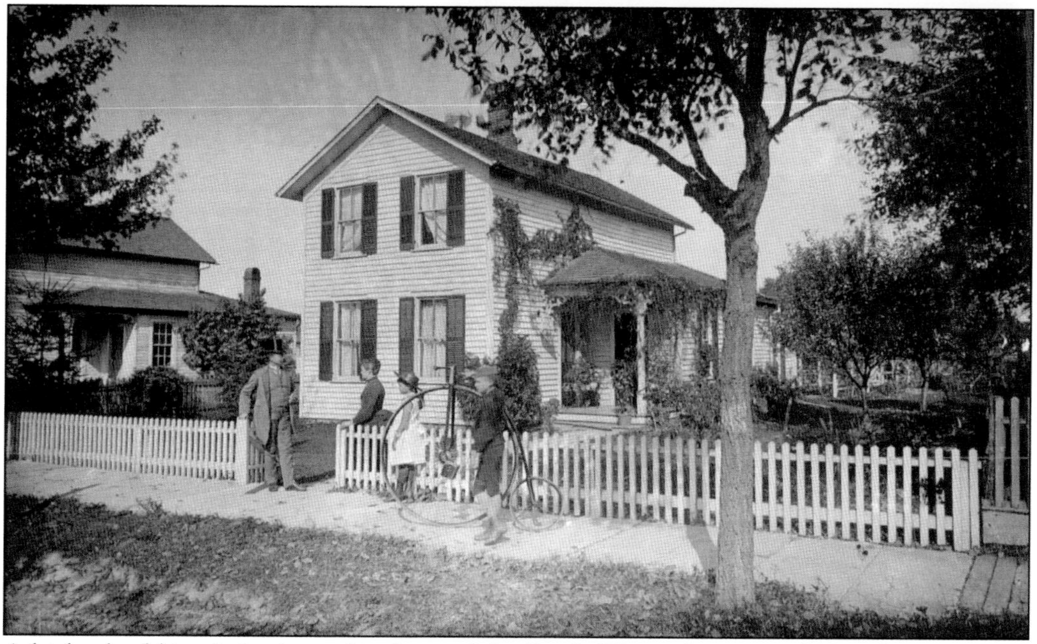

A high-wheel bicycle is pictured in front of the Frank Warner home at 95 Woodlawn Avenue. The house dates from around 1890.

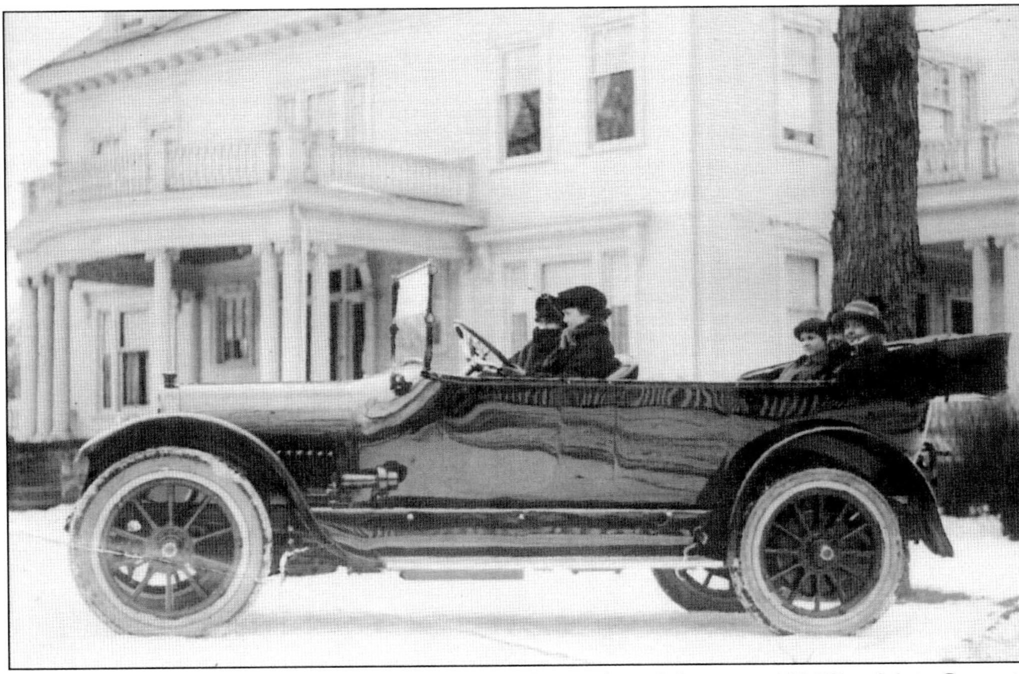

W.H. Merritt, a local dentist, built this Georgian Revival–style home at 123 West Main Street in 1906. It was constructed with a ballroom on the third floor. Music was played on the Victrola, and sometimes there were live musicians. The family had servants to provide for the formal affairs. Here are some ladies in their furs with a luxury automobile in front of the home. Today, it is the Georgian Manor Bed and Breakfast.

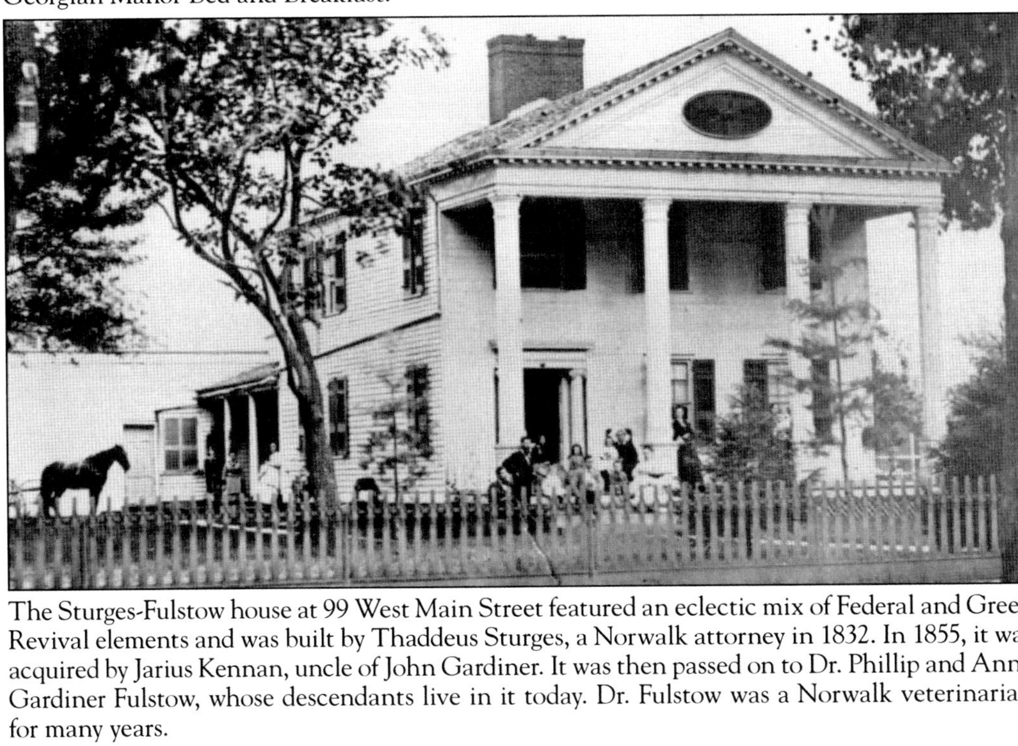

The Sturges-Fulstow house at 99 West Main Street featured an eclectic mix of Federal and Greek Revival elements and was built by Thaddeus Sturges, a Norwalk attorney in 1832. In 1855, it was acquired by Jarius Kennan, uncle of John Gardiner. It was then passed on to Dr. Phillip and Anne Gardiner Fulstow, whose descendants live in it today. Dr. Fulstow was a Norwalk veterinarian for many years.

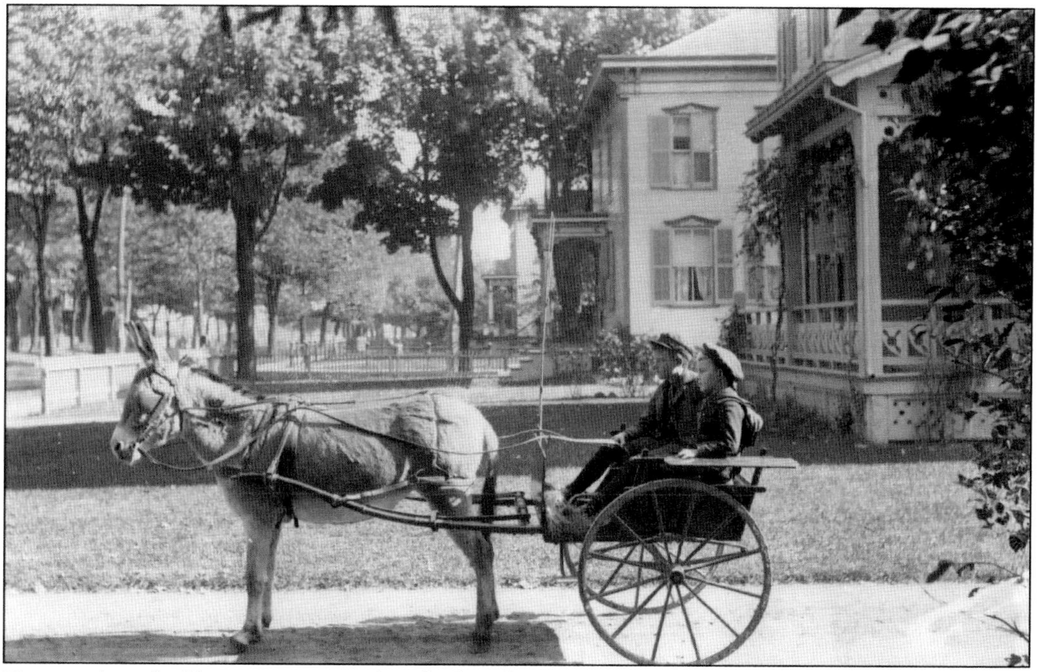

Two unidentified boys are pictured with their horse and wagon near 140 East Main Street and Garden Street.

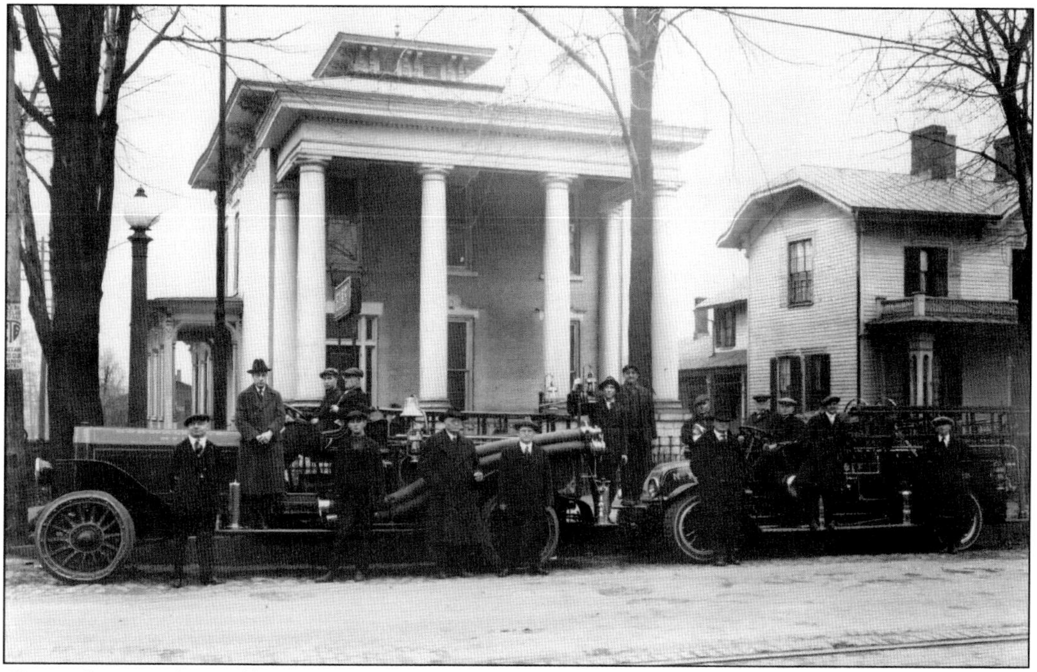

Shown here is the Williams House at 55 East Main Street. It was built by Theodore Williams, who was probably the first male child born in the village of Norwalk. He was president of the First National Bank of Norwalk and served for many years on the board of education. The house was later owned by the Elks Lodge and Mihali photographic studio. After that, it was used by the Towne and County Players. The fire trucks parked in front date the photograph to around 1915.

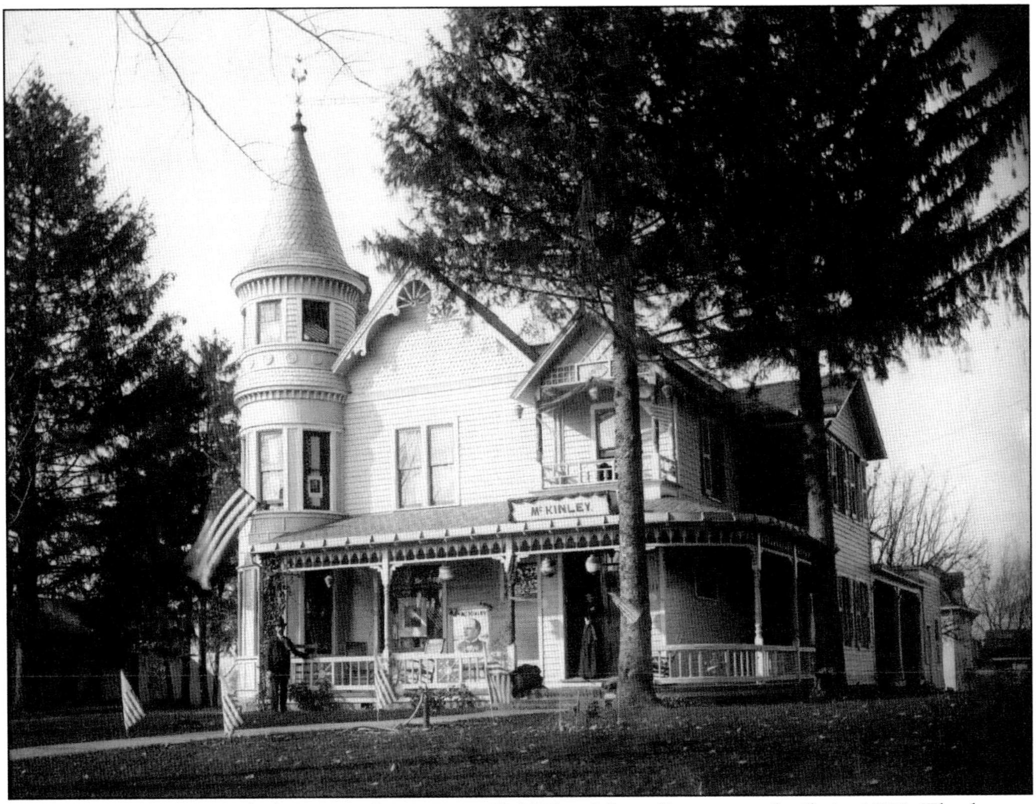


This Queen Anne–style home with tower at 184 West Main Street was built in 1874. The house is decorated for a Norwalk William McKinley political rally. It is no longer standing.

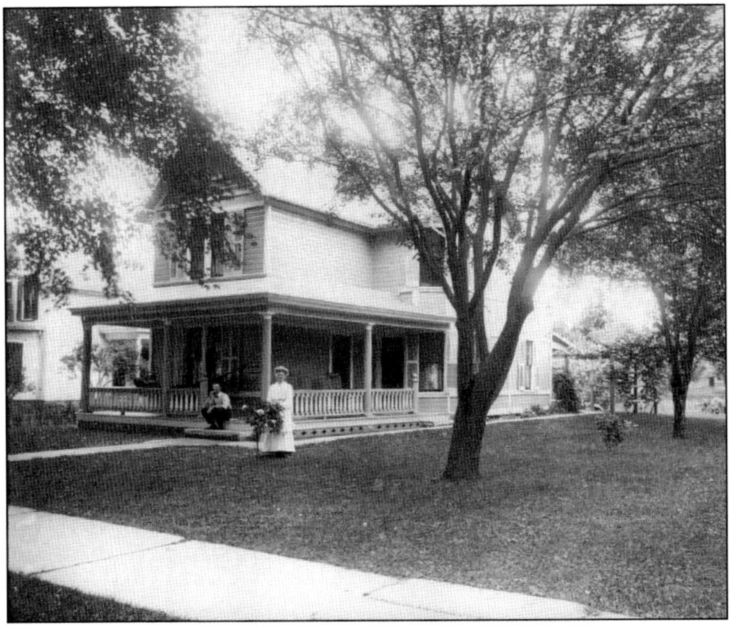

This home is at 12 Cortland Street and belonged to Henry and Anna (Heitzmann) Schumm. The peaceful residential neighborhood was quite attractive.

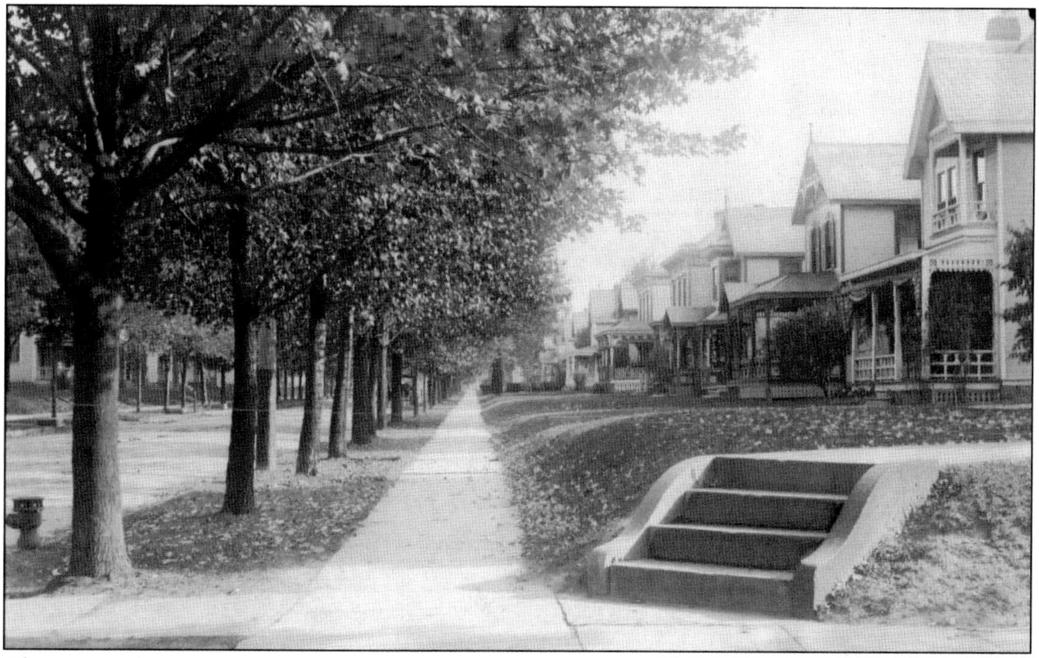

This is South Linwood Avenue. The elegant gingerbread on the homes was eye-catching along the tree-lined street. Notice the early fireplug.

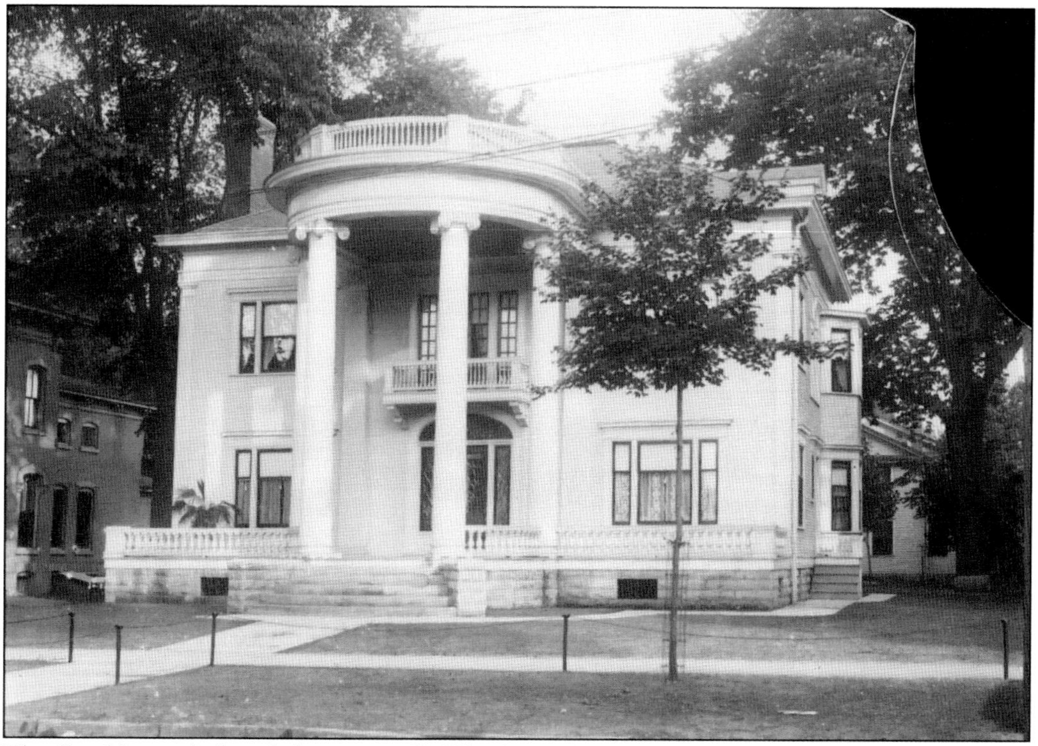

This "wedding cake"–style home is at 59 West Main Street. It was built in 1906 by A.S. Prentiss. It is a Sears "kit house." The pieces would arrive on site, prefabricated and numbered, and a contractor would assemble the house.

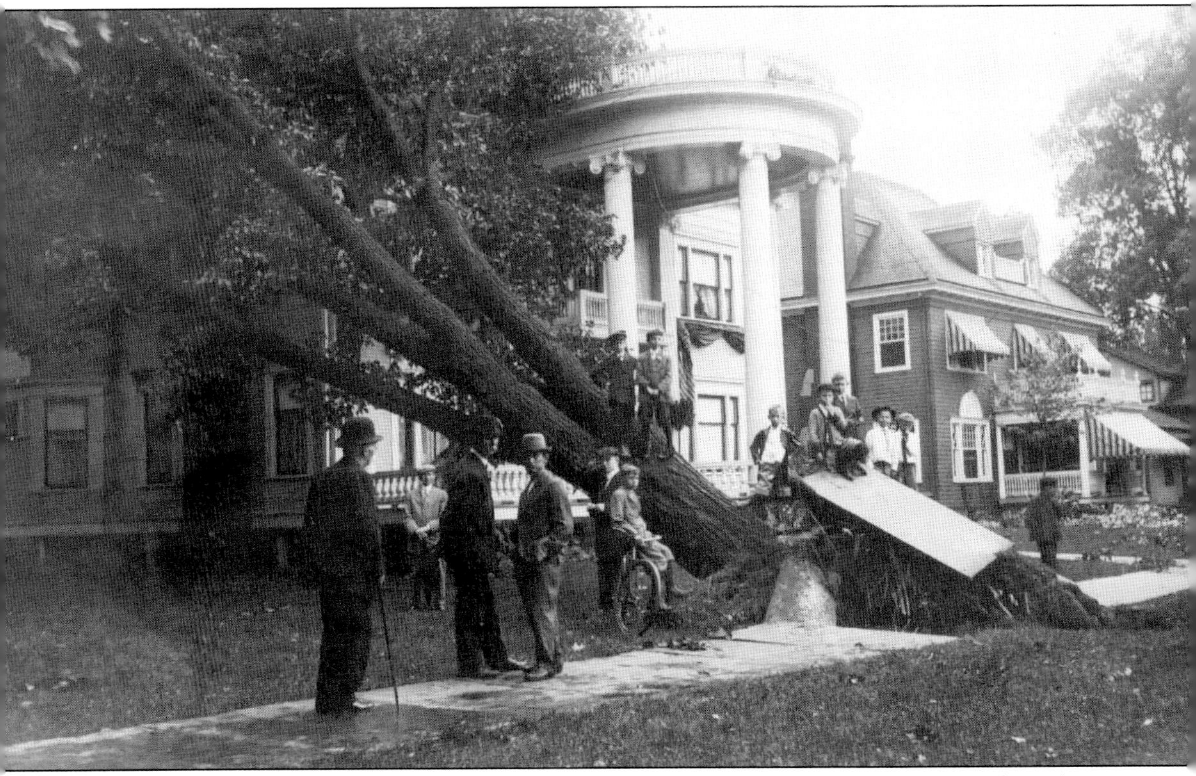

It looks like a storm has knocked over a tree in front of this home. The assembled crowd ponders its removal. There were no chain saws at the time, so axes and handsaws were the only options.

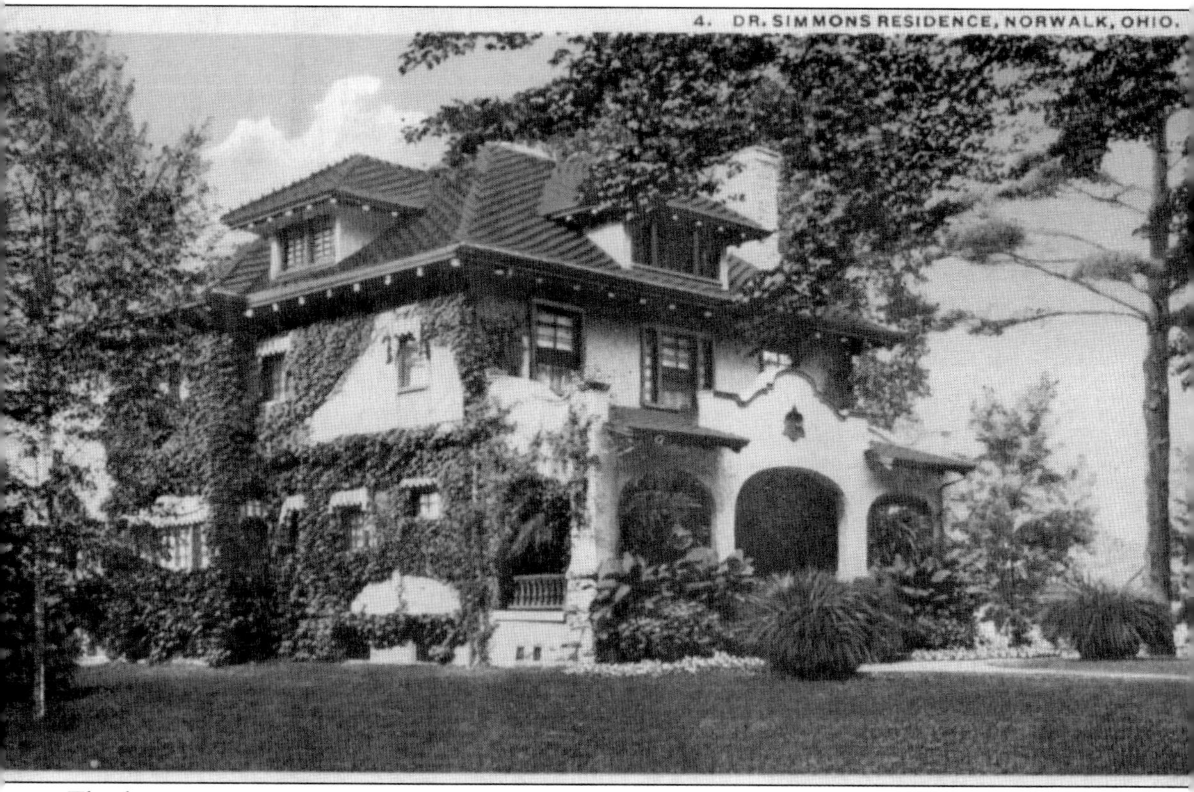


This house at 82 West Main Street was built by Dr. Sherman Simmons in 1906. The American four square–type house was very popular in the first three decades of the 20th century. The tile roof gives it a touch of Spanish style.

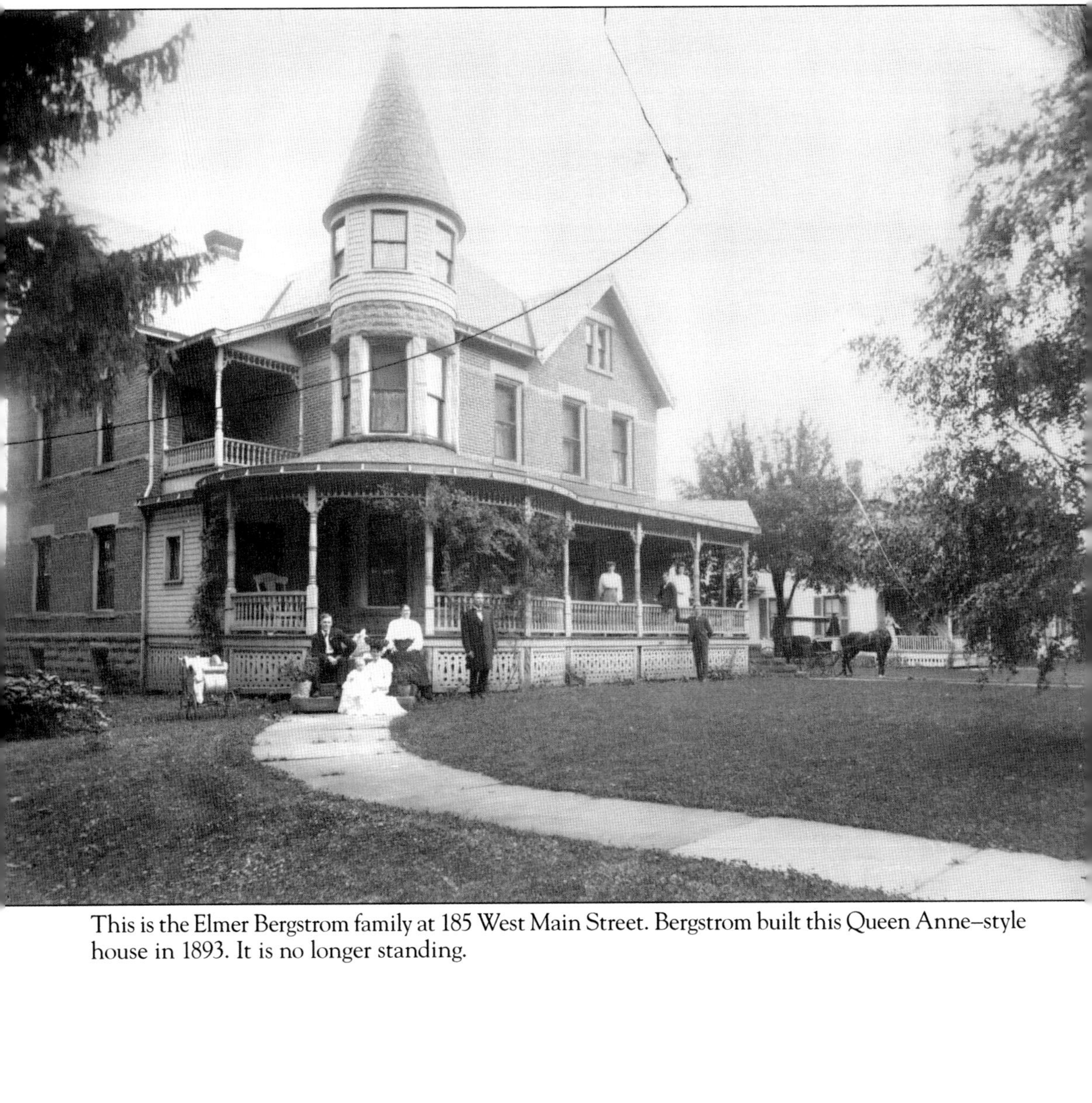

This is the Elmer Bergstrom family at 185 West Main Street. Bergstrom built this Queen Anne–style house in 1893. It is no longer standing.

*Eight*

# Assemblies and Parades

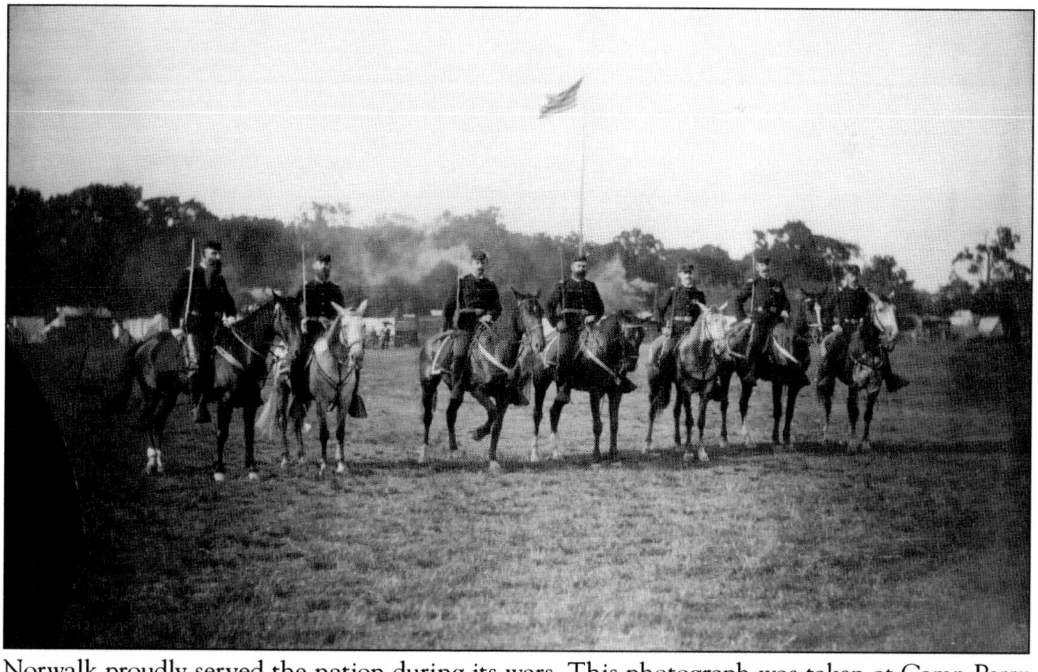

Norwalk proudly served the nation during its wars. This photograph was taken at Camp Perry in Ottawa County during a Civil War veterans' celebration.

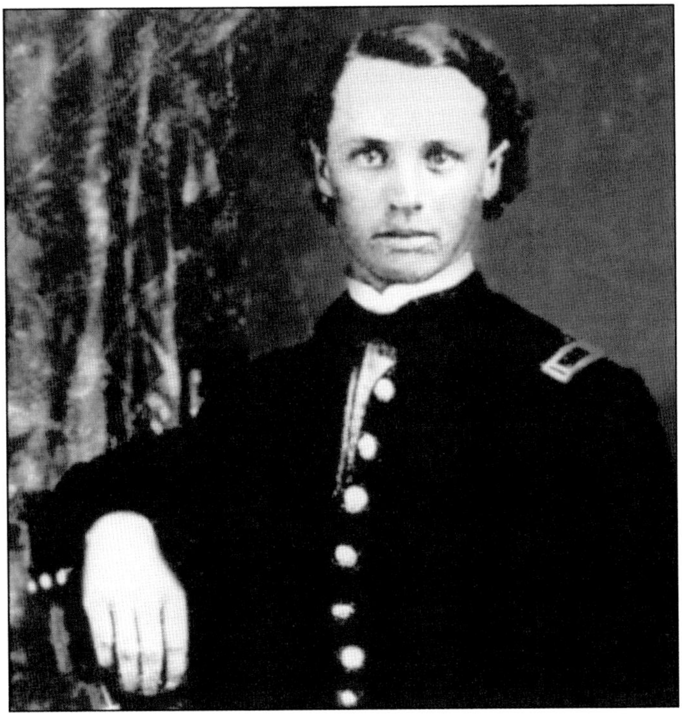

Lt. Asa Hillyer, seen here at age 27, a lawyer whose practice encompassed Norwalk and Monroeville, answered the call for volunteers to fill up the 101st Ohio Volunteer Infantry, forming at Camp Monroeville, on July 15, 1862. By December 10, Lieutenant Hillyer was promoted to the rank of captain. On December 31, the Union army was caught by surprise by Confederate forces under General Bragg near Stones River, Tennessee. Captain Hillyer was killed in the battle, and his body was returned home to his wife, Maria, and young son Eddy for burial. Supplied by Matt Burr, this photograph is part of the Brad Pruden collection.

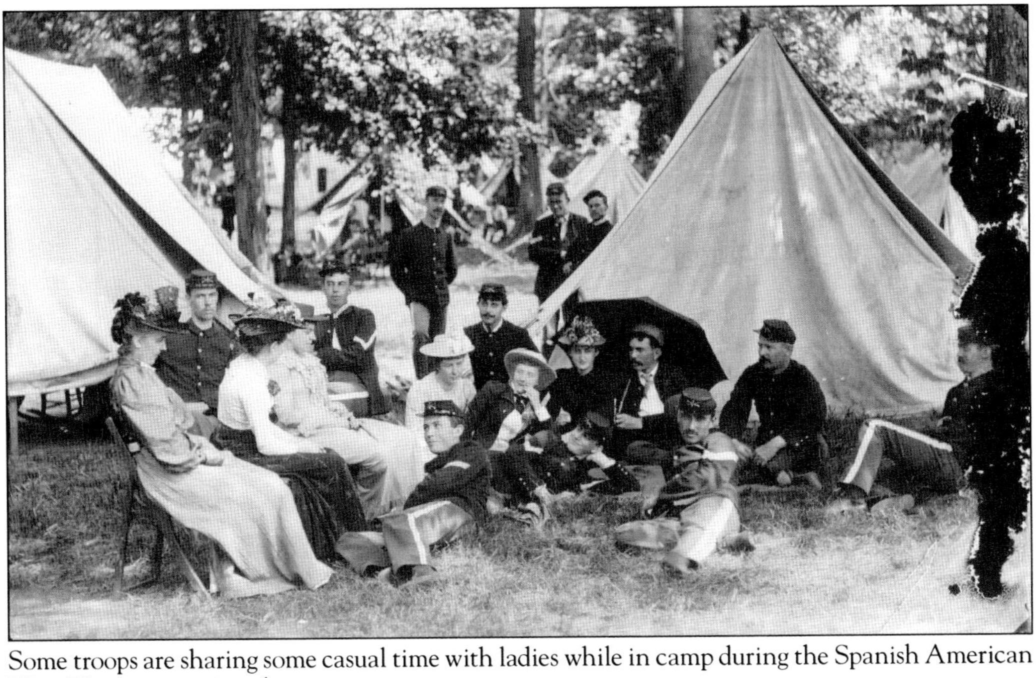

Some troops are sharing some casual time with ladies while in camp during the Spanish American War. The location is unknown.

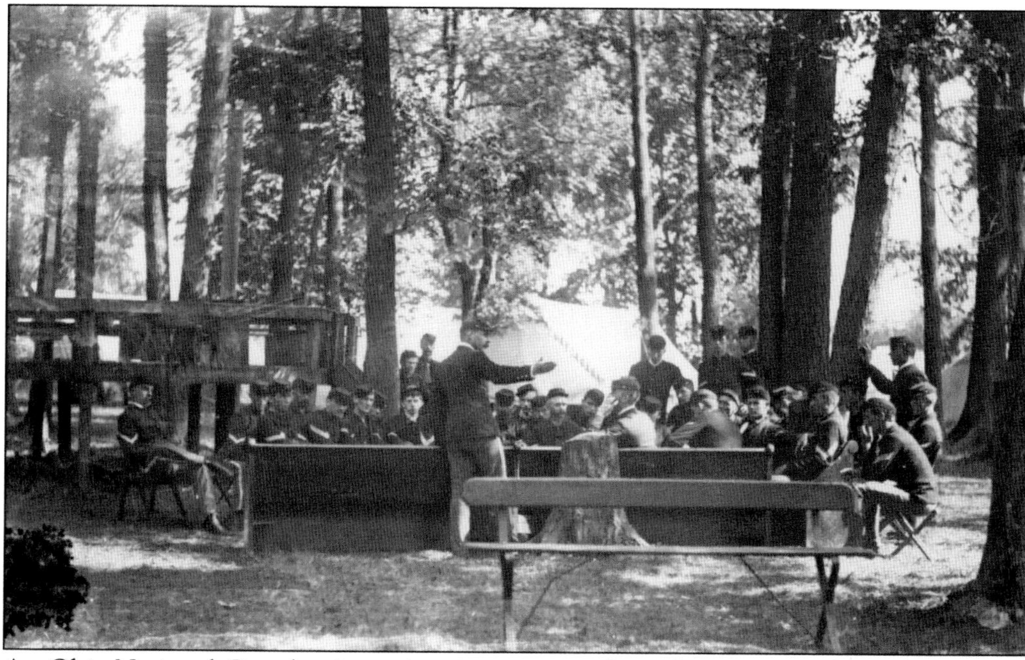

An Ohio National Guard unit receives instructions from their commanding officer in the 1890s.

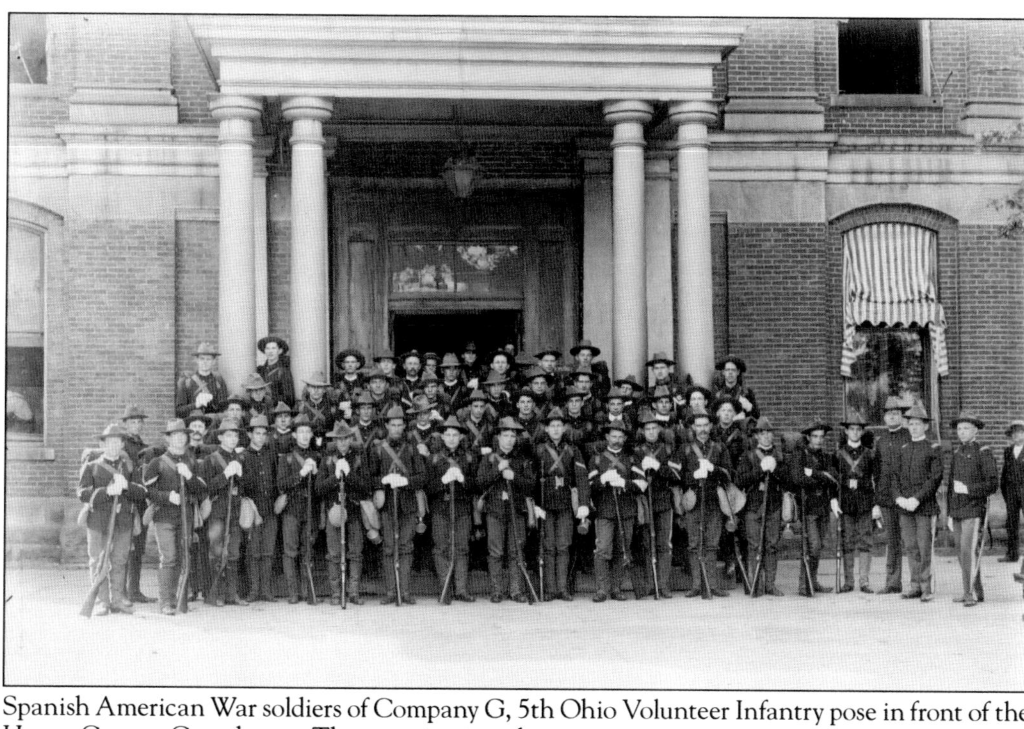

Spanish American War soldiers of Company G, 5th Ohio Volunteer Infantry pose in front of the Huron County Courthouse. The occasion is unknown.

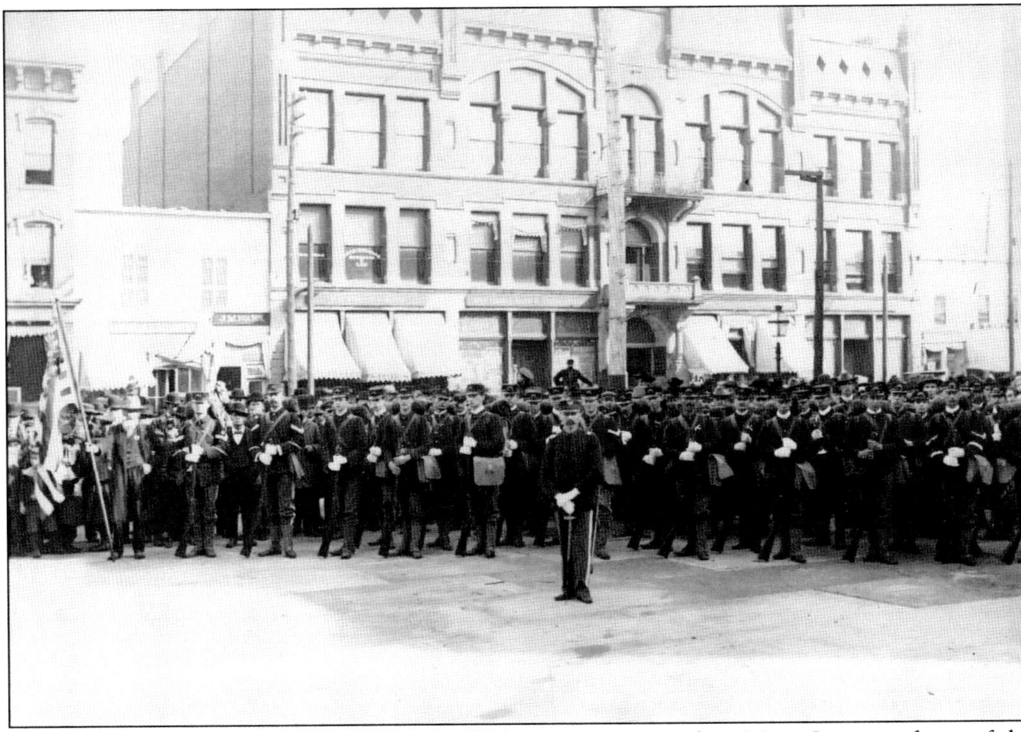

Troops of Company G, 5th Ohio Volunteer Infantry are pictured on Main Street in front of the Gardiner Building in 1898 for an unknown occasion.

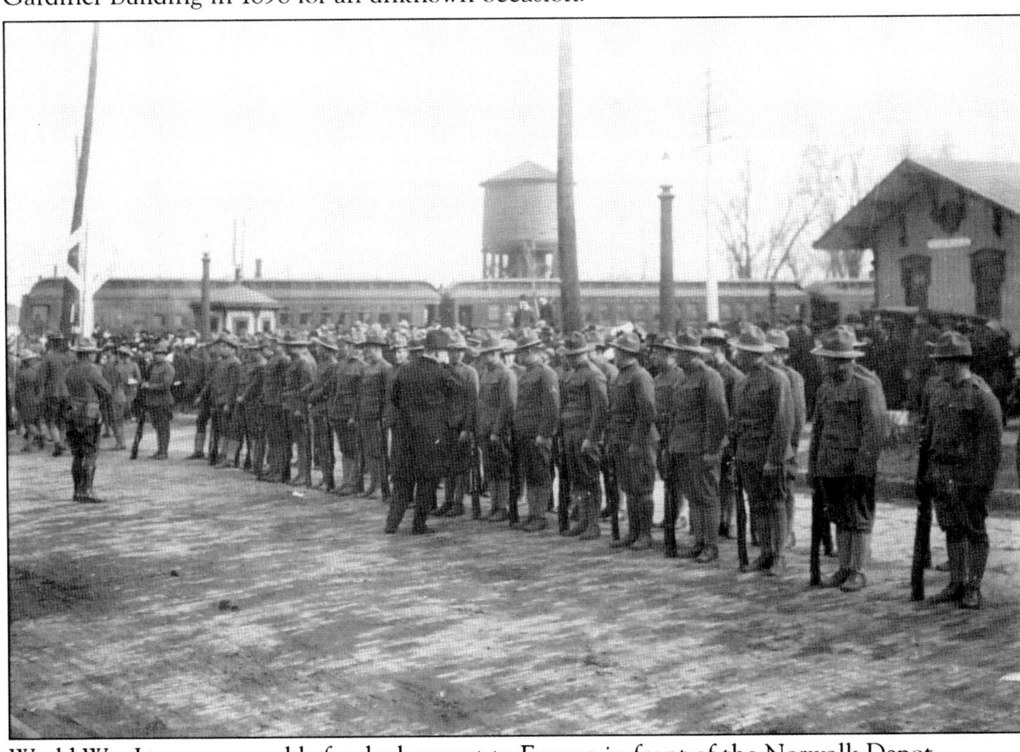

World War I troops assemble for deployment to Europe in front of the Norwalk Depot.

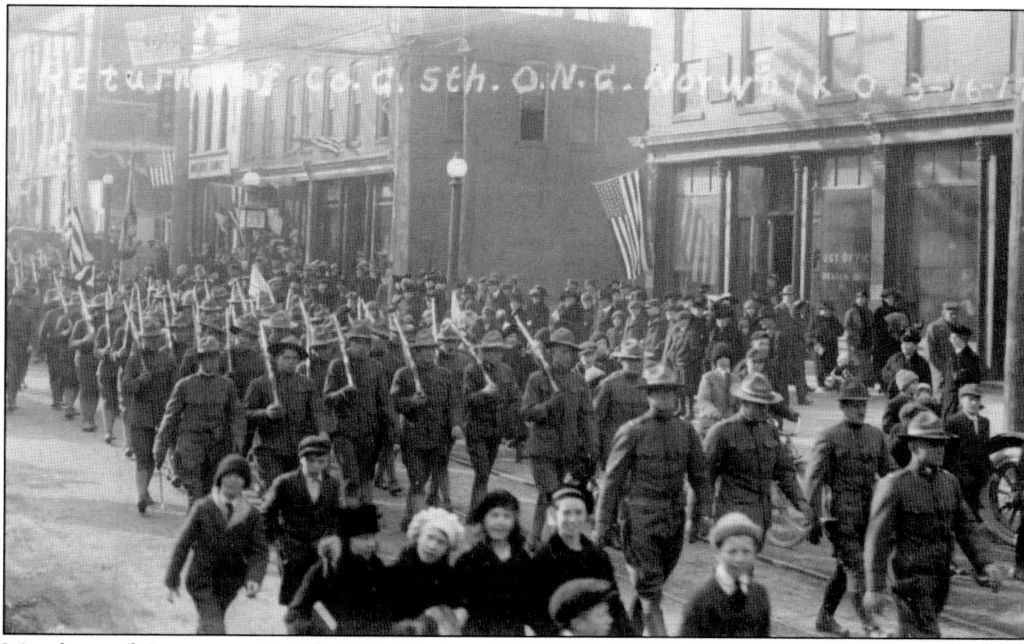

Members of Company G, 5th Ohio National Guard march down Whittlesey Avenue as they return home on March 16, 1917, after serving their county in World War I.

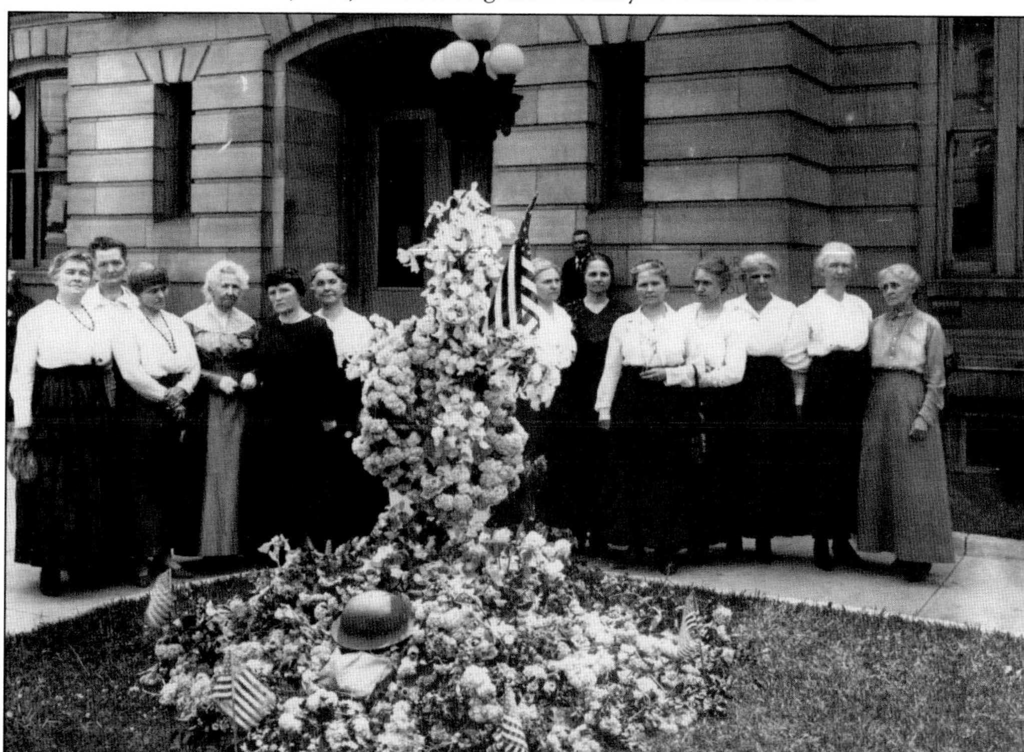

Grieving mothers placed this wreath in front of the courthouse on Decoration Day after World War I.

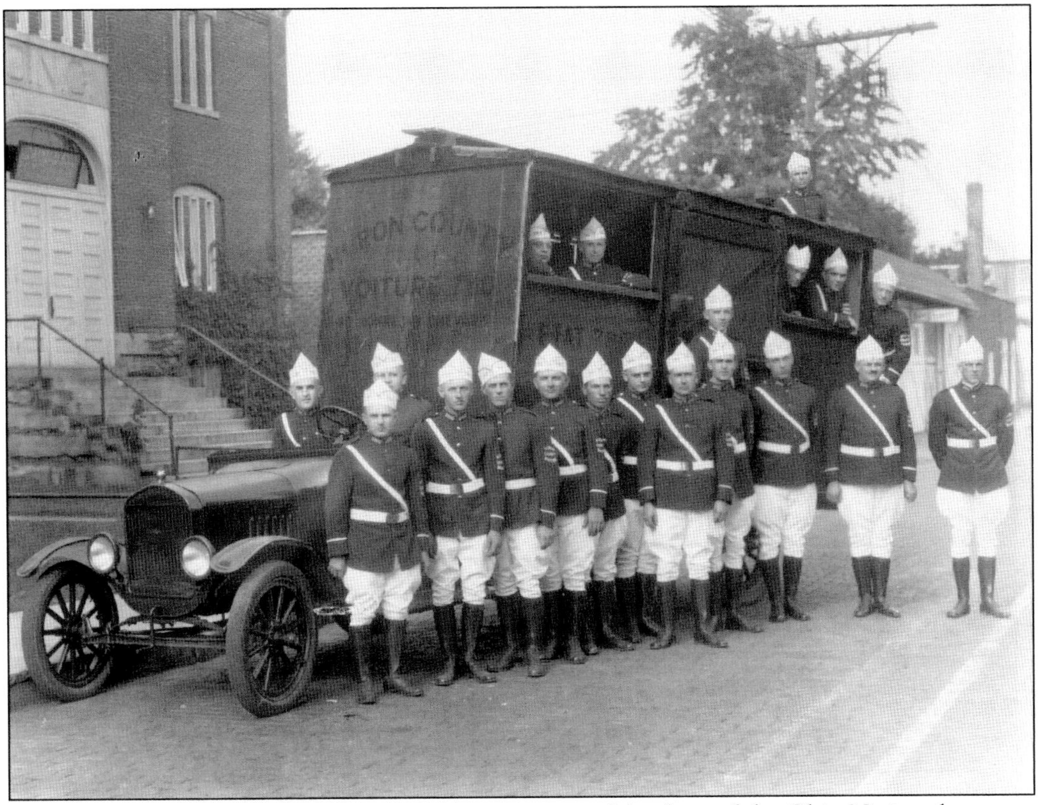

Members of the Ohio National Guard assemble outside of the armory on West Monroe Street in 1939.

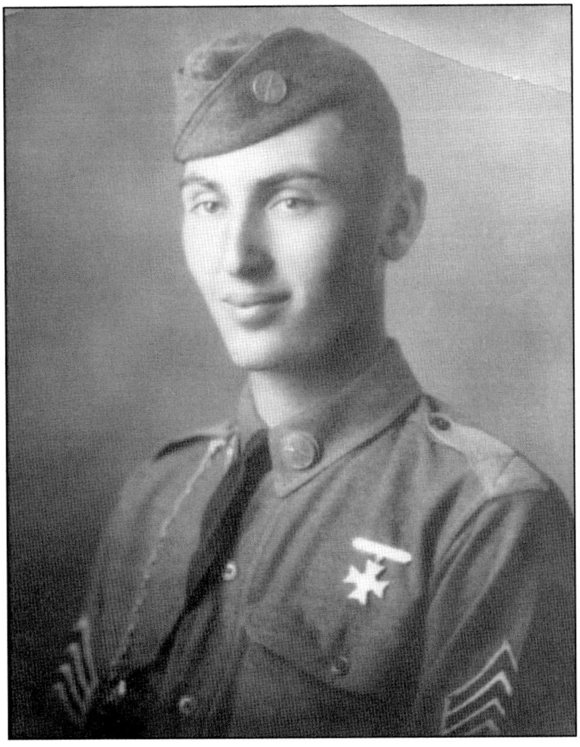

Sgt. Henry F. Schumm Jr. of Norwalk's Company G of the 145th Infantry of the Ohio National Guard is seen here in the early 1930s.

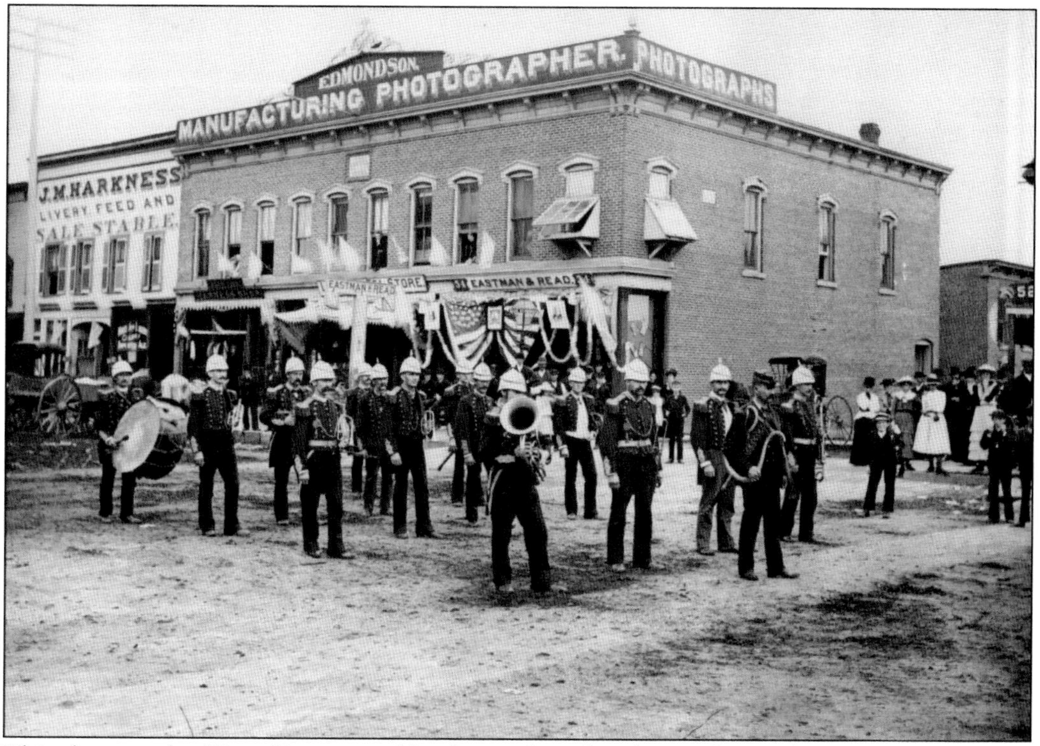


This photograph of Peter Reming and his famous brass band was taken at the corner of East Main and South Prospect Streets. The band was organized at the close of the Civil War and was active for about 25 years. They won several championships in band competitions throughout Ohio.

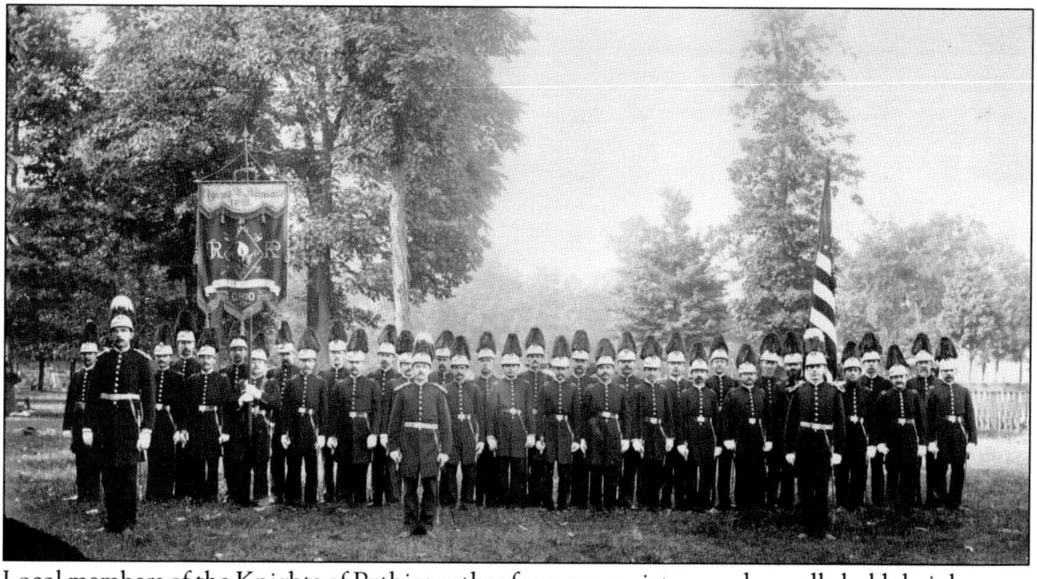

Local members of the Knights of Pythias gather for a group picture and proudly hold their banner. The Knights of Pythias were founded in Washington, DC, in 1864. It was the first fraternal order to be chartered by Congress. Their ideals are loyalty, honor, and friendship. They are also dedicated to the cause of world peace. The Norwalk chapter existed from 1906 into the 1920s.

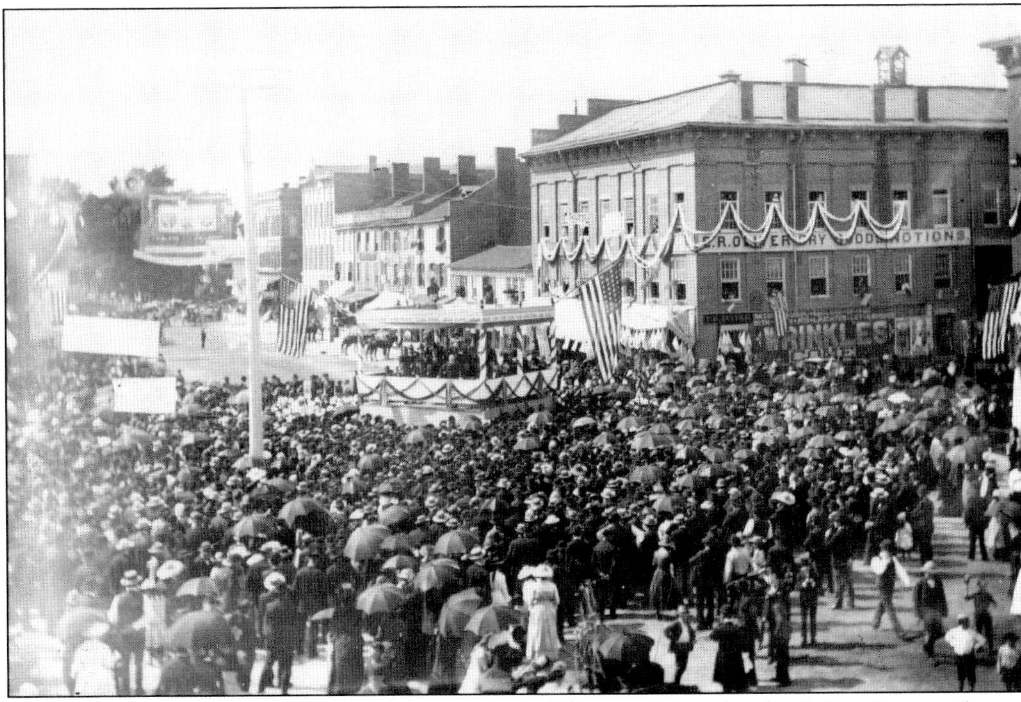

A crowd listens to Republican candidate James B. Blaine as he makes his bid to be president of the United States in 1884. He ran against Democrat Grover Cleveland. The picture was taken at Main Street between Benedict and Whittlesey Avenues.

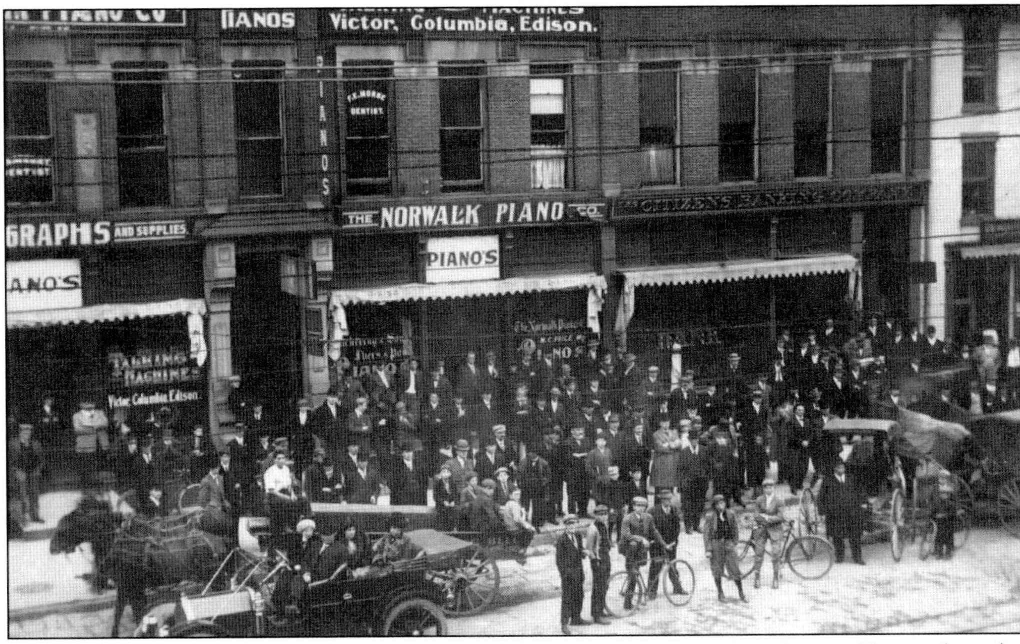


This crowd has gathered, possibly for a parade, about 1917 on East Main Street. Horses, bicycles, and automobiles all share the street with the interurban cars. Citizens Bank, Norwalk Piano Company, and the Victor, Columbia & Edison Talking Machine store can all be seen. This is an important glimpse of the area's contribution to the world at the time.

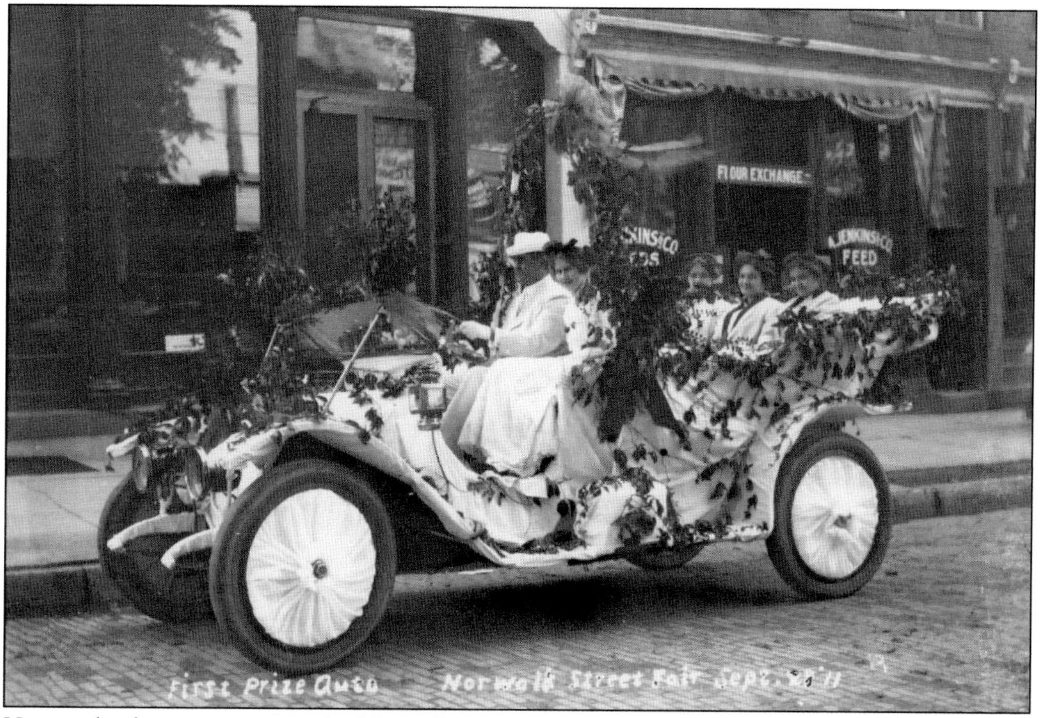


Here is the first-prize auto at the Norwalk Street Fair in September 1911.

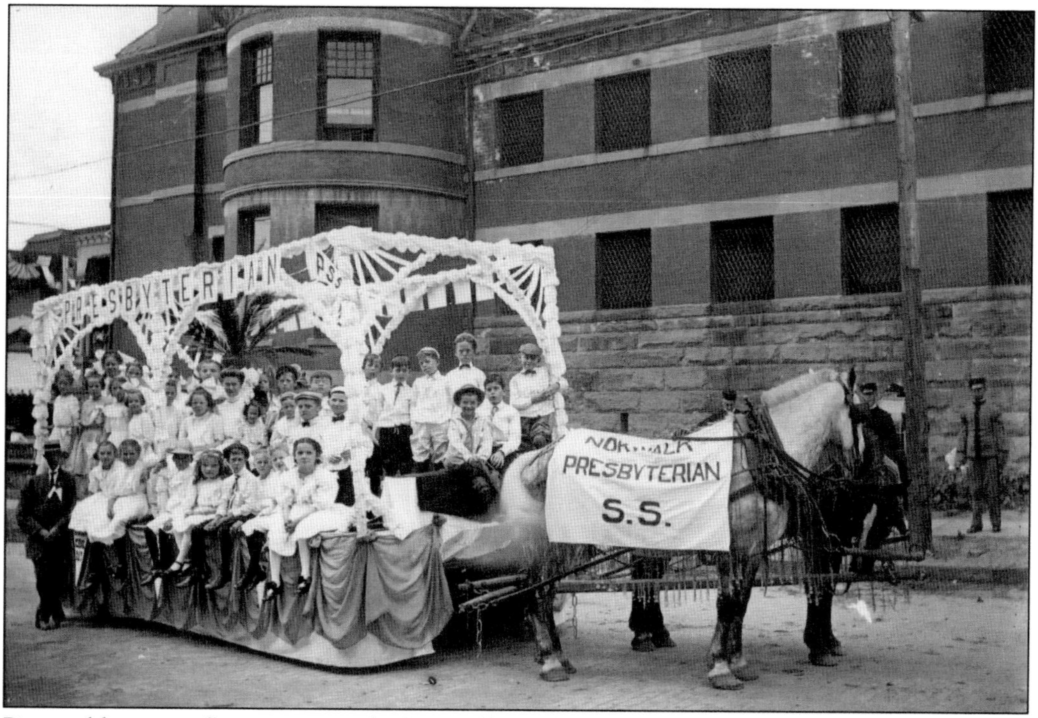


Pictured here is a float carrying the Norwalk Presbyterian Sunday school students in front of the Huron County Jail on East Seminary Street. The event was the Norwalk Street Fair, held in September 1911.

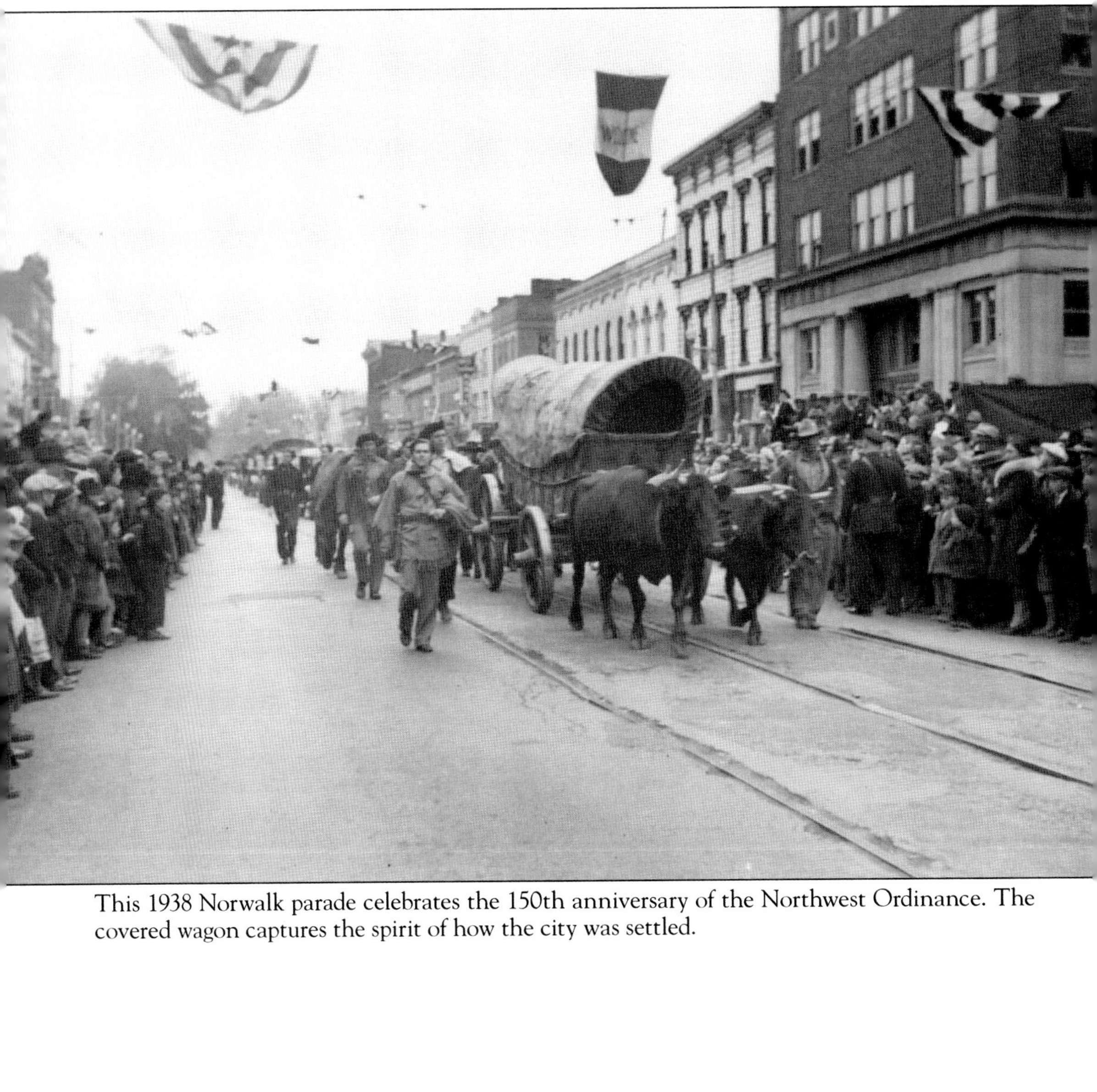

This 1938 Norwalk parade celebrates the 150th anniversary of the Northwest Ordinance. The covered wagon captures the spirit of how the city was settled.

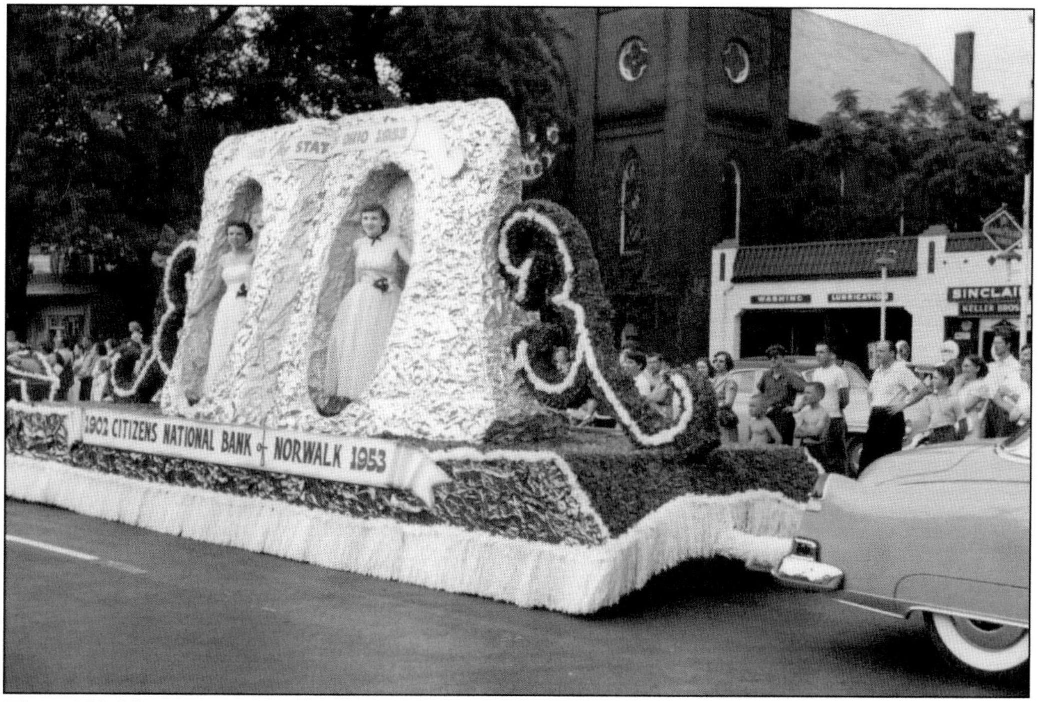


This 1953 Ohio sesquicentennial parade shows the Citizens National Bank float with the pageant queens on East Main Street in front of the Baptist church and the Sinclair station at the corner of North Foster Street.

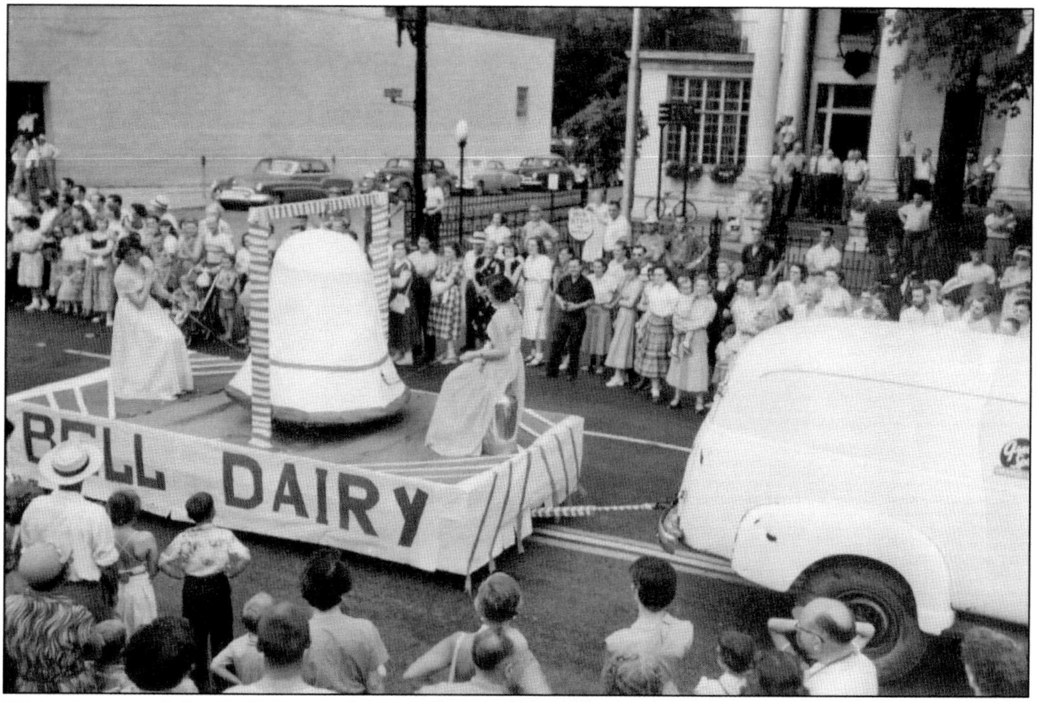


This picture of the Bell Dairy float in front of the Elks Lodge on East Main Street was taken during the 1953 Ohio sesquicentennial parade.

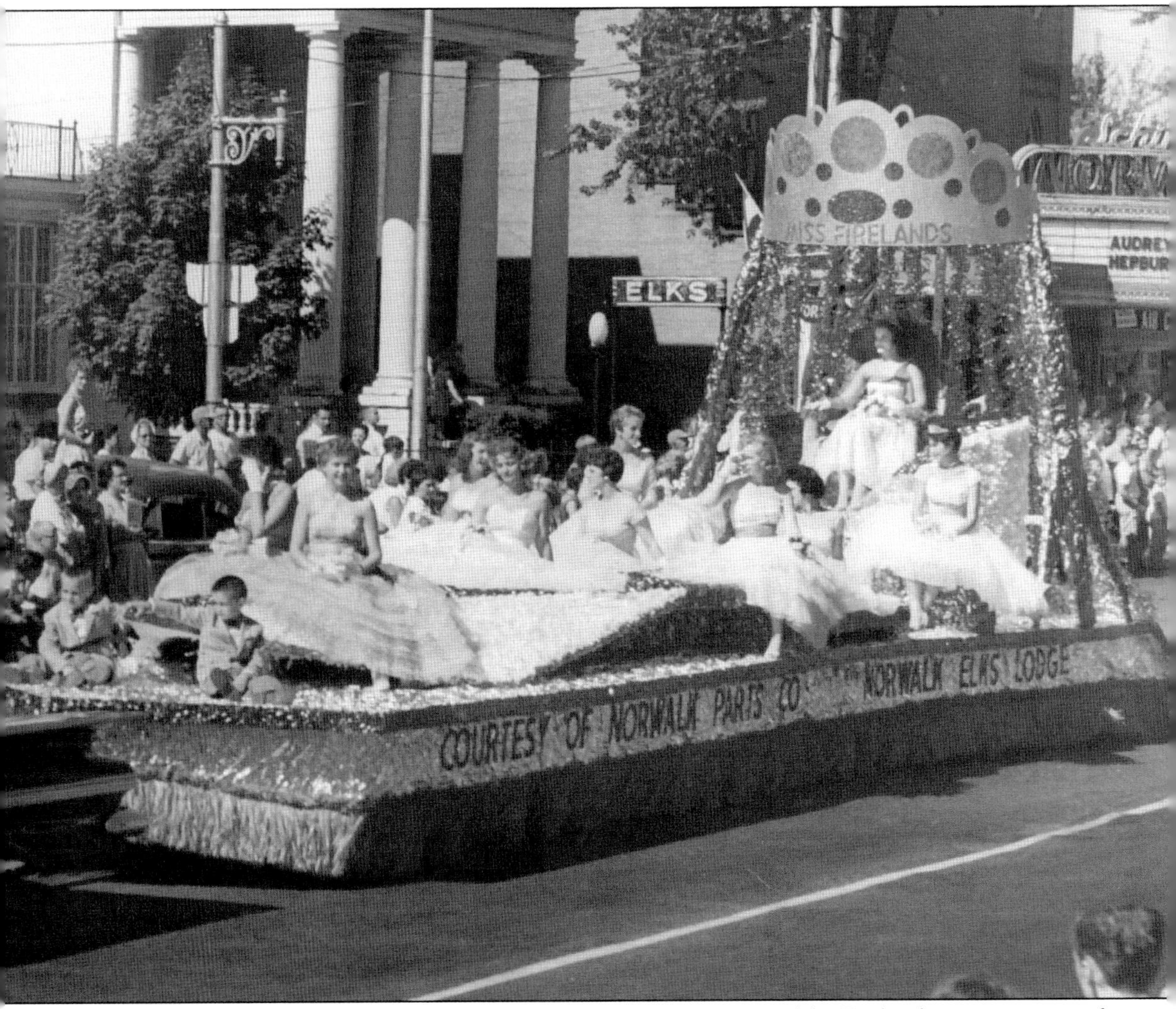


The queen's float passes through downtown Norwalk in 1959 as part of the Firelands sesquicentennial celebration. Queen Joan Sengstock reigns as the float passes Schine's Theater and the former Elks Lodge.

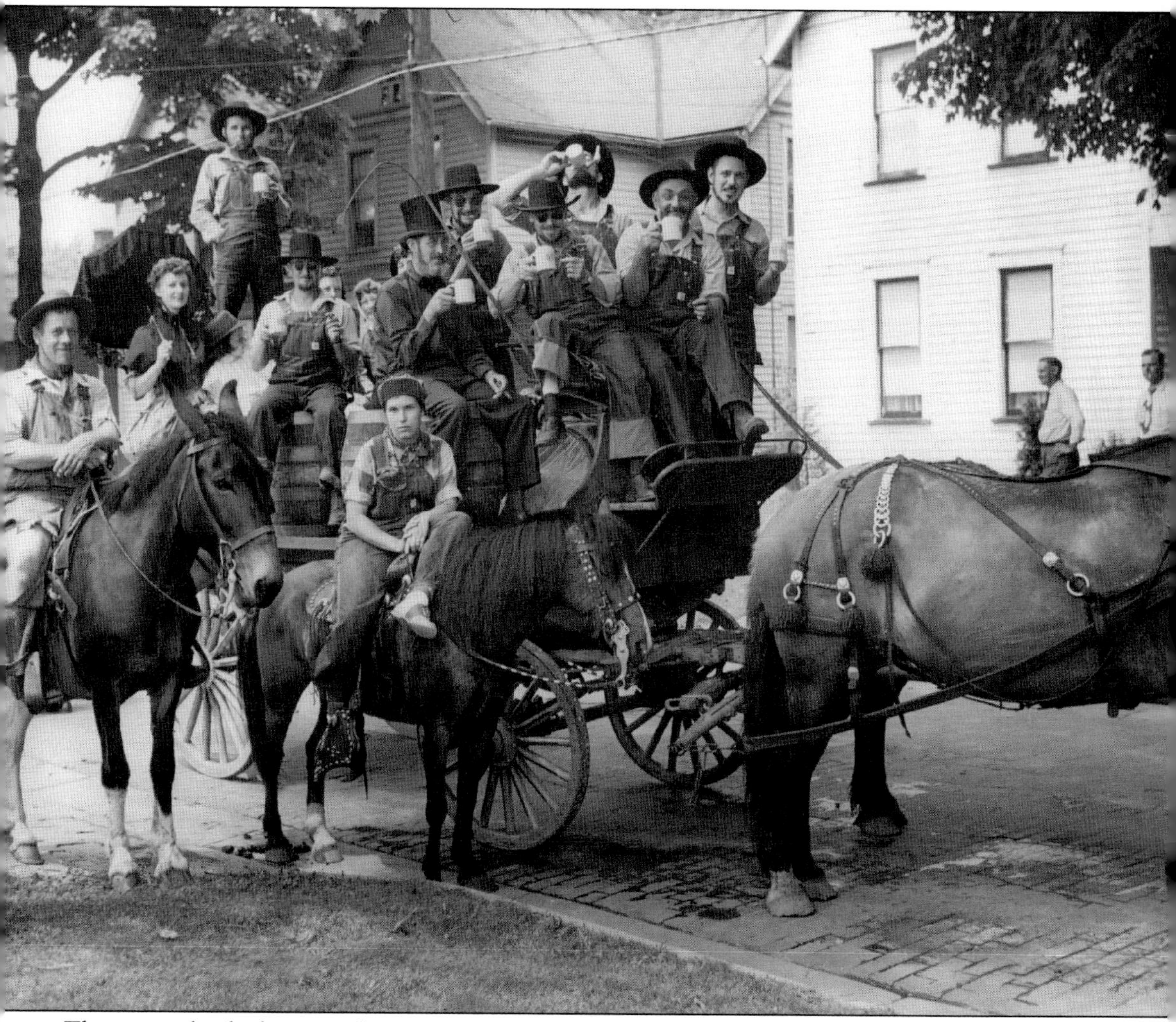

This wagonload of men and women are in good spirits enjoying the festivities during the 1953 Ohio sesquicentennial celebration.

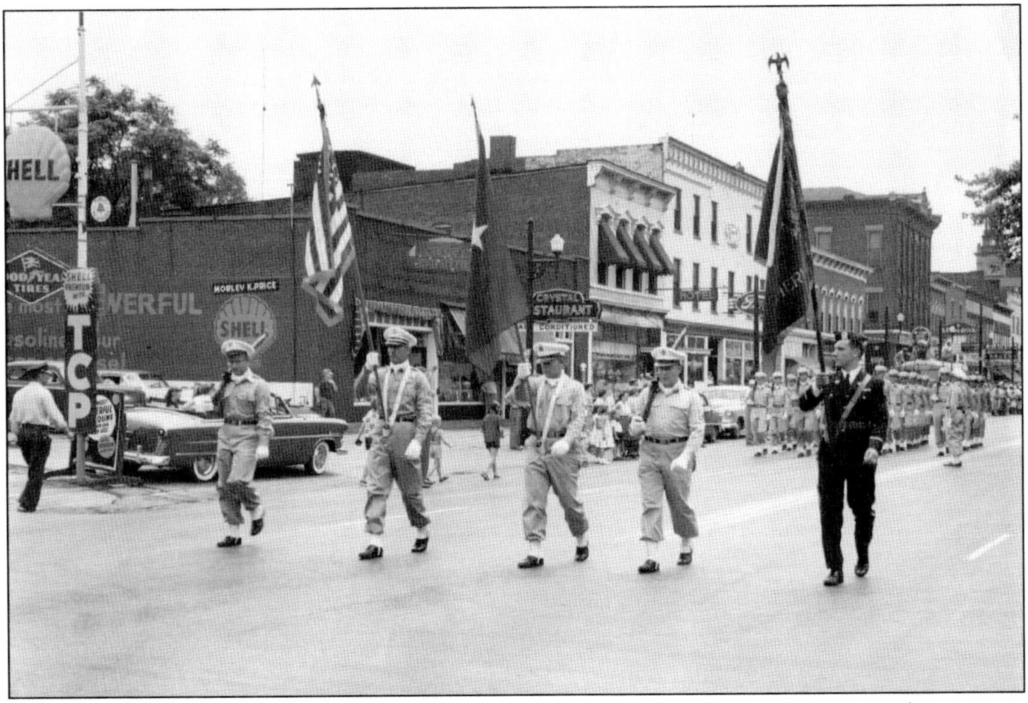


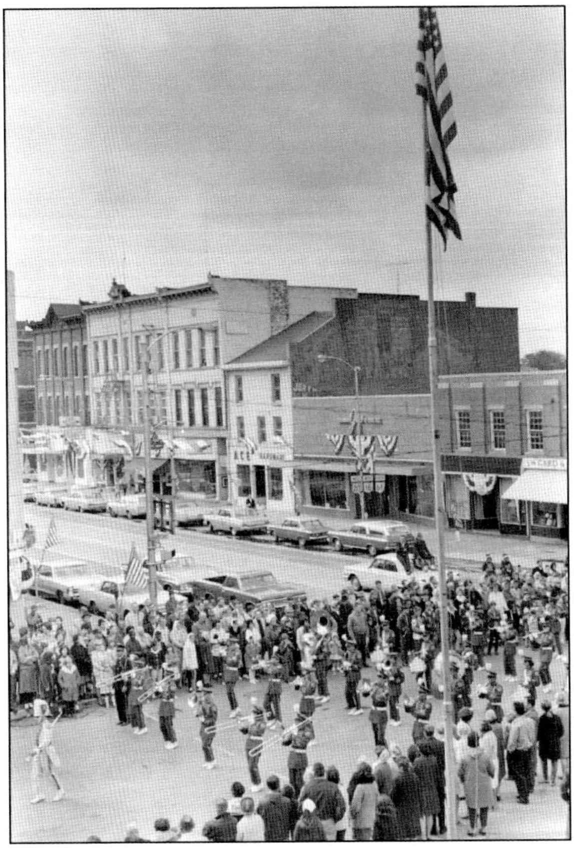


The 1963 Norwalk Memorial Day parade is led by military flag bearers. The Shell station is at the corner of South Foster Street, and the courthouse is at far right.

This parade in the early 1960s features a marching band crossing Main Street onto Benedict Avenue at the courthouse square.

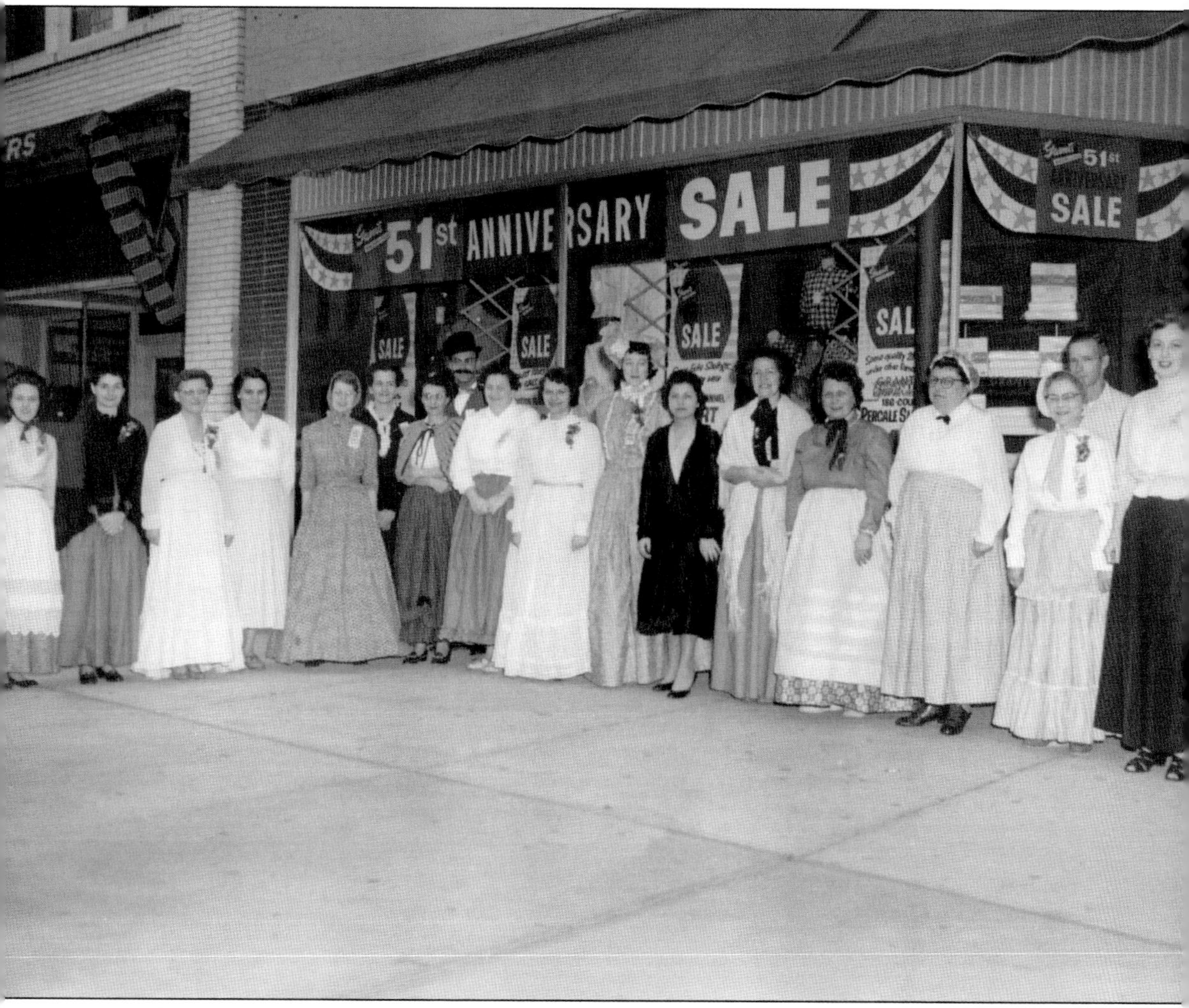


Here is the staff of Grants Department store celebrating the 51st anniversary with a sale in the late 1950s. Grants was a mid-20th century anchor store on Main Street.

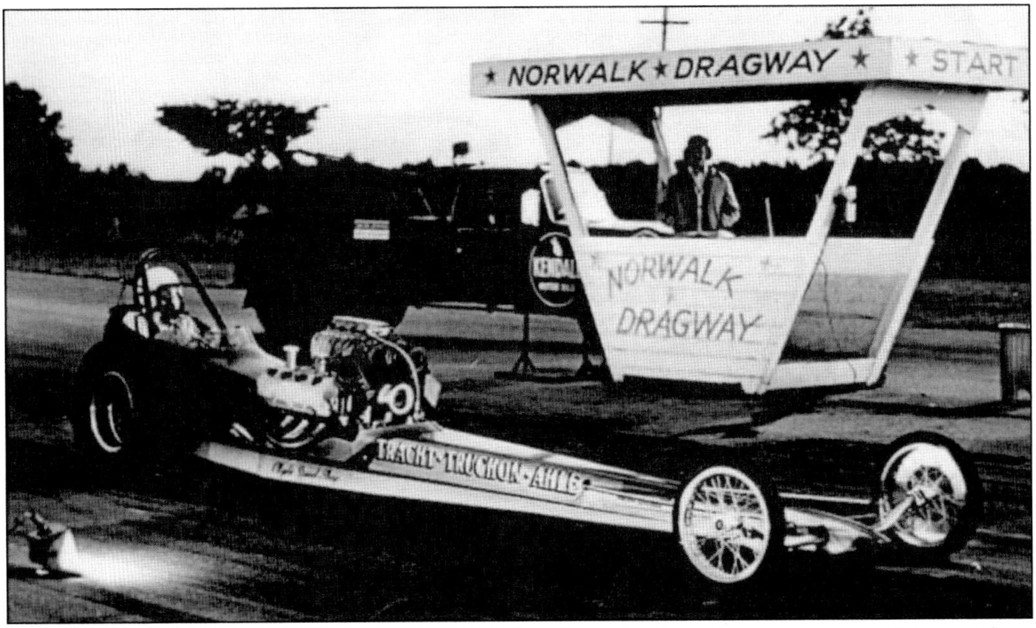


This front-end dragster, driven in the late 1960s by Norwalk's Jim Tracht, was one of the quickest entries at the Norwalk Dragway. The AA/Gas Dragster ran on nothing but gasoline. Its top speed was 194 mph. The Norwalk dragstrip was opened in the 1960s by Herzog and Shubert and was all but abandoned when it was resurrected in 1973 by William Bader Sr., Terry Gavin, and Clayton Joseph. The track struggled early on with no sanctioning body for assistance. Over the years, however, it acquired three different sanctions. From a $500 budget in 1974, the modern facility, Summit Motorsport Park, now has one that is set at $5 million.

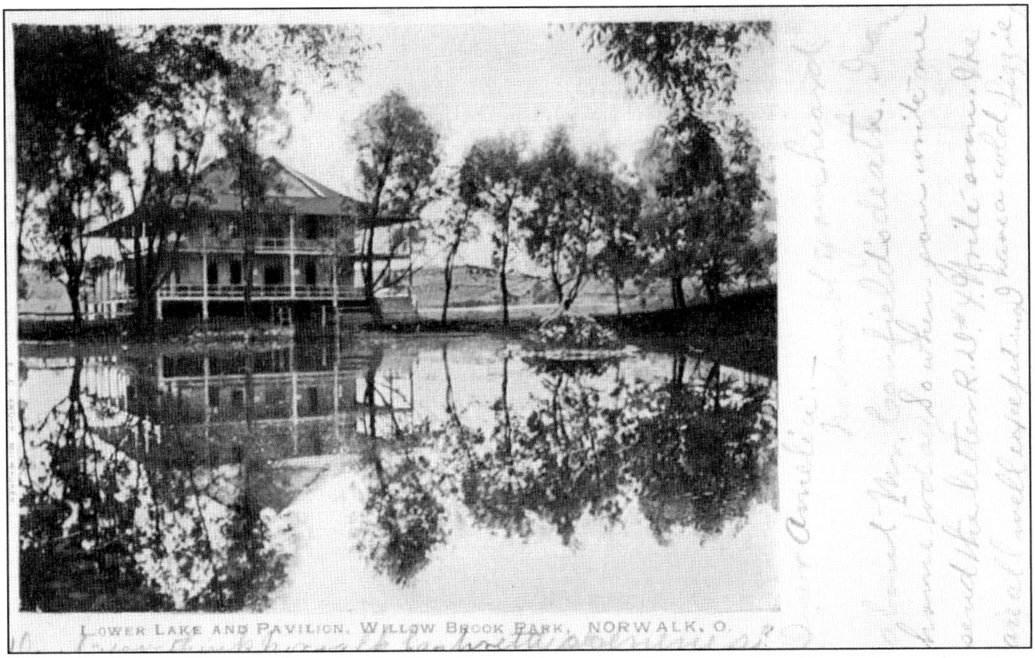


During the early 1900s, Norwalk's Willow Brook Park was a big attraction. It was located on East Main Street east of Old State Road. The park featured a pavilion and lake.

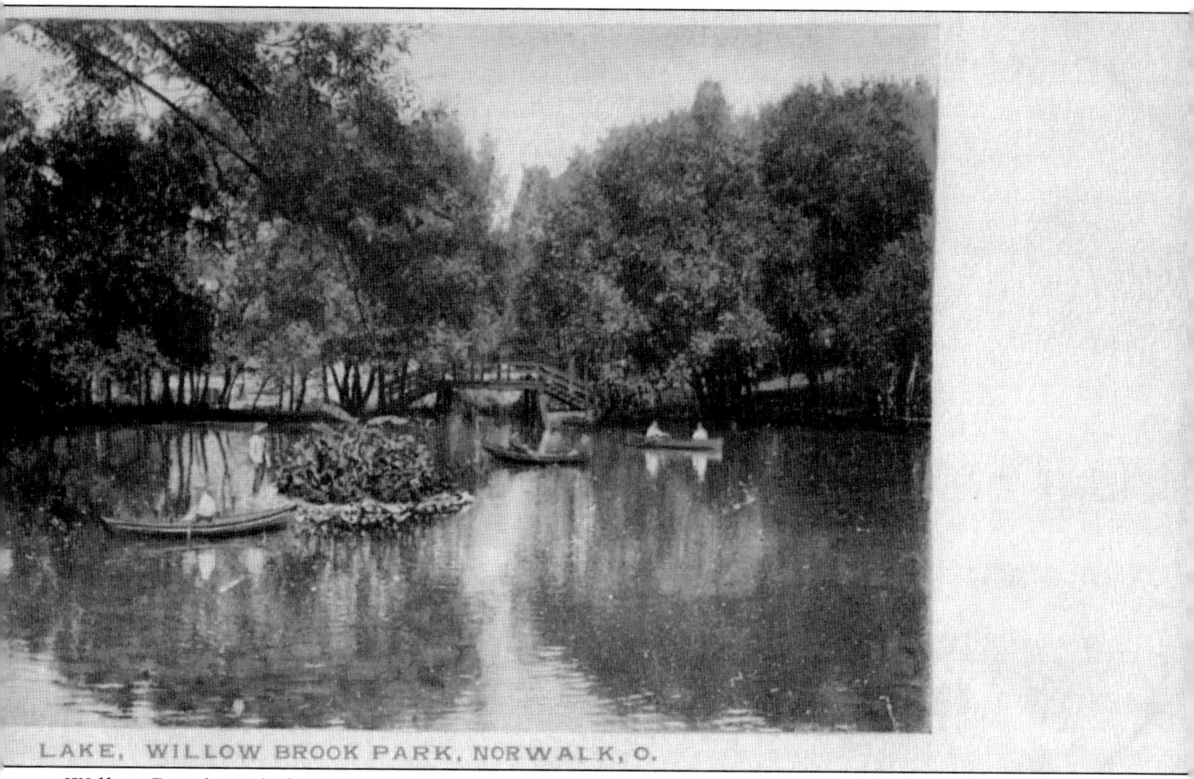


Willow Brook Park featured a large lake, which boaters could enjoy during the warm summer months. The park was also open in the winter for skating.

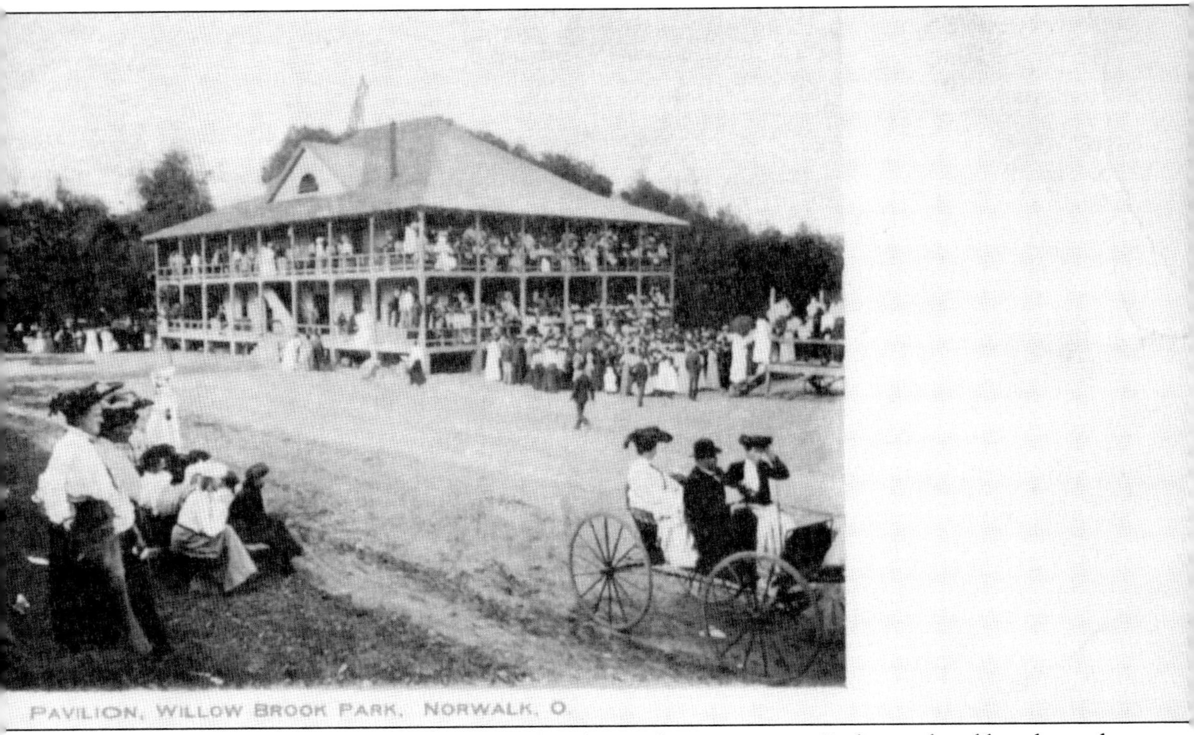


This postcard shows a family arriving in their horse-drawn carriage. Perhaps a local band was the attraction of the day that drew the large crowd shown at the pavilion.

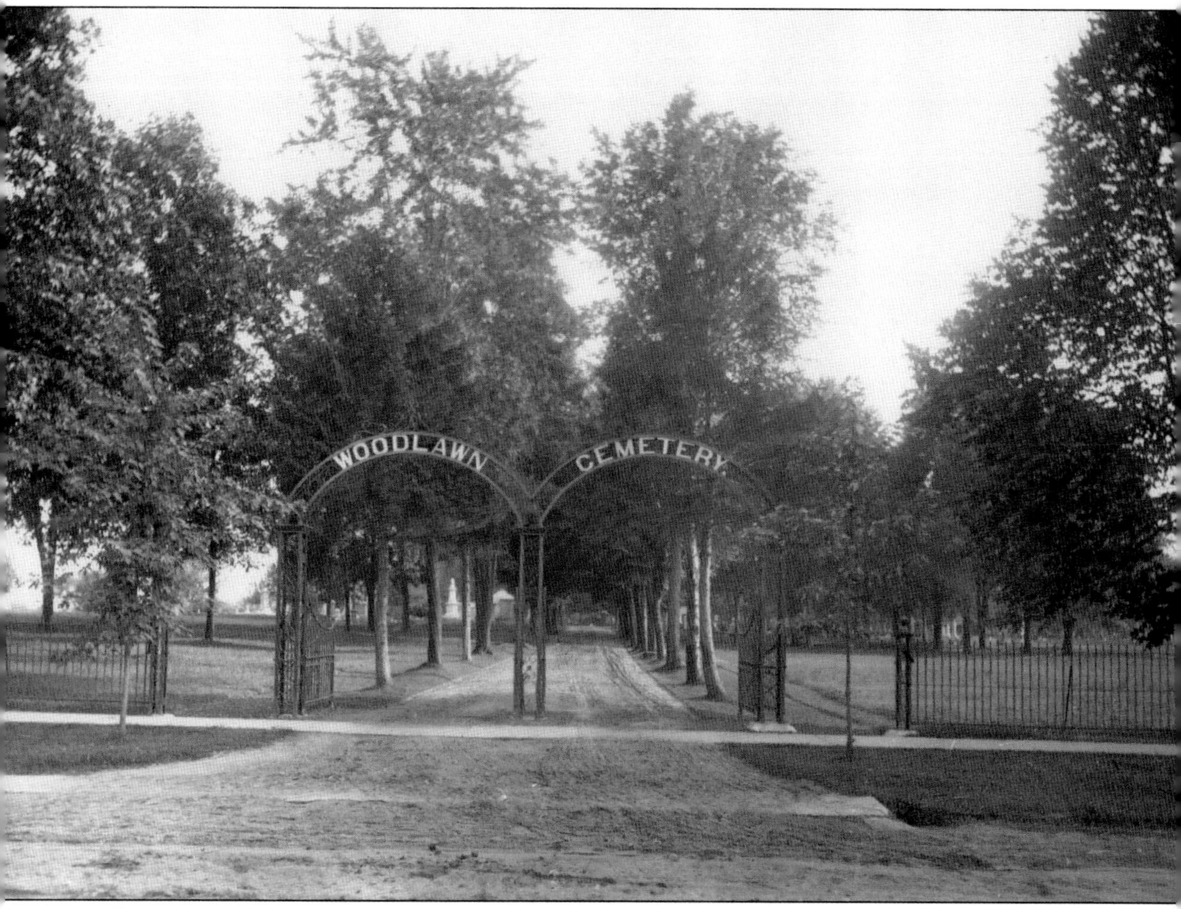


Woodlawn Cemetery is located on the city's south side. The cemetery is the final resting place for many of the pioneers who settled and established the city. The iron gate was removed after horse-drawn hearses were replaced in the early 20th century. Its peaceful setting is a great place to pass an afternoon.